••• **Trainer's Manual**

The CELTA
Certificate in Teaching English to Speakers of Other Languages
Course
Second Edition

Peter Watkins
Scott Thornbury
Sandy Millin

Shaftesbury Road, Cambridge CB2 8EA, United Kingdom

One Liberty Plaza, 20th Floor, New York, NY 10006, USA

477 Williamstown Road, Port Melbourne, VIC 3207, Australia

314–321, 3rd Floor, Plot 3, Splendor Forum, Jasola District Centre, New Delhi – 110025, India

103 Penang Road, #05–06/07, Visioncrest Commercial, Singapore 238467

Cambridge University Press & Assessment is a department of the University of Cambridge.

We share the University's mission to contribute to society through the pursuit of education, learning and research at the highest international levels of excellence.

www.cambridge.org
Information on this title: www.cambridge.org/9781009095396

© Cambridge University Press & Assessment 2022

The copyright in the material in this book is owned by or licensed to Cambridge University Press & Assessment, or reproduced with permission from other third-party copyright owners.

The contents of this book may be copied solely:

(i) under the terms of a valid licence from a collective licensing scheme operated by a reproduction rights organisation such as the Copyright Licensing Agency (UK), the Copyright Clearance Center (USA), the Copyright Agency Limited (Australia) and/or similar agencies in other territories;
(ii) where reproduction is permitted for personal reference or specific educational and teaching purposes under applicable copyright laws, including the UK's Copyright, Designs and Patents Act, 1988;
(iii) with the express prior written consent of Cambridge University Press & Assessment.

The worksheets in this book are designed to be copied and distributed in class.

First published 2022
20 19 18 17 16 15 14 13 12 11 10 9 8 7 6 5 4 3 2 1

Printed in Great Britain by CPI Group (UK) Ltd, Croydon CR0 4YY

A catalogue record for this publication is available from the British Library

ISBN 978-1-009-09539-6 Trainer's Manual Paperback
ISBN 978-1-009-37221-3 Trainer's Manual eBook
ISBN 978-1-009-09534-1 Trainee Book Paperback
ISBN 978-1-009-37220-6 Trainee Book eBook

Cambridge University Press & Assessment has no responsibility for the persistence or accuracy of URLs for external or third-party internet websites referred to in this publication and does not guarantee that any content on such websites is, or will remain, accurate or appropriate.

Contents

Introduction — 4

1 – Learners and teachers, and the teaching and learning context
1 Learning and teaching contexts — 7
2 Learners as individuals — 11
3 What do teachers do? — 15

2 – Language analysis and awareness
4 Introduction to analysing language — 19
5 Introduction to researching language — 24
6 Vocabulary — 32
7 Teaching vocabulary — 35
8 The sounds of English — 39
9 Stress, rhythm and intonation — 45
10 Teaching pronunciation — 50
11 Phrases and sentences — 56
12 Tense and aspect — 60
13 Language functions — 64
14 Text and discourse — 69
15 Presenting the meaning and form of new grammar items — 73
16 Checking the meaning of grammar items — 79
17 Practising new language items — 84
18 Providing feedback on learner production — 89
19 Teaching language items reactively — 95

3 – Language skills: listening, reading, speaking and writing
20 Focus on listening skills — 101
21 Focus on reading skills — 106
22 Focus on speaking skills — 112
23 Focus on writing skills — 117
24 Teaching basic literacy — 123
25 Integrating skills — 128

4 – Planning and resources for different teaching contexts
26 Lesson planning: defining aims — 133
27 Lesson planning: lesson design and staging — 137
28 Lesson planning: planning beyond the single lesson — 141
29 The online classroom v the face-to-face classroom — 146
30 Choosing and using teaching resources — 150
31 Teaching with limited resources — 155
32 Using educational technology — 160

5 – Developing teaching skills and professionalism
33 Organizing and managing a class — 163
34 Managing an activity — 168
35 Teaching young learners and teenagers — 171
36 Teaching at different levels — 176
37 Maintaining learner motivation — 182
38 Introduction to assessment — 185
39 Developing as a teacher — 190
40 Preparing for the workplace — 193

Teaching practice — 199
Classroom observation — 208
Review quiz — 209

Acknowledgements — 211

Introduction

What is *The CELTA Course*?

The CELTA Course is a coursebook for participants on the CELTA course. For more information about CELTA, visit the Cambridge English website:

https://www.cambridgeenglish.org/teaching-english/teaching-qualifications/

The CELTA Course is appropriate for either classroom use or a synchronous online programme, and covers all the main content areas addressed in CELTA. Much of the material could also be easily adapted to suit asynchronous delivery too. The book aims to provide trainers with ready-made lesson plans that can be tailored and adapted to meet the needs of their particular trainees. It thus saves on preparation time, as well as reducing the need to prepare and copy session handouts. It also provides a basis around which new centres can design and structure their courses. Finally, it provides trainees with a compact record of their course, which they can consult both during the course and afterwards.

What does *The CELTA Course* consist of?

The CELTA Course consists of two components:

- *Trainee Book*: this includes material to be used in input sessions on the course, plus advice concerning the practical and administrative aspects of the course, along with a file of useful reference material.
- *Trainer's Manual:* this includes guidance and advice as to how best to exploit the material in the trainee book, as well as, where necessary, photocopiable material to supplement sessions.

The bulk of the course comprises 40 units, each representing an input session of between 45 to 90 minutes. These are grouped under the five main topics of learning:

1. Learners and teachers, and the teaching and learning context
2. Language analysis and awareness
3. Language skills: listening, reading, speaking and writing
4. Planning and resources for different teaching contexts
5. Developing teaching skills and professionalism

The sequencing of units within these broad topics has been governed by a number of factors. These include:

- *developmental:* topics considered to be more fundamental – such as classroom management – are dealt with before topics that can be safely postponed until later in the course, such as preparing for the workplace
- *thematic:* topic areas that are related are usually sequenced together
- *conventional:* topics that – for whatever reasons – are conventionally dealt with early in most courses precede those that are conventionally dealt with later

However, it is not expected that trainers will necessarily follow the sequence of units in exactly the order that they are presented. (For more on how to use the course, see below.)

Each unit comprises a number of tasks, starting with a warm-up task and concluding with a reflection task.

As well as the input session tasks, the **Trainee Book** includes the following features:
- **Teaching practice:** This section consists of practical advice for trainees, as well as a bank of TP reflection tasks
- **Classroom observation:** This section consists of a bank of observation tasks for use in observing experienced teachers (as part of the course requirements) and TP
- **Guide to tutorials** and **Guide to written assignments:** These sections include advice as to how trainees should interpret the assessment criteria, and how they can best prepare for tutorials
- **Resource file:** This section includes:
  - a bank of 5-minute activities
  - a guide to the main English verb forms
  - a glossary
  - a recommended reading list and relevant website addresses

The **Trainer's Manual** consists of:
- a guide for each unit on how to set up activities, suggested variants, and expected answers to tasks
- optional (photocopiable) materials for some units
- **Teaching practice**: some guidelines on how to organize TP, write TP points, and give TP feedback
- **Classroom observation**: some suggestions as to how to get the most out of this component of the course
- **Review quiz:** a photocopiable review boardgame for trainees

How should *The CELTA Course* be used?

Each CELTA centre will design and run its courses according to its own particular circumstances and needs. Hence, *The CELTA Course* has been designed with flexibility and adaptability in mind. Course trainers are invited to select only those elements that meet the needs and syllabus specifications of their particular courses: it is not expected, for example, that they will do *all* the units and *all* the tasks in the book (for one thing, there is unlikely to be sufficient time on most courses), nor that they will do the units in the order that they occur in the book. To this end, the units have been written as far as possible as stand-alone entities.

When using the material, however, trainers should observe certain core principles that are intrinsic to the CELTA scheme. These are that the course is:
- **practical:** The CELTA is an introductory course, and as such it has to be very practical. This does not mean avoiding theoretical issues, but simply that input sessions should always be firmly grounded in classroom practice. This may mean starting with a discussion of classroom experiences, drawing out some basic principles, and returning to classroom practice through the analysis and evaluation of classroom materials.
- **integrated:** In keeping with the above point, emphasizing the interconnectedness, not only of theory and practice, but also of the different strands of the course, should be a priority. These strands include the input sessions, TP, classroom observation, and the written assignments. Trainers should seek every opportunity to draw connections, and to encourage trainees to make these connections for themselves. One way of doing this, for example, is to adapt some tasks so that they anticipate forthcoming teaching practice points, or to choose, as example material, extracts from the coursebooks the trainees are using in their TP. Likewise, TP reflection tasks

and classroom observation tasks can be chosen so that they tie in with areas of content that have been dealt with – or are about to be dealt with – in the input sessions. Similarly, opportunities to recycle themes that have been dealt with at an earlier stage in the course should be exploited. For example, when dealing with an area of language awareness, such as tense and aspect, there will be opportunities to review approaches to grammar presentation and practice.

- **experiential:** A core principle of the CELTA course is the notion that learning is optimized if it is driven by personal experience. To this end, trainers are recommended to include demonstrations of classroom procedures in the sessions, where the trainees experience classroom techniques as learners, and reflect on their experience. Many of the tasks in the book can be substituted with actual demonstrations, and these are flagged in the Trainer's Manual.

- **co-operative:** The course has been prepared for use as part of group study (as opposed to self-study), and as such exploits the communal and collaborative nature of the CELTA, where trainees frequently work together in pairs or small groups in order to compare experiences, complete tasks, debate issues, evaluate materials, or design lessons. For each task, the Trainer's Manual suggests an appropriate way of setting up the activity and how it might be conducted. There is an emphasis on pair and group work with a reporting-back stage, thus mirroring the learner-centred principles that trainees will usually be expected to apply in their own teaching. It is important that the training should take place in a space that is conducive to a variety of different working patterns, whether the course is run online or face-to-face.

- **reflective:** A key component of the experiential learning cycle is reflection; for this reason every unit ends with a reflection task. However, reflection can be built into the course at other points too. For example, after trainees have experienced an activity as if they were learners, they can then reflect on their experience in order to extrapolate principles that might apply when setting up the same or similar activities as teachers.

We hope that *The CELTA Course* provides support for both trainees and trainers throughout the course and beyond.

1 Learning and teaching contexts

Main focus
To raise awareness of the ways in which learning contexts can vary and the impacts that these variations will have on teaching.

Learning outcomes
- Trainees can describe a range of language learning purposes and situations, using standard abbreviations.
- Trainees understand how variations in context may impact on teaching, with regard to class size and the profile of learners.
- Trainees understand that different learners have different needs.
- Trainees develop an awareness of how learners' needs can be investigated via simple needs analyses.

Key concepts
- EFL, ESL, CLIL, EIL, ESP, EAP
- needs and needs analyses

Stage	Focus
A Warm-up	introducing some key variations in learning contexts
B Learners' purposes	defining EFL, ESL, CLIL, EIL, ESP and EAP
C Needs and needs analyses	identifying ways in which a teacher can investigate the needs of learners
D More differences	recognizing how class size and other variables will impact on learning and teaching
Key words for teachers	building of specialist vocabulary to talk about teaching
Reflection	trainees consider how they might apply what they have learned in the unit

A Warm-up

Encourage the learners to think back to a concrete situation in which they were either a learner or a teacher. Give them a little planning time to think about what they wish to say. The activity assumes some human interaction (rather than a lesson delivered entirely through a learning app).

As an alternative, this could be set up as a visualization task, with the questions being asked over appropriate music.

Give the learners time to compare the contexts they recalled before reporting back in open class.

1 – Learners and teachers, and the teaching and learning context

B Learners' purposes

1   Write *EFL* on the board and try to elicit what the letters might stand for. Write one or two further examples before setting up the matching activity.
    Answers: 1–d)   2–f)   3–a)   4–b)   5–c)   6–e)
    You could ask the trainees to identify an example of ESP from the list (EAP) in order to highlight how ESP acts as a generic term with specific examples branching from it.
    You may like to feed in more information about the types of learning context. This might include:
    ELT is a generic term that could cover all the other scenarios.
    EFL can be extended to cover short stays in an English-speaking environment when the learner is not a long-term resident in that country. So, a student who comes to the UK for a four-week summer course is also an EFL learner.
    ESL is one commonly used abbreviation for the phenomenon described. However, it may be broken down further. In the UK, ESOL is used to refer to the teaching of English to migrant or other minority groups, learning English in a host country. Learners may use their L1 at home but need English to have full access to the wider community – schools, health care and so on.
    CLIL is one content-based model of instruction and includes the explicit teaching of English to support learners so that they can also achieve in the 'content' subject.
    There is almost no end of examples of ESP courses, but as well as the examples given, common courses include: English for aviation, English for law, and English for hotels and tourism.

2   Give the trainees some time to read the profiles of learners and ask any questions that they need to. They could compare their answers before reporting back to you in open class.
    • Han is an EAP student.
    • Lucia is an EFL student.
    • Kazankiran is an ESL student.
    • Carmen is an ESP student, studying English for business purposes. It seems very likely that she also uses English as an international language.
    • Kah-Yee was a CLIL student. (Malaysia introduced CLIL in the early part of the 21st century, with mathematics being one of the subjects taught through English, but later the CLIL policy was reversed.)

C Needs and needs analyses

1   Invite the learners to look back at the profiles and consider which learners have the most predictable needs. Arguably, it is only Lucia who does not have easily anticipated needs. You may like to ask the trainees to speculate further about some of the needs of the other learners and what sort of content their course might include.

2   Focus the trainees on the questions. Allow them to discuss in pairs or small groups before reporting back.
    a   How might the needs of an ESL learner vary from those of an EFL learner?
        The needs of an ESL learner are likely to be more predictable. In some cases they may reflect day-to-day survival needs, such as making an appointment with a doctor, form-filling, and talking to a child's teacher. However, it is fair to say that people ought to have

1 Learning and teaching contexts

the opportunity to thrive, not merely survive, and so although these may be reasonable initial aims, they are unlikely to fulfil all of a learner's needs.

b **How might the needs of an EAP learner vary from those of an EFL learner?**
The needs of an EAP learner will reflect the type of texts they need to understand (e.g. lectures) and also produce (e.g. extended academic essays). This may mean that there is a case for teaching the genre features of those text types. In addition, the learner needs to be able to interact with their teachers in an appropriate manner.

c **What sort of language content would you expect a CLIL learner to receive?**
This will focus on the language needed for the subject they are studying. Again, there may be a need to study certain text types (e.g. if science is taught via English, they may need to study how to write a lab report). Particular vocabulary and grammar may accompany this (e.g. the passive voice may be taught in relation to a lab report).

d **Can you think of any implications for teaching if a student uses, or will use, English as an international language?**
There are several implications, including what 'counts' as an appropriate model of English on which to base feedback. However, more easily implementable actions might, for example, be things such as using listening comprehension texts that include speakers from a variety of L1 backgrounds.

3 Try to elicit from the trainees that they could investigate needs by surveying the learners, or by interviewing them.

Point out that if needs are known, courses can be designed to meet them, and this may prove very motivating for learners.

Put trainees into pairs and ask them to write questions that they could use to establish a learner's needs. You may like to start this in open class, by eliciting questions such as *How important is practising reading to you?*.

When the trainees have had some time, they can compare with another group before reporting back in open class. You may like to collate relevant questions on the board.

You could also point out that there are other sources of information, in addition to the learners themselves. For example, information could come from a learner's previous teachers, an HR department that knows the language demands of a company role, and so on. An alternative to this activity is to provide a simple needs analysis form for the trainees to analyse and comment on. You could use one that your centre uses and you are familiar with, for example.

D More differences

1 Direct the learners to the quote provided and ask them to speculate on other ways in which classrooms might differ. If necessary, provide an example to start. Trainees may comment on such things as the age of the learners, the numbers in a class, online v physical environments, the resources available, current English proficiency, groups that share a first language v those that don't, the experience and backgrounds of the teachers, and so on. The trainees may also comment on the differences brought about by variables within individual learners (such as their level of motivation). These types of difference are the subject of the following unit.

1 – Learners and teachers, and the teaching and learning context

2 Put trainees into groups of three or four and allocate each group a), b) or c). If you have time, groups could consider all three questions.
After sufficient time to generate some ideas, the trainees report back.

a The main difference would seem to be in terms of experience. It is unlikely that the young group has much actual business experience or can predict accurately what their specific needs will be in the future – and they may vary across the group anyway. However, the senior manager has a lot of experience and has probably taken part in similar meetings before. Their needs are therefore predictable. We might expect that the manager is involved in specifying the content, and to some extent planning, their own course. The degree of business knowledge expected of the teacher might also vary. This leads to a distinction between (paradoxically) 'general' ESP and 'specialized' ESP.

b The main differences are obviously in group size and the sharing (or not) of an L1. Teachers might feel more comfortable using pair and group work extensively with a relatively small group that can be easily monitored and have no option but to use English to communicate. They may feel more reluctant with a large group who might use their L1 to communicate. The group based in the UK might benefit from activities centring on places they have seen and will visit during their stay. This is unlikely to interest people who might never go to the UK.

c As in a), it is likely that the 1:1 learner can have a greater say in what they want to do in the lesson and what they enjoy doing. Activities can be designed to target particular language areas that are problematic for them or would be useful. With a class of 15, the teacher will need to think about how to set up pair and group work and how they might monitor breakout rooms efficiently. In both cases the teacher would probably want to include a balance of screen- and non-screen-based activities, so that learners do not spend the entire lesson looking at the screen.

KEY WORDS FOR TEACHERS

Remind the trainees of the need to be able to use teaching terms confidently and accurately. Ensure trainees have a range of resources from which they can check key language and teaching terminology. Remind them that there is a glossary at the back of the Trainee Book.

REFLECTION

Either focus the trainees on the sentence stems in their books or, if you prefer, dictate the stems. Give learners time to complete the stems before sharing with partners and reporting back.

While a range of answers are obviously possible, the completed sentences produced should reflect an appreciation of the diversity of learning contexts and the need to adapt teaching appropriately.

If time is short, trainees could choose two or three stems to complete, or you could allocate stems to different members of the group.

2 Learners as individuals

> **Main focus**
> To raise awareness of individual learner variation and the need to support strategic learning. The primary focus is on those variables over which the teacher has some control.
>
> **Learning outcomes**
> - Trainees can describe a range of language learning strategies and their importance.
> - Trainees understand how learning strategies can lead to learner autonomy.
> - Trainees can identify factors that are likely to maintain motivation.
> - Trainees understand that some learners will enjoy different activity types to others.
> - Trainees appreciate the need to embrace diversity and make classrooms safe and supportive spaces.
>
> **Key concepts**
> - language learning strategies
> - motivation
> - learner training
> - learner autonomy
> - learner preferences
> - learner identity

Stage	Focus
A Warm-up	introducing some key factors in individual variations in learning
B Learner preferences	identifying different learner preferences
C Motivation	recognizing factors that can impact on motivation
D Language learning strategies	identifying a variety of learning strategies
E Learner training	identifying opportunities for learners training and how training might be best achieved
Key words for teachers	building of specialist vocabulary to talk about teaching
Reflection	trainees reflect on various dimensions of individual difference

A Warm-up

1 With books closed, describe the scenario to the trainees. Allow them to think for a few moments before discussing in pairs and reporting back their ideas.

Accept all reasonable suggestions.

Motivation, learner preferences and learning strategies are dealt with in the unit. The trainees may also suggest factors such as age and aptitude, which are not dealt with in detail here because the teacher has no control over them.

If a trainee suggests *learning styles*, explain that you will return to that in the next section of the lesson.

1 – Learners and teachers, and the teaching and learning context

2 This would be an opportunity to point out that learning English is simply harder for some people than others because of the 'distance' between their L1 and English. For example, a French learner of English, such as Sophie, will recognize many cognates, see similar grammar patterns and recognize the script and writing conventions of English. On the other hand, a Chinese learner of English (Zhao) will not derive this support from their L1 and will have to learn things, such as the Roman script, that some other learners take for granted. Also, a learner who has already successfully learned other languages will have an advantage – again, Sophie and also Safia. They will, for example, have probably developed successful learning strategies and also may be more resilient if they sense a lack of progress because they will be confident in their ability to learn another language.

B Learner preferences

If a trainee has suggested learning styles as an explanation for individual differences in task A, explain that while different learners may **like** different classroom activities, there is very little evidence to suggest that those preferences impact directly on learning (Lethaby and Harries, 2016). However, doing things we enjoy, may impact on motivation to study and our willingness to invest in particular activities.

1 Ask trainees to reflect on a language learning experience they have had. Encourage them to recall it in as much detail as possible and share one or two thoughts about what they liked and did not like. They then complete the questionnaire individually.
2 Trainees share their responses with others in small groups. Ask them to report back particularly on the contrasts that they found in their groups.

They should understand that within any one class it is likely that there will be learners who like different types of activities. Some, for example, may enjoy communicating with others in small groups, while some may prefer a more conventionally studious approach and enjoy the study of language. Teachers generally plan a variety of activity types within a lesson, and may also consider how a single activity could be used to meet a variety of preferences. For example, a communicative piece of group work could be followed by a focus on, and study of, the language that was produced in that group work. It is also worth noting that learners may not always enjoy the same activities as the teacher.

C Motivation

Note: Motivation is dealt with in more detail in unit 37.

1 Direct the trainees back to the learning experience they recalled for task B and then ask them about the factors that contributed to motivation or diminished it. This can be done in open class.
2 Ask the trainees to read through the list and explain any points that are unclear to them, before giving them time to make their selections.
3 The trainees may already agree on some of the same points, but it is unlikely that they will agree on all four. If there is time, the pairs could again be combined with a view of agreeing on another list of four. The outcomes of these discussions can be reported back in open class.

2 Learners as individuals

D Language learning strategies

1 Write *I get very nervous and anxious in English lessons …* on the board. Elicit how this might impact on learning. Ask trainees to suggest any potential solutions.
  Ask trainees to focus on the other difficulties, again thinking of solutions where possible.
2 Trainees match difficulties and solutions and then quickly check answers with a partner. Confirm answers.
  Answers: A–3) B–5) C–2) D–1) E–4)
3 Focus the trainees on the questions. Explain that there may be more than one learner for each question, and each learner may fit more than one category.
  Answers:
   i A and C
   ii E and perhaps C, although their anxiety may also be treated by avoidance strategies.
   iii B (Trainees might also suggest D, who has taken action to target their listening skills, but difficulties in this area are common at low levels and are not necessarily an indication that learning is not working.)
  You may wish to point out that deliberate strategies to control emotion are often referred to as 'affective strategies'.
  Those strategies that plan and monitor success of an activity (as in person B) are referred to as 'metacognitive strategies' and those actions that are designed to lead to learning (such as downloading a vocabulary learning app) are 'cognitive' strategies.
4 Depending on time, this could be set up as an all-class activity or as group work. Accept any plausible suggestions and prompt and elicit if the trainees struggle to think of ideas.

  What advice would you give these learners?
  a I need to improve my grammar – what can I do?
    There are plenty of online sentence-level grammar exercises, admittedly of varying quality, that a simple search would produce. In order to make such searches, learners need to have some awareness of metalanguage – the language used to describe language. For example, they need to know the names of verb forms or terms such as 'countable/uncountable noun', and so on.
    There are also more text-level exercises a learner could do. For example, some studies have shown that extensive reading can lead to improved grammar production. Also, learners could record themselves during pair work in a lesson and later transcribe what they said, checking it for accuracy.
  b I want to improve my vocabulary – what can I do?
    Again, reading will help grow the number of words known and also the quality of knowledge in terms of things like collocation and register restrictions. There are also plenty of vocabulary practice activities online. One important factor in remembering new words is the spacing of practice. So, vocabulary should be recycled, and learners should review their notes regularly.
  c I want to improve my speaking – what can I do?
    The learner could access pronunciation materials, look for opportunities to join groups online, arrange a skills swap with someone who wants to learn their language, or make recordings of their speaking, amongst other things. There are a number of online sites that connect people wishing to practise their respective languages, e.g. HelloTalk.

E Learner training

1 It would be a good idea to prepare for this by looking at the coursebook(s) before the session so that trainees can be directed to particular pages. If the coursebook(s) do not have any examples of learner training, you could supply some material that does. Alternatively, you could extend activity 2 and have the trainees suggest what might be useful to add. Assuming there is learner training material in the coursebook(s), ask trainees to identify the strategies presented. Not all strategies will appeal to all learners equally, so many materials will present two or three strategies together, so that learners can experiment with all of them and select what appeals to them.
2 This can feed forward into future planning. Learning strategies can be simply explained, they may be demonstrated, or the teacher may recount examples of their own language learning experiences. Often the best way to present a learning strategy is simply for the teacher to explain it, or if possible, demonstrate it.

KEY WORDS FOR TEACHERS

Remind the trainees of the need to be able to use teaching terms confidently and accurately. Encourage them to experiment with one or more of the vocabulary-learning strategies you have discussed in the lesson.

REFLECTION

1 Answers will vary, and will obviously depend on how well the trainees know their learners by this point in the course.
2 Trainees may, amongst other things, suggest: age, ethnicity, gender, sexual orientation, physical and mental (dis)abilities, beliefs, attitudes, and experiences.
If the trainees need support in thinking of ideas, they could be prompted by being asked to think about differences between people generally in society, as the members of a class are a subset of the wider population.
3 Suggestions may include: respecting all members of the class; giving equal opportunities to speak and voice opinions/beliefs to all members of the class; ensuring that the classroom is a safe and supportive environment, free of hostility and bullying; using material that represents the lives and identities of all the people in the class.
4 Trainees may make a variety of suggestions. One obvious advantage of understanding more about the learners is that the teacher can make better informed decisions about what topics and material should be included and/or avoided in lessons. In order to do this, teachers might individually interview learners about their lives and experiences, or ask them to write short autobiographies as a writing task. Of course, these strategies are only likely to succeed when there is a degree of trust between the teacher and learners.

Reference

Lethaby, C. and Harries, P. (2016). Learning Styles and Teacher Training: Are we Perpetuating Neuromyths? *ELT Journal*, 70,1, pp.16–27.

3 What do teachers do?

> **Main focus**
> To raise awareness and give an overview of the various roles that teachers have to perform. These roles will be returned to and focused on in more detail throughout the course.
>
> **Learning outcomes**
> - Trainees can identify a range of roles that teachers perform.
> - Trainees understand the difference between real questions and display questions.
> - Trainees can anticipate the roles they will play in a given activity or lesson.
>
> **Key concepts**
> - checking understanding of new language
> - checking understanding of instructions
> - real questions v display questions
> - monitoring
>
> Note: these concepts will be returned to and dealt with in more detail in subsequent units.

Stage	Focus
A Warm-up	introducing some key facets of a teacher's job
B Roles of teachers	looking in detail at roles teachers play
C Observation	seeing how roles are performed in a real teaching situation
D Anticipating roles	anticipating what skills will be required in given activities
Key words for teachers	building of specialist vocabulary to talk about teaching
Reflection	trainees reflect on how they can use their new knowledge going forward

Note: for task C you will need a suitable recording of a lesson, or section of a lesson. There are many ELT lessons available on online services such as YouTube. Several ELT methodology books also include recordings of lessons. Alternatively, you could set the observation task before this lesson, either as part of the observation programme of the course, or to be completed during a TP lesson.

A Warm-up

1 Read the statements below, inviting speculation on what job they describe after each one. The job is a member of an airline cabin crew. If the trainees guess before you get to the last sentence, invite them to speculate on what the other prompts would be.
I greet people.
I check documents.
I help people.
I sometimes have to provide emergency first aid.

1 – Learners and teachers, and the teaching and learning context

> I demonstrate safety procedures.
> I check safety procedures are followed.
> I serve drinks and food.

2 Use the prompt to elicit from trainees some of the key parts of a teacher's job. For example, planning, giving instructions, eliciting information, explaining new language, monitoring progress.

Alternative warm-up

Give the trainees the following list of jobs: *sports coach, actor, social worker, tour group leader, lecturer, salesperson, driving instructor, nurse, guitar teacher.*

Ask trainees to complete the following sentence stem in as many ways as they can in four minutes, using one of the jobs in the gap. The trainees can use each job more than once, or indeed use jobs not in the list.

A teacher is like a _____ because …

B Roles of teachers

1 Explain the matching activity. Give learners a couple of minutes to complete the exercise individually before briefly comparing with a partner.
   Answers: 1–c) 2–a) 3–b) 4–e) 5–f) 6–d)
   Draw trainees' attention to the fact that 'focusing on language' need not necessarily come in the form of a teacher explanation. It may be elicited from the learners, using skilfully crafted questions. For example: 'I used to live in Athens. What sort of word comes after *used to*? Do I live there now?'

2 Trainees can work individually before comparing their answers.
   Answers:
   i   Which two are eliciting language from learners? A, F
   ii Which one is building rapport? D
   iii Which one is checking an exercise? E
   iv Which two are part of managing the class? B, C

You may also want to feed into the discussion:

A Elicitation is part of focusing on language, as well as supporting engagement in the lesson.
B Gives instructions and invites participation through using a question. (You may wish to highlight the nomination of a learner to speak, rather than waiting for a volunteer.)
C Gives an instruction but this time to an individual, and it seems that this is principally about ensuring focus and so relates to controlling the class.
D Taking interest in an individual is a way of building rapport.
E Checking answers to an exercise completed by the learners. You may wish to highlight the phrase *the answer for question 3 is …*, as this ensures that learners can follow and be confident that they know the correct version.
F Again, eliciting is part of focusing on language.

C Observation

To reduce the burden of the observation, you could assign specific sections of the form to different trainees, so that they do not feel overburdened.

1. Explain the task to the trainees and ask them to complete the sheet as they watch. If you are using a recording of a lesson, you may want to stop the video every few minutes to discuss specific moments in the lesson.
2. Allow the trainees time to compare and discuss before reporting back. You may want to highlight specific examples of good practice or comment on how things might have been improved.
3. Asking questions is a key part of a teacher's job. You may wish to highlight how questions can be used:
   - to promote genuine communication ('Has anyone been to New York?' – real question)
   - to elicit language from learners ('What is the word for the person who flies a plane?' – display question)
   - to check understanding of new items of language ('Does *used to live* refer to the past or the present?' – display question)
   - to check instructions to activities ('Do you have to write full sentences, or just notes?' – display question)
   - to politely control the class ('Can you listen now?' – this does not function as a question at all: the implied meaning is 'stop talking')

Display questions are often used to either elicit language from learners or to check understanding. Typically teachers 'follow up' the student response with confirmation/praise.

T: What's the past form of *sink*?
S: Sank.
T: Good.

If a wrong answer is given, a teacher will often invite contributions from other class members.

T: What's the past form of *sink*?
S: Sanked.
T: Nearly, not quite; can anyone help?

Also, you may wish to highlight that if a teacher asks a question, it is a good idea to leave a little time for learners to process it and respond, before the teacher continues talking.

It may be a good idea to confirm the list of questions from the observation that the trainees must address, before they report back their ideas on which questions were real and which were for display purposes.

D Anticipating roles

Ensure that the trainees understand the situation and the instruction. It is not important for them to see the actual material to be used at this stage – the instruction should be sufficient for this task.

If you prefer, use some guidance for TP from your own course instead.

Trainees may offer a variety of answers. Accept only those that they can justify.

Before the lesson the teacher will need to:
- plan the lesson
- provide (either design or find) an additional activity, as per the instruction

1 – Learners and teachers, and the teaching and learning context

The teacher is also likely to need to:
- research the new language item to be taught

During the lesson it seems very likely that the teacher will need to:
- give instructions
- focus on the new language item
- check understanding of new language
- check answers to the exercise
- monitor group work
- elicit feedback on the communication generated in the group work
- offer corrective feedback on the group work

The teacher is also likely to:
- motivate and encourage
- control the class and/or individual behaviour

KEY WORDS FOR TEACHERS

Remind the trainees of the need to be able to use teaching terms confidently and accurately.

REFLECTION

1. How do the roles of a language teacher compare with those of:
   - a maths teacher?
     Roles that are linked to classroom management, such as instruction-giving and monitoring, are likely to be the same. Both teachers will need to build rapport with a class. Both will need to focus on new subject content, be able to explain new concepts and correct errors. Both may use elicitation to help learner engagement.
     It is likely that the maths teacher will use fewer 'real' questions. They may use them to build rapport but are less likely to use them to elicit new 'content' that can be analysed and worked on, in the way a language teacher might.
   - a tour guide?
     A tour guide will need to give clear instructions but will not need to monitor any form of group work. They are unlikely to need to correct errors (unless a tourist volunteers information that is plainly incorrect). A tour guide will need to establish rapport with the group, as will the language teacher. The tour guide will focus on new content but is unlikely to try to elicit that content. A tour guide is unlikely to have to motivate and encourage members of the group.
2. Answers will vary. As trainees offer suggestions, ask them to justify and also give examples where they can.
3. Focus the trainees on the observation sheet and explain the task. You may wish to add other roles for the trainees to consider, if there are things you particularly wish to highlight. Encourage discussion in small groups before the trainees report back in open class.
4. If there is time, allow the trainees to think ahead to their next teaching practice, or one section of their teaching practice. They should identify which roles will be most important to that particular piece of teaching.

4 Introduction to analysing language

Main focus
An introduction to some core principles and processes in the analysis of language for teaching purposes.

Learning outcomes
- Trainees understand how language can be analysed from the perspective of text, of grammar, of vocabulary, and of pronunciation.
- Trainees understand how language is broken down and organized into a teaching syllabus.
- Trainees are aware that language analysis involves identifying parts of speech.
- Trainees understand the way English grammar is in large part realized through grammar (function) words, including auxiliary verbs.

Key concepts
- meaning, concept; grammatical form
- context, function, style
- spoken and written form; pronunciation, spelling
- parts of speech
- content (or lexical) v grammar (or function) words
- auxiliary verbs

Stage	Focus
A Warm-up	raising awareness of the different levels of language analysis and mapping linguistic features in terms of their scope
B Basic concepts and terminology	introducing key concepts through a matching task
C Syllabus decisions	understanding how language systems are organized for teaching purposes
D Parts of speech	developing the capacity to categorize words according to their class
E Content words v grammar words	distinguishing between content and grammar words, and understanding the role and importance of auxiliary verbs
Key words for teachers	building of specialist vocabulary to talk about teaching
Reflection	trainees self-assess their language analysis skills and set learning goals

A Warm-up

1 The activity can be done in pairs. Note that the activity avoids specialist terminology at this stage, and assumes that the trainees will be familiar with the terms used. If they are in doubt, point out that the meanings of the terms will be refined during the course of the unit, and in subsequent units, and/or refer them to the glossary.
Answers: 1 sounds; 2 syllables; 3 words; 4 phrases; 5 sentences; 6 texts

2 – Language analysis and awareness

You may want to point out that the pyramid does not distinguish between spoken and written language, 'sounds' being specific to the former, and 'sentences' more typical of written language; 'utterances' is sometimes preferred when describing spoken language. 'Texts' can refer to both spoken and written text. Note also that the terms are not mutually exclusive: that texts can consist of a single sentence, or even a single word (*STOP*), and that words, too, may consist of a single syllable (*cat*) or sound (*I, a*).

2 Some suggestions might include:
Level 1: vowels and consonants and letters (of the alphabet); suprasegmental features of pronunciation, such as intonation, word stress
Level 2: suffixes/prefixes and other morphemes
Level 3: multi-word units
Levels 4 and 5: clauses, which might most easily be categorized as intermediate between phrases and sentences
Level 6: different kinds of text types, such as conversations, speeches, signage, novels
At this early stage, you will need to use discretion as to what degree of detail is appropriate for your trainees. If your class finds it difficult to think of ideas for this, give them a language feature (such as *clauses*) and ask them where they would put it in the pyramid. Alternatively, you could set this task as a pre-session task, where they could use online resources to familiarize themselves with the terminology.

B Basic concepts and terminology

1 Answers:
1–e) 2–a) 3–g) 4–j) 5–b) 6–i) 7–d) 8–c) 9–f) 10–h)

2 Answers:
a a set of instructions of the recipe type
b it is found on the outer wrapping of a teabag, hence it would be found anywhere that tea is prepared
c to instruct
d semi-formal, but with some features of advertising text, such as the positive-sounding words *perfect, freshly drawn, gently*
e words relating to tea and tea-making (*cup, tea, bag, water, milk, sugar*); words with positive associations (see previous point)
f imperatives (*use, add, leave*); ellipsis (i.e. words that are omitted, as in *Leave [it] standing; [It] Can be served*; *-ing* words (also called *participles*, i.e. *boiling, standing, stirring*) to describe actions extended in time; absence of an article (called *zero article*) before the uncountable nouns *water, milk, sugar*

Note: Trainees should not be expected to identify all these grammar points, but it may be worth pointing them out so as to demonstrate the potential of even short texts to embed a significant amount of grammar. You should also make the point that this level of analysis is useful for teachers, but is not necessarily appropriate for learners, except at quite advanced levels.

3 The activity aims to raise awareness about the effect of grammatical and lexical choices on meaning, i.e. that lexicogrammar is a tool to 'make meaning', rather than being simply a set of 'rules'. Trainers need not go into any detail in terms of explaining these effects, but they could refer trainees to resources that they can consult if interested (see also unit 5 Introduction to

4 Introduction to analysing language

researching language). The following answers are only suggestive (and, again, you could make the point that learners may not need to understand these distinctions, but that analysing texts in this way is a useful way of developing teachers' language analysis skills):

2. In *teabag, tea* tells us what kind of *bag* it is (cf *toothbrush, bookcase, handbag*, etc.). *A bag of tea*, on the other hand, tells us how much tea there is, and follows the same pattern as *a bottle of milk, a kilo of bananas, a piece of work*. This is both a lexical distinction and grammatical distinction with a significant effect on meaning.
3. *Freshly drawn* has positive connotations (as if the source of water was from a well) and therefore suits the 'promotional' register of the text.
4. The *-ing* grammatical suffix on the participle denotes an activity in progress ('the water is boiling'), while the *-ed* suffix is (usually) grammatically passive and implies completion: 'the water is boiled / has been boiled'. This is a significant grammatical distinction.
5. In this context, there is little difference in meaning, although when used to talk about persons, *leave* + object + *to*-infinitive usually means 'to allow someone to be responsible for doing something', as in *I'll leave you to lock up*. This is a grammatical distinction.
6. The omission (or ellipsis) of the subject pronoun *it* is a feature of the register of texts such as recipes, where the omitted item is easily recoverable from context and/or when space is at a premium.
7. *Can* is a modal verb implying (in this case) theoretical possibility; *should*, another modal verb, denotes desirability or mild obligation, which is a significant difference in meaning. Although individual words, modal verbs are usually classed as grammar items.

Note: Vocabulary is dealt with in unit 6. Text organization is dealt with in unit 14.

C Syllabus decisions

You may wish to use the syllabus in any of the coursebooks the trainees are currently using, in which case you could select a range of syllabus items accordingly. There is some variation in the way that syllabuses are segmented and exemplified. In the example given, for example, the vocabulary strand is articulated in terms of lexical sets or fields (*Describing trends, preparing food*) which may easily be confused with functional language.

1. Key:

present and past passive	Grammar
make an apology and explain what happened	Functional language
saying /s/ or /z/ at the end of a word	Pronunciation
reported questions	Grammar
talking about time and money	Vocabulary
was/were going to	Grammar
stressing long words	Pronunciation
keep your listener engaged	Functional language
I wish	Grammar
saying long or short vowel sounds	Pronunciation

2 – Language analysis and awareness

2 The main points to note here are that syllabus choices are determined by such factors as:
- *utility:* more useful items taking precedence over less useful ones
- *frequency:* more frequent items taking precedence over less frequent ones
- *complexity:* less complex items taking precedence over more complex ones, although the criteria for complexity tend to be somewhat vague
- *cohesion:* items that are easily related tend to be grouped together, e.g. the lexical set of food items is often taught alongside quantifiers such as *some/any, how much/many*
- *convention:* coursebook syllabuses tend to replicate one another

Note: the topic of planning a series of lessons is dealt with in unit 28.

D Parts of speech

Note: You might like to model the classroom use of a literary text, by asking the trainees to read the text silently, and then answer questions like: *Where do you think this was written? What kind of text is it? What feelings does it evoke? Do you like it?*

It may also be a good idea to do the first line of the text with the whole class, before asking the trainees to continue in pairs or small groups. If time is short, give each group one line to work on.

Answers:

In	the	empty	doorway	many	petals	are	scattered
prep.	det.	adjective	noun	det.	noun	verb	verb

As	they	fall	they	blend	with	the	song	of	the	birds
conj.	pronoun	verb	pronoun	verb	prep.	det.	noun	prep.	det.	noun

Slowly	the	bright	spring	sun	appears	in	the	window
adverb	det.	adjective	noun	noun	verb	prep.	det.	noun

And	a	thin	line	of	smoke	drifts	from	the	incense	burner
conj.	det.	adj.	noun	prep.	noun	verb	prep.	det.	noun	noun

Note that *spring* and *incense* are technically not adjectives: they have no comparative form, for example. They are nouns that (like adjectives) modify other nouns, hence they are called noun modifiers, and are an extremely productive feature of English grammar.

E Content words v grammar words

You might want to point out that – like all distinctions in grammar – the difference between grammar words and content words is a fuzzy one. Grammar words can still impact meaning but the choices of which words can fill any 'slot' are strictly limited. Whereas for content – or open class – words there are very many words that would be grammatically acceptable.

1 1 The content words are underlined:

In the <u>empty</u> <u>doorway</u> many <u>petals</u> are <u>scattered</u>;
As they <u>fall</u> they <u>blend</u> with the <u>song</u> of the <u>birds.</u>
<u>Slowly,</u> the <u>bright</u> <u>spring</u> <u>sun</u> <u>appears</u> in the <u>window</u>
And a <u>thin</u> <u>line</u> of <u>smoke</u> <u>drifts</u> from the <u>incense</u> <u>burner.</u>

2 There are 20 content words out of 39 words in total, i.e. just over 50%.

3 This proportion is typical of most texts, with a bias towards function words in spoken language and up to 60% content words in more technical or academic writing. The proportion of content to grammar words is a handy measure of lexical density, which in turn is an indicator of a text's readability.

2 The grammar words (also called function words) tend to be the most frequent words in English (of the 100 most frequent words, 80 are grammar words, according to Davies & Gardner, *A Frequency Dictionary of Contemporary American English*, Routledge, 2010); like most high frequency words, they are shorter on average than content words (they have been 'eroded' over time); their frequency – which is a function of their usefulness – means that they are repeated often, even over relatively short stretches of text (there are five instances of *the* in the 39-word poem); they tend not to be stressed in spoken language, where their 'weak forms' are preferred; and they form what is called a 'closed set', i.e. unlike content words, they rarely permit new coinages, so there are many fewer members of the set of grammar words than there are of the set of content words.

At this point you may wish to point out that English is not a highly inflected language and therefore does not 'have a lot of grammar', compared to languages such as Turkish or Portuguese. On the other hand, its grammar is, in large part, concentrated in its function words, and these, therefore, should be an important objective in teaching.

3 a Trainees may find the explanation dense and opaque, mainly due to the concentration of information, and the assumption of familiarity with grammatical terminology. On the other hand, the use of examples, and the clear layout are 'user-friendly', and it is a model of concision. The assumption is that learners will have met many of these concepts previously, so this might be a useful summary.

b Most learners will have been introduced to present continuous, present simple and past simply at beginner and elementary levels (A1 and A2) and, also at these levels, some of the more common modal verbs (*can, would, have to* …) in their more frequent uses. At a slightly later stage they will have met perfect and passive forms, as well as the less frequent modal verbs (*might, ought to*).

c Other uses of auxiliaries include:
short answers: *Do you live here? Yes, I do.*
question tags: *You live here, do you?*
emphasis: *I do live here.*

KEY WORDS FOR TEACHERS

Use the key words to review some of the main 'takeaways' from the session.

REFLECTION

1 Ask trainees to answer the questions individually; depending on the nature of the group, you may also suggest they compare their responses, but it is important that they should not feel that the exercise is evaluative.

2 Allow trainees to compare and report their answers; if there is a consensus on any particular topic, it may be worth scheduling a short 'clinic' to address it.

Topic 2 – Language analysis and awareness

5 Introduction to researching language

Main focus
To enable teachers to better understand the range of ways in which they can find out about language points they will cover with students in lessons.

Learning outcomes
- Trainees become familiar with resources they can use to find out information about language they plan to teach.
- Trainees understand the concept of modality and some key features of modal and semi-modal verbs.

Key concepts
- concept, meaning, form, pronunciation
- context, model sentence
- modal verbs

Stage	Focus
A Warm-up	trainees familiarize themselves with key elements of language analysis which they may need to research, and sources for this information
B Researching language using coursebooks	trainees learn about what information a coursebook might provide about language
C Researching language using teacher's books	trainees learn about what information a teacher's book might provide about language
D Researching language using reference books	trainees learn about what information reference books might provide about language
E Putting it all together	trainees summarize their knowledge of modals of obligation and consider the process of researching language
Key words for teachers	building of specialist vocabulary to talk about teaching
Reflection	trainees consider the role of language research in the planning and teaching process

A Warm-up

1 Trainees will need a copy of the language analysis form used at your centre to complete this activity. You may wish to familiarize the trainees with the form yourself first, or you can use this activity to allow trainees to identify the key parts of the form themselves.
Answers will vary, depending on the form you use at your centre.

2 Answers may include:
- the coursebook
- the teacher's book
- the workbook

5 Introduction to researching language

- grammar books
- other reference books, for example *Learner English* by Swan and Smith
- reputable websites, for example https://dictionary.cambridge.org/grammar/british-grammar/
- trainees' prior knowledge – it's perhaps worth emphasizing that they may already know some of the information they need without requiring further research
- colleagues, for example within a strong professional network or a supportive staffroom

B Researching language using coursebooks

Tasks B, C, D and E of this unit are based around a single TP point: modals of obligation drawn from *Empower B1+*. You may wish to replace the content with material you are using on the course, although some of the tasks would probably need quite a lot of adaptation if you choose to do this.

> **Trainer tip**
>
> Rather than having trainees work through tasks B, C and D in order, you may decide to set up a jigsaw activity, where you divide the trainees into two groups, with each group working on task B or D. As it is much shorter, allocate task C to groups which finish faster. Task B is probably more suited to trainees who need support with language analysis, while task D is more suited to trainees who are already able to analyse language somewhat independently.
>
> Trainees would aim to complete as much of the language analysis form as possible from their sources, then compare notes in task E and discuss which resources were more or less useful for them. If you choose to use a jigsaw approach, tell the trainees that their TP tutor has given them a grammar lesson to teach on the topic of 'modals of obligation' (this information appears at the beginning of task B in the Trainee Book, if they forget this).
>
> Note: there is no specific reference to using the internet to research language items during this unit. For many trainees, that may be the default. The aim of the unit is to show them other reliable places where they can find useful information. You may wish to include a step where you help the trainees to decide which internet sources are and are not reliable, perhaps combined with task D.

1 Text-based presentations are covered in more depth in unit 15, but you may wish to ask trainees the following question, to draw their attention to the contextualization of the target language:
   - Why is it beneficial for learners to encounter new language in context first, rather than as decontextualized words or phrases? Compare your answer with a partner.

Contextualizing language is beneficial for learners as it can help their understanding of the meaning of the target language, and how and when it can be used. Taking model sentences from a longer text which learners have previously interacted with may also reduce any negative feelings learners may have about studying grammar, and create smoother transitions between stages in the lesson.

The answers to i) are:
   - obligation: *have to (move), mustn't (do), can (do), don't have to (spoil)*
   - advice: *ought to (be prepared)*

Answers to ii) will depend on the trainees. This activity may help you to learn more about which trainees are more or less confident about discussing grammar.

2 – Language analysis and awareness

2 Encouraging trainees to try out activities which they will expect learners to do during the lesson can help them to identify trainees' own gaps in their knowledge of the target language, as well as potential problems which learners might face when completing activities. Remind trainees to think about *why* the answers are correct, not just *what* the answers are.

Answers to the coursebook activity are:
1 *ought to* and *should*
2 *don't have to*
3 *must* and *have to*
4 *can't* and *mustn't*
5 *can*

Of course, language may be used more flexibly than this coursebook exercise suggests. For example, if a boss says 'I think you should attend the meeting', it is probably necessary to attend. To some extent, context determines how language is interpreted. It is potentially worth pointing out that the rules in this coursebook exercise are somewhat decontextualized – they do not refer back to the text which the learners have already looked at.

If you wish, you could ask trainees some extra reflective questions at this point:
- Did you match the words to the rules correctly?
- Did you find any of them challenging?
- Did you need to look at the text to help you?
- If you had any problems, what does that tell you about possible problems learners might have with this grammar?

3 Grammar summaries in coursebooks or workbooks often contain a lot of information which trainees may be tempted to copy out wholesale onto their language analysis form. This activity introduces the idea of summarizing this information in their own words.

If you are short of time, you may wish to divide up the verbs between the trainees.

Verb	Use	Notes / Possible problems
must	when we make the rules	no past or future form – use *have to* instead questions with *must* are very rare
have to	when we talk about other people's rules	don't use contractions more common than *must*, especially in spoken English
have got to	when we talk about other people's rules	used in spoken English means the same as *have to*
mustn't	when something is not allowed, often when we make the rules	[no information in the summary]
can't	when something is not allowed, often about other people's rules	[no information in the summary]
couldn't	for things which were not allowed in the past	[no information in the summary]
don't have to	no obligation – it's not necessary to do something	[no information in the summary]
should	give advice and recommendations	more common than *ought to*
ought to	give advice and recommendations	less common than *should*

5 Introduction to researching language

C Researching language using teacher's books

You may wish to point out that the amount of additional information which teacher's books provide about grammar can vary, with some adding no extra information, and others (like this one) providing information about problems which learners might have with a particular grammar point. It's unusual for teacher's books to include additional information about vocabulary or functions, but trainees should always check, just in case!

1 Trainees will encounter the idea of pure modals and semi-modals in section D. Acceptable answers here might be 'bare infinitive', 'infinitive without *to*', or 'verb 1', depending on what terminology you prefer. One problem learners might have is including *to* when it is not needed.
2 Learners may contract *have to*, or make mistakes with word order.
3 Learners may not be able to distinguish between the negative forms *mustn't* for obligation and *don't have to* for lack of obligation, because both *must* and *have to* express obligation in their positive forms.

D Researching language using reference books

If trainees have access to reference books, you may choose to set up this activity differently, to simulate more closely how trainees could do research for their own TPs. Trainees can list the questions from A which they still don't have an answer to, then look at their reference books to try to find those answers. Fast finishers can look up extra information to supplement what they have learned from the coursebook and the teacher's book. Afterwards, trainees could reflect on how easy it was to find the information they were looking for and what other information they managed to find.

To use the activity in the Trainee Book, briefly introduce the two books which the excerpts are taken from: *Grammar for English Language Teachers* by Martin Parrott (GELT), and *Learner English* by Michael Swan and Bernard Smith (LE), which is subtitled 'A teacher's guide to interference and other problems' and which includes information about problems which speakers from many different language backgrounds might have when learning English. The excerpts provided are a representative sample – there is a lot more information connected to modals of obligation in both books. You may wish to only use a selection of the excerpts to reduce the amount of processing, or to use all of them with a more confident group of trainees.

If you are running a face-to-face course, divide the excerpts on pages 30–31 of the Trainer Manual between the trainees. If you are running an online course, you could distribute the information in one of the following ways:

- Type up the information, ready to send a direct message or email to each trainee.
- Type up the information and turn the whole text white except for the excerpt number. In the input session, share a link to the whole document. Trainees can highlight their excerpt, while leaving the text white. That way they will be able to see their excerpt, but nobody else will.
- Take a separate photo of each excerpt, ready to send a direct message or email to each trainee.
- Scan the page, then cover each excerpt with a numbered shape. Share a link to the document. Give trainees a time limit to uncover their excerpt, read it and remember it, without reading any of the others!

2 – Language analysis and awareness

Once trainees have their information, ask them to speak to as many people in their group as possible. They should read their excerpt and decide together which question(s) each one answers.

Answers:
Excerpt 1: b, c
Excerpt 2: c, f
Excerpt 3: c
Excerpt 4: a, b
Excerpt 5: a, e
Excerpt 6: d
Excerpt 7: d, g
Excerpt 8: e
Excerpt 9: c, f
Excerpt 10: g
Excerpt 11: e
Excerpt 12: e

E Putting it all together

1 Answers to the first question will vary. Answers to the second question should include the coursebook (specifically the page being used to introduce the language and the grammar summary, generally found at the back of the book), the teacher's book, and reference books.

2 Answers will vary, but hopefully they will be positive!

If time permits, you may want to set up the following scenario, to help trainees research language more quickly.

> A colleague has called in sick. You are going to teach a lesson on third conditionals to upper-intermediate students in 15 minutes. You have ten minutes to find out what you can about this pattern. Complete a language analysis form with as much information as you can.

KEY WORDS FOR TEACHERS

Remind the trainees of the need to be able to use teaching terms confidently and accurately.

REFLECTION

If you are short of time, you may wish to ask trainees to focus on one or two of the statements which they feel most strongly about. It might be worth mentioning some of the following points:

Research before planning: It's useful to do at least some research before you start planning, particularly about which aspects of the language are likely to be new or familiar to the learners. Many trainees plan their lessons first, then complete the language analysis as something of an afterthought. By encouraging them to do research before or during the planning process, they may feel more confident when deciding how to approach language they are teaching. By considering the meaning/use at the beginning of the planning process, trainees can make sure they create/choose useful contexts or practice activities for the specific areas they want to focus learners' attention on in the lesson.

Vocabulary/Grammar: The basic questions in task A can also be used to research vocabulary, though the sources used may vary a little, for example looking at a good learner dictionary for definitions.

Grammar books: While grammar books are undoubtedly useful when researching language, some trainees can find them overwhelming and spend a long time trying to process the information they read. By using the coursebook and teacher's book first, and then trying to fill in gaps with a grammar book, they may find it easier to process information, and they are more likely to approach what they read in a targeted way.

Comprehensive knowledge: This is not necessary. However, teachers should always make sure they have completed all of the activities they expect their learners to do, and that they know *why* the answers are correct, not just *what* the answers are. Any extra information they find out may be useful in answering learners' questions.

Teach everything you know: The aim of this statement is to make sure that trainees can differentiate between language analysis and predicting problems, and the actual teaching which they do. It's important to focus in on the areas which learners (might) have trouble with, rather than regurgitating everything the teacher has learned about a particular grammar point or set of vocabulary.

Answer all of the learners' questions: As with 'comprehensive knowledge', the teacher should be able to answer most questions directly related to the activities which learners are doing. However, they should not be afraid to tell learners that they don't know something. At this point, a more confident teacher may choose to show learners how they can find out that information within the lesson. Otherwise, they can tell learners that they will find out. To maintain the learners' trust, it's important that the teacher remembers to follow up on these questions in a later lesson.

Possible problems: By considering problems which learners might have, teachers are more primed to notice them if they do happen in the lesson. They should also have considered ways to address those problems if they arise, meaning that they do not feel put on the spot as much as they might if they hadn't considered possible problems. This level of preparation can also build learners' trust, as they see that the teacher is prepared for problems and knows how to resolve them.

2 – Language analysis and awareness

Excerpt 1 It is helpful to consider modal verbs under the following broad headings: • 'pure' modal verbs: *I **can** swim. They **may** come.* These all have the same formal characteristics. • semi-modal verbs: *I **ought to** go now. We **have to** arrive by 6.00.* These forms are very closely related to 'pure' modal verbs in terms of meaning but may not share all of their formal characteristics. (GELT 153)	**Excerpt 2** **Formal characteristics of modal verbs** *Can, could, may, might, must, shall, should, will* and *would* are 'pure' modal verbs. They: • are not inflected in the third person: *He **must** go.* NOT **He musts go.* • are followed by the 'bare infinitive': *I must **go**.* NOT **I must to go.* • are negated by the addition of *n't* or *not*: *I can't, I can**not**.* NOT **I don't can.* • are inverted with the subject to form a question: ***Should I** do it?* • have no past form: NOT **I musted go.* (GELT 154)
Excerpt 3 *Ought* is similar to the pure modal verbs, except that we use the full infinitive (i.e. with *to* after it) rather than the bare infinitive. *You **oughtn't to cook** vegetables so long.* (GELT 154)	**Excerpt 4** **Ought to and should** The meaning of these two modal verbs is the same. *Ought to* is more common in British than American English, and more common in speaking than writing. Nonetheless, *should* is used roughly seven times more frequently than *ought to*. We choose between the two verbs partly on the basis of personal preference, and partly to avoid repetition. (GELT 157)
Excerpt 5 Some learners use *must* to express any degree or kind of obligation, and in doing so may inadvertently sound rude or dictatorial. In this case, teachers may want to 'ban' it in order to promote some of the alternatives which more often express obligation (e.g. *have to, should, ought to* and *had better*). (GELT 158)	**Excerpt 6** In most contexts, we stress some other part of the sentence, and then we 'weaken' the modal verb (i.e. we say it very fast and very softly). The vowel is often reduced to /ə/ or is practically omitted. The final consonant is also often left out, especially if the verb which follows begins with another consonant. The weak form rather than the strong form is the most neutral. (GELT 163)
Excerpt 7 In most contexts modal verbs are pronounced in a very weakened form and learners may fail to hear or identify them. (GELT 163)	**Excerpt 8** Avoidance: Many learners find other ways of expressing what they want to say, even when they understand the meaning of modal verbs and can use them appropriately and accurately in controlled exercises. […] This problem is common among speakers of Latin-based languages. (GELT 164)

Photocopiable   © Cambridge University Press & Assessment 2022

Excerpt 9	Excerpt 10
Learners often use full infinitives after pure modal verbs instead of bare infinitives. *You must to do it.* [...] Learners may over-generalize the rules for forming questions and negative statements which involve adding *do* or *did*. *She doesn't must finish it.* (GELT 164–165)	Learners may over-emphasize modal verbs in contexts where they would normally not be stressed. This may give the impression that they are contradicting something that has already been said and can lead to people misinterpreting their attitude. (GELT 165)
Excerpt 11	**Excerpt 12**
French uses forms of the single verb 'devoir' to cover the notions of obligation and deduction expressed in English by *must* and *should*. (LE 60)	There are no modal verbs in Arabic. Their function is performed by normal verbs, often impersonal, or prepositions followed by a subjunctive (present) tense: I must go: *From the necessary that I go.* / *On me that I go.* (LE 203–204)

All excerpts taken from *Grammar for English Language Teachers* (GELT), 2nd edition, or *Learner English* by Swan and Smith (LE). The page number is in brackets.

Photocopiable   © Cambridge University Press & Assessment 2022

Topic 2 – Language analysis and awareness

6 Vocabulary

Main focus
To learn principles of word formation and word meaning.

Learning outcomes
- Trainees understand the main ways that words are related in terms of meaning.
- Trainees understand the main ways that words are formed.
- Trainees can apply this knowledge to identifying the objectives of teaching activities.

Key concepts
- sense relationships: synonyms, antonyms, lexical sets
- collocation
- word formation: affixation, compounding
- multi-word units and phrasal verbs

Stage	Focus
A Warm-up	trainees experience a brainstorming task
B Lexical meaning	analysing words in a text in terms of their meaning relationships
C Word formation	identifying the main ways that words are formed in English
D Vocabulary focus	identifying the focus of coursebook activities
E Lexical difficulty	identifying sources of difficulty in understanding words
Key words for teachers	building of specialist vocabulary to talk about teaching
Reflection	applying language analysis to a selected text

A Warm-up

1–3 You can set this activity up by drawing a 'spidergram' on the board – i.e. a central hub from which several lines radiate. Write *gardening* in the centre; elicit some words as examples and then trainees brainstorm more related words, in pairs or groups. They then compare, and make connections between some of the words. The activity prepares them both for the text that follows, and for the discussion of lexical sense relations.

B Lexical meaning

1 Answers: 1–d) 2–a) 3–e) 4–b) 5–c)
2 Other examples of synonyms: *necessary, essential; lop off, cut off;* of antonyms: *stop, continue;* of collocations: *stands to reason* (*green matter* may be a collocation in some registers, but the two words do not normally co-occur with significant frequency, like, for example, *grey matter*); of word families: *transported, transportation;* of lexical sets: *food, water, minerals, sunlight, chlorophyll, nourishing* (i.e. words associated with growth); *lop off, cut off, stub, swelling, rot, decay, deadly,* etc. (words associated with ill health).

C Word formation

1 Answers: 1–b) 2–c) 3–d) 4–a)
2 This task aims to introduce trainees to phrasal verbs, but does not pretend to be exhaustive: it focuses primarily on their idiomaticity and their possible separability. At this level, it should not be necessary to go into any great detail, e.g. regarding transitive v intransitive verbs, or the obligatory separability in the case of pronoun objects. You may need to explain 'idiomatic meaning', i.e. meaning that is not the sum of the meanings of the individual components, and hence not easily inferred from them. Note that the issue of idiomaticity is a question of degree, some phrasal verbs being more idiomatic than others. Note also that the examples are restricted to phrasal verbs that share the same meaning: there are other meanings of 'set off' and 'get on', for example, that behave differently, e.g. 'to set off a fire alarm' or 'to get on a bus'. For the purposes of this activity, consider only the usage illustrated in the examples. You may want to do the first two examples with the whole class, before putting the trainees into pairs or small groups.
Answers:

Phrasal verb	Idiomatic		Syntax	
	yes	no	parts are separable	parts are not separable
set off	✓			✓
give back		✓	✓	
look after	✓			✓
get on	✓			✓
knock over		✓	✓	
make up	✓		✓	

D Vocabulary focus

1 The coursebooks target the following areas:
   a collocation, specifically words and phrases that co-occur with *make* and *do*
   b affixation, specifically prefixes which form opposites (or antonyms) of the words they are attached to
   c multi-word items, or chunks, specifically those constructed around *way*
2 The main thing to emphasize is that learners will need opportunities to practise the new items in one way or another. Activities might include:
   a gap-fill exercises, where students insert the correct choice of collocate; question-and-answer interaction, e.g. *Who does the shopping in your home?*
   b peer testing; writing a text to include as many of the negative adjectives
   c dictionary work to find more examples; dialogue writing to include as many of the phrases as possible.

2 – Language analysis and awareness

E Lexical difficulty

1 As preparation for this exercise, it might be helpful to brainstorm some of the factors that make a word difficult or easy to understand. These might include: low frequency (hence lack of prior exposure); idiomaticity, e.g. when a word is being used figuratively, or when the meaning of a chunk cannot be easily inferred from its components; insufficient clues in the context; absence of a similar word (known as a cognate) in the learner's L1.

- *bark:* difficult – there are minimal contextual clues, and there is the possibility of it being confused with its homonym, i.e. the sound a dog makes
- *chlorophyll:* moderately easy – although it is a low frequency and specialized term, it is likely to be similar in the learners' L1, and also it is glossed in the text (*green matter*)
- *lop off:* moderately difficult – a low frequency and somewhat informal phrasal verb but sufficient context to infer an approximate meaning
- *parent:* moderately easy – the word will be familiar to most learners in its literal sense, although not necessarily when used figuratively, as here
- *pruning:* difficult – low frequency, specialist word, insufficient context information, especially on the first occurrence
- *stub:* moderately difficult – low frequency, although the cumulative effect of four occurrences should help understanding
- *sunlight:* easy – easily deducible from its high-frequency component parts

2–3 Words that are essential to even a superficial understanding of the text are *pruning* and *branch(es)*. Most other words that are necessary to understanding the gist of the text can be worked out from context, but it may help to elicit the parts of a tree in advance of reading.

KEY WORDS FOR TEACHERS
Use the key words to review some of the main 'takeaways' from the session.

REFLECTION
Coursebook texts may already have a vocabulary focus, but – as this unit has tried to demonstrate – there is often more lexical 'potential' in a text than space typically allows. So you should encourage trainees to look for other, possibly less salient, features of the lexical content of the text, e.g. compounds, affixation, phrasal verbs, chunks, etc.

7 Teaching vocabulary

Main focus
To give a variety of ways of teaching the meaning, form and use of new lexical items.

Learning outcomes
- Trainees understand some ways of conveying the form and meaning of new lexical items.
- Trainees understand the importance of context in word choice and how context can impact on meaning.
- Trainees are able to analyse vocabulary practice activities.

Key concepts
- word knowledge: meaning, form, use; spoken and written form
- conveying meaning: visual aids, realia, mime, demonstration, definition
- recycling of items
- eliciting
- checking understanding; concept checking

Stage	Focus
A Warm-up	introducing the topic
B Meaning, form and use	focusing on meaning form and use, as applied to vocabulary
C Presenting techniques	introducing ways of presenting vocabulary
D Eliciting vocabulary	summarizing basic principles for eliciting new language
E Checking understanding	introducing concept-checking questions
F Practising techniques	introducing some simple ways of practising vocabulary
Key words for teachers	building of specialist vocabulary to talk about teaching
Reflection	trainees reflect on what they have learned by planning a short vocabulary activity

A Warm-up

Allow the trainees a little time to think about the two questions before discussing them in groups and briefly reporting back to the class. For question 1, it is likely that most members of the group will choose 'words and phrases'. This can be exploited to demonstrate that people instinctively value vocabulary linked by topic, and also 'chunks' of language which go beyond single words and have an immediate communicative value. The quote from David Wilkins also highlights how important vocabulary is to communication.

2 – Language analysis and awareness

B Meaning, form and use

1 Here is an example from Vietnamese: *bạn bè* (= friend). However, you could substitute this for a word from another language you know. The aim is to give trainees a focus as they think about the different aspects of word knowledge.

Write the trainees' suggestions on the board as they make them. When they have finished, introduce the concepts of meaning, form and use. The trainees could then say which of their suggestions apply to each category.

2 Learners will always need to know something about form (and generally both written and spoken form). They will always need to know about meaning.

Other information about the word may not always be necessary, but teachers should consider issues such as:
- common collocations (e.g. the word *traffic* collocates with *heavy* – *heavy traffic*.)
- connotation (part of meaning)
- part of speech / word class
- grammatical information (e.g. whether a verb requires an object)
- formality

The level of detail of information required may depend on the lexical item and whether it is likely to be used productively or solely for receptive purposes. Some of the additional information may be picked up automatically if the learners have frequent encounters with the new word.

3 The teaching implications of the above might include:
- it is not enough to teach just the form of the word, or just its meaning
- teaching for production (i.e. speaking and writing) involves more steps than teaching simply for recognition
- to teach all aspects of a word's form, meaning and use can be quite a lengthy process; this means that, given the number of words that learners need, some of the work of vocabulary learning has to be entrusted to them, e.g. through extensive reading, learner training, etc.

C Presenting techniques

1 The aim of this section is to give trainees a very simple summary of some of the options they have when teaching vocabulary. You may prefer to demonstrate some or all of the techniques by briefly 'teaching' the trainees a few words, as if they were learners of English. This would probably make the techniques more memorable. In any case, ensure that the trainees understand what the techniques involve before completing the final column. Techniques 1–4 focus on meaning, 5–7 on form and 8–9 on use (although arguably the piece of authentic communication might be used in a variety of ways).

2 Answers will vary.

3 If time is short, you could divide the class into groups and they each look at one or two sets of words. The key point to note is that some items might lend themselves to one presentation technique more than another. Concrete nouns will lend themselves to using visuals of some sort (Group 1). Physical actions might be mimed (Group 2). However, for more abstract concepts, such as those in Group 4, definitions might be preferable. In the reporting back stage, you could select some specific examples from the list and elicit alternative ways in which the items could be taught.

7 Teaching vocabulary

D Eliciting vocabulary

1 Allow the trainees a few minutes to discuss their ideas in small groups before comparing with you.
   a not good advice – eliciting needs to be done quickly and efficiently or it will slow the lesson down too much. The prompts should be as transparent and as clear as possible.
   b good advice – finding the right prompt can be difficult for inexperienced teachers when they are under pressure in a lesson
   c good advice – perhaps the single most important piece here
   d not good advice – you cannot elicit something which is unknown
   e good advice – this often 'triggers' the word for learners, but in line with c), above, it should not be allowed to slow the lesson

2 You could replace these words with ones that are likely to occur in teaching practice over the next few sessions.
   Allow the trainees a few minutes to discuss their ideas in small groups before comparing with you.
   a a watch (noun) – the teacher could point to his/her own watch and ask 'What's this?'
   b a game show – through a definition – a type of television programme where ordinary people answer questions and do things to win prizes. Or perhaps through examples, if there are suitable ones familiar to the whole group.
   c a hurricane – through a definition or through a picture
   All of these could be potentially elicited through translation. For example, 'In Spanish it's *'un huracan'*.

3 The point of this exercise is to stress the need for trainees to avoid obsessing over elicitation. As teachers, it is perfectly acceptable to tell the learners what words mean. The missing words are: *involve, giving, elicit, quickly, prepared, guessing*.

E Checking understanding

1 Allow the trainees some time to discuss the techniques before discussing them in open class. You may wish to point out the following:
   a Translation: fairly quick and in some ways efficient – it relies on the teacher having a fairly expert knowledge of both languages and also assumes that the class shares a common language. It may encourage learners to see words as having direct equivalents in other languages and this is not always the case.
   b Teacher monitoring: as long as learners get plenty of opportunities to practise using the new language, this may be all that is necessary. In this way more time can be devoted to meaningful practice, which is likely to be more beneficial.
   c 'Do you understand?': learners may be embarrassed about saying that they do not understand – or they may genuinely think that they do understand (in the case of 'false friends', for example) and therefore not get the clarification they need.
   d Example sentence: this can be effective, as long as learners think of sentences that actually do give some demonstration of meaning. It is easy to think of sentences that do not demonstrate this. For example, 'the teacher just asked me to use the word *pogo* in a sentence'.
   e Short, easy-to-answer questions: can be useful as long as they are well-designed and appropriate. See below for details.

2 – Language analysis and awareness

2 Answers:
   i   The teacher asks the questions in order to check understanding.
   ii   a) No b) Yes
   iii The answers are short and easy for the learners to give, if they understand the word being checked.
3 Trainees could work in small groups to think about the language and to prepare appropriate questions.
   Questions may vary, but sample ones are given below.
   1 Do you use a briefcase for work or for holidays? (work)
   2 Do you put clothes in a briefcase? (no)
   3 Was the car badly damaged or a bit damaged? (badly) Could it be repaired? (no)
   4 Is there a coast between countries? (no) Do all countries have coasts? (no) Do islands have coasts? (yes)
4 Asking such questions is particularly useful if the teacher judges that there is a high risk of learners misunderstanding, as in the case of so called 'false friends'. Arguments might also be made for using these questions when the stakes are very high (such as when teaching English for air traffic control or medical purposes).
   It is probably not worth taking up too much time with such questions when any misunderstanding will be revealed in subsequent activities. Also, if the meaning is very obvious (imagine the word *apple* being taught through the use of a picture), there is little point in using valuable time.

F Practising techniques

1 Start by emphasizing the need to provide practice opportunities for new language items, including vocabulary. Where vocabulary is taught before a reading or listening text, the practice might be considered to be the encounter with the word in the text.
   Allow the trainees to discuss the practice activities in small groups before conducting class feedback. All the activities are intended as relevant and useful. The key point is that trainees appreciate the need to provide practice activities. Some, such as the discussion (1), are more communicative than others and some activities may draw on different skills (reading and writing versus speaking and listening, for example).
   Activity 5 draws attention to the need for new vocabulary to be recycled over time, as this will help the learners remember the new items.
2 Trainees work in groups. You may wish to assign each group a set of words to work on. Encourage trainees to provide more than one type of practice activity where they can.

KEY WORDS FOR TEACHERS

Remind the trainees of the need to be able to use teaching terms confidently and accurately.

REFLECTION

Put the trainees into groups and allow them time to prepare their responses. Remind them that they are not limited to individual words and that they can include collocations and phrases. Encourage them to plan in as much detail as possible. When the groups have had a chance to plan, invite them to report back. Or, if time allows, they could briefly 'teach' the lessons to the other groups.

8 The sounds of English

Main focus
To learn how English sounds are classified, described and represented.

Learning outcomes
- Trainees understand the difference between (spoken) sounds and (written) letters.
- Trainees are able to read and write phonemic transcription of consonant and vowel sounds.
- Trainees are aware that different languages have different phonological systems.
- Trainees understand the principle behind minimal pairs activities.

Key concepts
- phoneme: vowel, schwa, monophthong, diphthong; consonant
- phonemic script
- minimal pairs
- contrastive analysis

Stage	Focus
A Warm-up	experiencing an activity focusing on sound discrimination
B Sounds v letters	focusing on the difference between letters (graphemes) and sounds (phonemes)
C Consonant sounds	introducing and practising the way consonant sounds are represented
D Vowel sounds	introducing and practising the way vowel sounds are represented
E Contrasting languages	comparing the phonology of two languages and using a minimal pairs activity
F Review	a quiz of some of the main content of the session
Key words for teachers	building of specialist vocabulary to talk about teaching
Reflection	comparing trainees' accents with a standard, and considering implications for teaching

A Warm-up

1 Write the following names on cards, or photocopy and cut up the table. Distribute the cards so that each trainee has one. If there are more than 20 trainees, you may have to invent more names, e.g. *Joan Bird, Jean Bird*, etc. Tell the trainees that these are their 'new names', that they should memorize them, and keep them secret. Then 'call the class register', i.e. call out names randomly; when the trainees hear their 'name', they answer 'Present'. In the event that more than one trainee answers to the name, call it out again until the problem is resolved.

2 – Language analysis and awareness

1 Jan Bird	2 Jan Baird	3 Jan Burt	4 Jan Beard
5 Jon Bird	6 Jon Baird	7 Jon Burt	8 Jon Beard
9 Jen Bird	10 Jen Baird	11 Jen Burt	12 Jen Beard
13 Jim Bird	14 Jim Baird	15 Jim Burt	16 Jim Beard
17 Jem Bird	18 Jem Baird	19 Jem Burt	20 Jem Beard

Photocopiable © Cambridge University Press & Assessment 2022

If you are working online, display all the names, call out the names randomly and, using the chat window, the trainees write the number of the name they hear.

2 a In discussing this activity, point out that while trainees may find the activity unproblematic, learners are more likely to fail to discriminate many of these names, since they may not share the same sound differences in their first language.
  b The language targets the phonological system of English (as opposed to the grammar or vocabulary systems, for example) and, specifically, the pronunciation of individual sounds, especially vowels, as well as the way some consonant sounds are 'assimilated' into adjacent sounds, e.g. *Jen Baird* can sound like *Jem Baird*.

B Sounds v letters

1 Dictate the following words: *letter, sound, vowel, consonant, phoneme*.
2 Note that *phoneme* is the technical term for a sound, and specifically one that makes a difference in meaning, such as the *–ir-* sound in *bird*, and the *–ear-* sound in *beard*.
3 Answers:

Word	Number of letters	Number of sounds*
letter	six	four (/letə/ or /lɛtɚ/)
sound	five	four (/saʊnd/)**
vowel	five	four (/vaʊəl/)**
consonant	nine	nine (kɒnsənənt/ or /kɑːnsənənt/
phoneme	seven	five (/fəʊniːm/ or /foʊniːm/)***

*BrE and AmE respectively, where there is a difference
** /aʊ/ is a diphthong (see below)
*** /əʊ/ and /oʊ/ are also diphthongs

Point out that, depending on your regional accent, you may not pronounce the word identically to other speakers, and that the above transcriptions are only a guide.
4 Establish the fact that there is no one-to-one match between letters and sounds in English. In focusing on pronunciation, it is important to distinguish between the way words are written and the way they are actually pronounced.

C Consonant sounds

1 Make sure that trainees know that consonant sounds are formed when the airflow from the lungs is obstructed by the moveable parts of the mouth, including the tongue and lips. At this stage of their training, it is probably unnecessary for trainees to know the terminology

for describing the manner and place of consonant production (such as *bilabial plosive, palato-alveolar fricative*, etc.), since this terminology is rarely if ever used in teaching materials. It is sufficient to know that consonant sounds are produced at various points in the mouth, from the lips to the soft palate – and beyond.

/m/ at the lips (bilabial)
/v/ at the teeth and lips (labiodental)
/n/ at the tooth ridge (alveolar)
/t/ behind the tooth ridge (post-alveolar)
/r/ at the hard palate (palatal)
/k/ at the soft palate (velar)

2 Answers:
1 met; 2 deck; 3 then; 4 hedge; 5 breath; 6 fetch; 7 next; 8 yet; 9 shred; 10 shrink
Point out that, in these examples, the vowels are either written /e/ (as in *ten*) or /ɪ/ (as in (*tin*)). Note that it is customary to write phonemic symbols within slashes.

3 Answers:
a /sent/ b /edʒ/ c /θɪn/ d /θɪŋ/ e /θɪŋk/ f /ðɪs/ g /fɪkst/ h /dʒest/ i /jeld/ j /stretʃt/
You may wish to distribute different words to pairs/small groups, to save time. Nominate representatives from each group to write the transcriptions on the board.

D Vowel sounds

1 Let the trainees explore the changes in tongue, lip and jaw position individually and then compare in pairs. Point out that in performing this activity they have done a 'guided tour' of what is called the 'vowel space', i.e. the area of the interior of the mouth delimited by the tongue's highest and lowest points, and its most forward and back positions. If you wish, you can visualize the vowel space in this way:

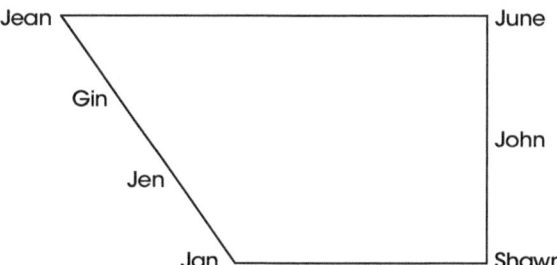

Thus the vowel in *Jean* is produced with the tongue close to the roof of the mouth and maximally forward, without actually being in contact with any other part of the mouth. By contrast, the vowel in *Shawn* is produced with the tongue set low and back. Note that in American English, the vowel in *John* and *Shawn* is the same: /ɑː/. The movement of the lips can be described in terms of spreading (*Jean, Jan*) and rounding (*June, John*). Again, it is not necessary, at this level of training, to go into any more detail as to the precise features of the individual vowels.

The system of phonemic transcription that we have adopted is the one that is used in the *Cambridge Advanced Learner's Dictionary*, Cambridge University Press, 2005. While the conventions for transcribing British English (known as RP, or Received Pronunciation) are

2 – Language analysis and awareness

well established, the American system of transcription is less standardized. Many learners' dictionaries, such as the *Cambridge International Dictionary of English,* include transcriptions of words in American, as well as British, English. Trainees who speak other varieties of English will need to be aware that their accent will not always match these conventions.

You may also wish to point out:

1 that the vowel sounds followed by the sign ː, i.e. /iː/, /ɑː/, /ɔː/, /uː/ and /ɜː/, are known as *long vowels,* in contrast to the *short vowel* sounds, which are not so marked
2 that the vowel sound /ə/ (*schwa*) is the unstressed, neutral vowel sound at the end of words like *sister,* for example, or at the beginning of words like *ago*
3 that the symbols /ɚ/ and /ɝ/ represent the 'r-colouring' of most American accents, i.e. that the vowels /ə/ and /ɜ/ in words like *father* and *bird* respectively are modified by the /r/ that follows them, which is not the case in RP, where the /r/ in such words is not articulated
4 that standard American uses vowel + /r/ combinations for the three British English diphthongs represented in the words *dear, sure* and *fair,* i.e. /dɪr/, /**ʃur**/, and /fer/

2 Answers:
a *Batman* b *King Kong* c *Airplane* d *Jaws* e *The Birds* f *Psycho* g *Pulp Fiction* h *Vertigo* i *The Shining* j *Jaws 2*

3 Answers:
British English: a /ʃrek/ b /ben hɛː/ c /snætʃ/ d /stɑː wɔːz/ e /haɪ nuːn/ f /bleɪd rʌnə/ g /məmentəʊ/ h /mɪstɪk rɪvə/
American English: a /ʃrek/ b /ben hɝː/ c /snætʃ/ d /stɑːr wɔːrz/ e /haɪ nuːn/ f /bleɪd rʌnɚ/ g /məmentoʊ/ h /mɪstɪk rɪvɚ/

4 Check the trainees' transcriptions, especially where they are likely to be negatively influenced by the spelling of a word. Allow for some variability, according to individual accents. Check, also, that the *schwa* sound is being transcribed correctly.

E Contrasting languages

In this section Thai has been chosen to contrast with English, since it has a significantly different sound system, but you may prefer to choose a language that is more relevant to your training context – in which case you will need to change the paired examples accordingly. Note that in both charts, International Phonetic Alphabet (IPA) symbols have been used: the Thai symbols are *not* letters of the Thai alphabet. Technical terms (alveolar, fricative, etc.) have been simplified or removed entirely.

1 You should do the first two or three examples with the class. Remind trainees that the difficulties are those that a speaker of Thai would encounter when learning English, not those that a speaker of English would encounter learning Thai – such as the aspirated plosive (or stop) sounds /pʰ/, /tʰ/, and /kʰ/ or the 'pre-palatal affricates' /tɕ/ and /tɕʰ/, none of which are phonemic distinctions in English.
   a pat v bat: this should not be a problem, as a similar distinction exists in Thai.
   b fan v van: the /f/ v /v/ distinction does not exist in Thai, so this might be a problem.
   c right v light: Thai has both an /l/ and a /r/ equivalent, so this should not be a problem.
   d mess v mesh: Thai does not have an /s/ v /ʃ/ distinction, so this is likely to be a problem.
   e sin v sing: not a problem.

f latter v ladder: not a problem.
   g back v bag: Thai does not have a similar distinction, so this could be a problem.
   h sigh v thigh: Thai has no /θ/ sound, so this may be a problem.
2 The extract targets the /s/ v /θ/ distinction.
3 The activity is a classic 'minimal pairs' activity, in which a contrast is made between two sounds that make a difference in meaning in English but which might not make a difference in the learners' language.
   a The teacher can voice the two sounds, first in a word, and then in isolation, while matching each with its corresponding picture (e.g. mouse v mouth), and exaggerating the way the sounds are articulated; cross-sectional diagrams of the mouth could also be used to illustrate the different settings of tongue and teeth.
   b Sound discrimination can be tested by saying different words from the set, either in isolation or in the sentence context, and the learners circle, or point to, the one they hear – or point to its associated symbol on one side of the board or another.
   c Production might involve students repeating the sounds after the teacher (or a recorded model); producing the sound in response to the teacher pointing at a picture from the set; and then testing each other, in pairs, as in stage b above.

F Review

This activity could be set as a kind of race, with trainees competing in small groups to be the first to produce all the correct answers.
   a 26
   b RP: 44 (24 consonants + 20 vowels); General American 40 (24 +16)
   c *thought* = 3; *six* = 4; *coaching* = 5
   d At least five in RP: /ɔ:/ as in *tall*, /æ/ as in *cat*, /eɪ/ as in *ate*, and /ə/ and /ɑ:/ as in *banana* (/bənɑ:nə/). Four in American (*tall* = /tɑ:l/).
   e Consonants are produced by interrupting or obstructing the airflow; for vowels, the airflow is simply modified, but not interrupted.
   f /s/ is voiceless; /z/ is voiced
   g *schwa*
   h /ɪ/ is a monophthong, while /aɪ/ is a diphthong.
   i /z/
   j /ɜ:/ or /ɝ/
   k True (Shakespeare wrote *Macbeth*)
   l False (New York is *not* in Texas)

2 – Language analysis and awareness

KEY WORDS FOR TEACHERS

Use the key words to review some of the main 'takeaways' from the session.

REFLECTION

1. This activity could be set as a homework task, where trainees research information online about the pronunciation of their own variety of English, and share this in a subsequent session. Obviously, this may include non-native varieties, as well as native. Note that many of the differences between a speaker's accent and the RP or General American (GA) descriptors are likely to be *phonetic* rather than *phonemic*. That is, they will be different realizations of the same contrasts: the pronunciation is different but the meaning is not affected. For example, in Scottish English:
   - the vowel in *boat* is articulated as the monophthong /o/, not the diphthong /əʊ/ as in RP. Nevertheless, the phonemic contrasts between *boat* and *boot*, or *coat* and *cot*, are still maintained, so the differences are phonetic, not phonemic.
   - Likewise, because Scottish English is 'r-coloured', the RP diphthong /iə/ as in *beer* is realized as a monophthong + /r/: /ir/. But the meaningful distinction between *beer* and *bear* is still present: again the differences in pronunciation are phonetic, not phonemic.
   - On the other hand, in most varieties of Scottish English the phonemic contrast between /æ/ and /ɑ:/ does not exist, so that *Pam* and *palm* are pronounced the same.
   - Likewise, the RP distinction between /ʊ/ and /u:/ does not exist, so that *look* and *Luke* are not distinguishable: these differences are phonemic.
2. It is important to emphasize that, with regard to teaching, there is no disadvantage in *not* being an RP or GA speaker – even where learners themselves might aspire to speak one of these varieties. In other words, there is no reason that teachers should attempt to adapt their own accent accordingly. At the same time, and regardless of the variety of English the teacher speaks, it is generally useful for learners to be exposed to as wide a variety of English accents as is practicable, from both English and non-English L1 speakers. The teacher can draw learners' attention to any significant differences between the accents of different speakers.

9 Stress, rhythm and intonation

Main focus
To learn how suprasegmental features of pronunciation (such as stress, rhythm and intonation) influence meaning and intelligibility.

Learning outcomes
- Trainees understand the basic mechanics of stress, rhythm and intonation.
- Trainees understand how stress, rhythm and intonation influence meaning.
- Trainees understand how these principles can be incorporated into the design of classroom materials and activities.

Key concepts
- word stress, syllable
- sentence stress
- new v given information
- strong and weak forms
- rhythm
- intonation, pitch
- grammatical, attitudinal functions of intonation

Stage	Focus
A Warm-up	experiencing communication using only intonation
B Stress	working out some regularities in word stress placement, and learning how sentence stress distinguishes between given and new information
C Rhythm	learning how low-information words are accommodated into the rhythm of an utterance, including the distinction between strong and weak forms
D Intonation	distinguishing between the grammatical and attitudinal functions of intonation
Key words for teachers	building of specialist vocabulary to talk about teaching
Reflection	discussing the relative importance, and ease, of teaching segmental and suprasegmental features

A Warm-up

In setting this activity up, it may help to write the following on the board:
A: Well
B: Well
A: Well
B: Well

2 – Language analysis and awareness

A: Well
B: Well

Challenge trainees to imagine a conversation consisting of only these words. Then ask them to read the instructions in their book.

This activity demonstrates how much meaning can be conveyed by means of intonation alone. It is worth pointing out, though, that the kinds of meaning that are conveyed are fairly limited and that they are also reinforced by facial expression, gesture and voice quality. Most students would have little trouble doing this activity, assuming they understood the words of the paraphrased dialogue, and that they were relatively uninhibited. Attitudinal features of intonation – such as expressing uncertainty or surprise – are probably universal.

B Stress

1 This activity demonstrates that word stress in English, while not 100% regular, is generally fairly predictable. Proficient speakers are able to assign stress correctly, not because they know the rules (which are complex), but because of their previous encounters with similar words. Some general tendencies that can be extracted from these examples are:
   - In two-syllable words the stress tends to be on the first syllable, especially where the second syllable is a suffix (**paw**ler, **ved**dish, **mal**mer).
   - Polysyllabic words tend to be stressed on the antepenultimate syllable, i.e. the third-to-last: **pan**diful, **loom**itive, **im**belist.
   - However certain suffixes, such as –ic, -tion, 'attract' the stress. The stress falls on the penultimate syllable: loo**mi**tion, imbe**lis**tic.
   - This accounts for stress shift in word families: **ge**on, geo**net**ics, etc.

   You could ask trainees to think of real word examples for these different tendencies.

2 a Check that trainees have correctly identified the main stress in the words they have selected.

   b Techniques for highlighting word stress include:
   - providing a clear, even exaggerated, model
   - asking learners, *'Where's the stress?'*
   - 'finger-coding', i.e. using the fingers of one hand to represent the syllable structure of the word, and drawing attention to the stressed syllable
   - drilling the word
   - tapping out the stress pattern, humming it, or using any other non-linguistic way to show the pattern, such as using different coloured Cuisenaire rods
   - writing the word on the board with an indicator of prominence, e.g. a small box, above the stressed syllable
   - grouping words with the same stress pattern together

3 a Answers:
   i Don't worry | be **hap**py.
   ii You win some | and you **lose** some.
   iii You can run | but you can't **hide**.
   iv It's not what you know | it's **who** you know.
   v Don't just stand there | **do** something.
   vi The bigger they are | the harder they **fall**.
   vii Two steps forward | one step **back**.
   viii You scratch my back | and I'll scratch **yours**.

9 Stress, rhythm and intonation

b   Utterance stress (unlike word stress) is variable, and can shift according to the speaker's assessment of what the listener needs to focus on. As a general rule, *new* information – as opposed to *given information* – is stressed, as in examples like this, where an explicit contrast is indicated. Note that this is a particularly difficult skill for many learners to master, since – in many languages – sentence stress plays a less influential role in distinguishing new information than does word order, for example.

4   The exercise focuses on the way that speakers' choice of utterance stress indicates what they consider the new (hence important) information. If trainees are in doubt as to the meaning of stress shift, set up an exchange between yourself and a trainee of the type:
A: *Where do you LIVE?*
B: *In X. Where do YOU live?*

C Rhythm

1   Point out that this is another example of a classroom activity that trainees could do with their students. The object is to maintain the same rhythm, stressing the high-information words, while *accommodating* intervening syllables by reducing them in different ways. These ways include the use of *contractions* (*should've*) and of *weak forms*, e.g. /ʃəd/ rather than /ʃʊd/. The 'squeezing' and 'swallowing' of the low-information words can be a problem for students when listening, as these words are difficult to perceive. And failure to use weak forms and contractions can make their spoken language sound stilted, while failure to stress the high-information words can make their message difficult to unpack.

You could point out that English is sometimes classified as a *stress-timed* language, i.e. one where the stressed syllables occur at regular intervals, so that intervening syllables are accommodated to fit the rhythm. This contrasts with *syllable-timed* languages (like Spanish or Chinese) where the syllables are given approximately the same length. (This distinction has been challenged by some theorists, who argue that stress timing only occurs under certain conditions, and is not generally perceptible in normal speech).

2   The activity focuses on the difference between *strong forms* and *weak forms*, a distinction that affects most of the common *function words* in English – such as auxiliary verbs, determiners, prepositions and conjunctions. The use of weak forms is an important factor in achieving a native-like *rhythm* (see above).

This may be an opportunity to remind trainees that there can be discrepancies between speech as spoken and speech when written down (through phenomena such as the use of weak forms, assimilation, elision and catenation in speech), causing learners problems in comprehension. Playing recordings of authentic speech, e.g. taken from the internet, and comparing these with transcriptions is one way of raising awareness about this issue.

D Intonation

Note that this section on intonation deliberately avoids a detailed discussion of the different pitch direction and pitch span distinctions that are often related to differences in grammatical meaning, since most trainees (and students) find these difficult to perceive. Nor does it discuss the *discoursal function* of intonation, i.e. the role of intonation in the management of talk, since this is seldom if ever represented in teaching materials. For a more detailed analysis, see *English Phonetics and Phonology* (3rd edition), by Peter Roach (Cambridge University Press, 2000).

2 – Language analysis and awareness

1 Note: Punctuation has been purposefully removed, in order to allow different possible intonation patterns. If trainees are having difficulty coming up with alternative expressions of these sentences, you can model them yourself. These are the possible variants (| = a tone unit division):
   a 1 | The people who left suddenly | started running |
     2 | The people who left | suddenly started running |
   b 1 |When shall we eat grandma?|
     2 |When shall we eat,| Grandma?|
   c 1 |The mouse,| which ate the cheese,| escaped.|
     2 |The mouse which ate the cheese| escaped.|
   d 1 |He's a nurse.|
     2 |He's a nurse?|
   e 1 |Sigrid is not Swedish,| is she?| ↑
     2 |Sigrid is not Swedish,| is she?| ↓
   f 1 |I'll have it with ham↑| basil, ↑| olives, ↑| pineapple … ↑|
     2 |I'll have it with ham, ↑| basil, ↑| olives, ↑| pineapple. ↓|
   g 1 |Hi!!!!| (with broad pitch span)
     2 |Hi.| (with narrow pitch span)
   h 1 |Thanks a million!!!| (with broad pitch span)
     2 |Thanks a million.| (with narrow pitch span)

2 The objective of this activity is to highlight the *grammatical* and *attitudinal* roles of intonation. The grammatical role includes the way that intonation serves to 'package' information by segmenting utterances into *tone groups*, as in the example about Chinese opera, and in the utterances (a), (b), and (c). Utterances (d) and (e) can be used to show how intonation helps distinguish between statements and questions, including question tags (e) – another grammatical function. Utterance (f) can be used to show the distinction between *completion* (falling tone on the last word) or *incompletion* (rising tone), as in lists. It is the example that most closely represents the discoursal function of intonation. Finally, examples (g) and (h) can be expressed in a variety of different ways to convey the speaker's attitude, ranging from *high involvement* (using a broad pitch span and high *key*) or *low involvement* (the opposite). Intonation helps to package information, and to make distinctions between statements and questions, certainty/uncertainty, completion/incompletion, and high and low involvement. Arguably, failure to use intonation in these ways can distort the speaker's message and lead to misunderstandings, as well as threatening interpersonal communication, such as when speakers seem to be conveying low involvement (but for a contrary opinion, see the J.C. Wells quote in the panel).

3 The exercise focuses on the empathetic use of falling intonation in question tags to signal agreement. The activity that is missing, and which would prepare students to do the interactive task, is a 'read aloud' task, where they read a number of sentences, attempting to apply the appropriate intonation to the question tag. Point out the gap-fill activity is purely grammatical and doesn't involve intonation, and that the dialogue activity is freer than the one that follows, but might usefully be included at a later stage.

9 Stress, rhythm and intonation

KEY WORDS FOR TEACHERS
Use the key words to review some of the main 'takeaways' from the session.

REFLECTION
Points to emerge from this discussion are:
1 There is still some debate as to which features of pronunciation are critical in ensuring communication, a current view being that suprasegmental features, such as stress and rhythm, are more important than segmental features, such as the pronunciation of individual phonemes. However, the issue is complicated by the fact that few, if any, features operate in isolation (so it is difficult to single out what exactly has caused a communication breakdown), and also the fact that such variables as the *listener's* proficiency, previous exposure, and first language, also play a role.
Given that many English users need English to interact, not with native speakers, but with other non-native speakers, the goals of pronunciation teaching are in the process of being re-defined. Research suggests that – for successful communication between non-native speakers – features such as the pronunciation of individual vowel sounds and intonation are less critical than consonant sounds and the correct placement of sentence stress. However, what is clear is that the majority of learners are better served by aiming for 'comfortable intelligibility' when they speak, rather than aiming to sound like a native speaker.
2 'Learnability' will be influenced by factors such as the learner's L1, and the amount of natural exposure they get, but most (adult) learners always have difficulty mastering the full range of English vowel sounds, using intonation in a native-like way, mastering a stress-timed rhythm, and placing stress correctly in sentences. Perhaps the 'easiest' area is word stress, since learners steadily accumulate exemplars (rather than rules) through exposure and practice.

Topic 2 – Language analysis and awareness

10 Teaching pronunciation

Main focus
To explore a variety of techniques and activities for teaching different features of pronunciation and consider when it might be appropriate to use them.

Learning outcomes
- Trainees review principles and issues of pronunciation teaching.
- Trainees are aware of how these principles are realized in teaching activities.
- Trainees know how to integrate pronunciation teaching into their classes.

Key concepts
- intelligibility
- reception v production
- standard (British/American/etc.) English
- English as a Lingua Franca / English as an International Language
- contextualized v decontextualized

Stage	Focus
A Warm-up	considering issues related to the teaching of pronunciation
B Pronunciation activities	identifying the objective of a range of activities, and evaluating them
C Techniques for teaching pronunciation	considering at what stages in a lesson a teacher might focus on pronunciation, and how they can do this
D Anticipating problems	identifying typical problems associated with some common language areas and designing a teaching strategy
E Planning pronunciation work	identifying areas of pronunciation teaching that could be integrated into activity sequences
Key words for teachers	building of specialist vocabulary to talk about teaching
Reflection	recapping key points from the session and considering how to apply them to trainees' own teaching

A Warm-up

1 You may decide to allocate one area to each pair or group of trainees. The following points could be mentioned:

| Speaking | Non-standard pronunciation may compromise intelligibility, or, in the case of intonation, convey an inappropriate attitude. |
| | Learners who know they have a strong L1 accent may be unwilling to communicate. |

Listening	Learners unfamiliar with the sound distinctions in English may confuse words (e.g. *heat/hit*).
	The way fluent speech is articulated does not always correspond to its written forms, and, along with its speed, can cause processing overload and incomprehension.
Reading	Sound-spelling relationships are not always transparent in English. Learners may fail to recognize the written form of words which they know the spoken form of.
	As we read, we sometimes sound out words or phrases to help us understand or we hear them in our heads. This can be more challenging for learners with pronunciation problems.
	Learners may fail to recognize the spoken form of words which they know the written form of. Along with the speed of fluent speech, this can cause processing overload and incomprehension.
Writing	Learners may spell words phonetically if they do not know spelling patterns associated with particular sounds, including transferring spelling patterns from their first language(s) at times.
	If they cannot distinguish between similar sounding words, learners may write the wrong word, for example *cap* or *cup*.
Grammar	They may not perceive sounds that indicate grammatical distinctions, such as the difference between *I can help you / I can't help you*; *I go there a lot / I'd go there a lot*.
Vocabulary	As with reading and writing, learners may not be able to connect the spoken and written forms of vocabulary to each other; they may not realize that they are reading or hearing a word which they are already familiar with.
	Being able to pronounce a word as well as read it provides an extra way for the brain to process it, and therefore increases the chance that learners will remember it.

2 The following points should be made:
   a Standard British or American English is the most common model used in coursebooks and dictionaries, but their status has been challenged on the grounds that they do not represent the majority of English accents, and, more importantly, because for learners who are learning English as an International Language (EIL) / English as Lingua Franca (ELF), it may be an inappropriate model. Nevertheless, in the absence of a viable alternative, it is likely to remain the dominant model. This does not necessarily mean, though, that teachers should adopt standard British or American English for teaching purposes.
   b The prioritizing of intelligibility over accuracy is associated with the communicative approach. Given that few adult learners will achieve native-like pronunciation (or may even want or need to), 'comfortable intelligibility' may be a more appropriate goal. It is also more realistic, as there are some features of pronunciation (such as intonation and the pronunciation of individual sounds) that are considered resistant to instruction.

2 – Language analysis and awareness

c As can be seen from A1, pronunciation can have on impact on all areas of a learners' English. Pronunciation is therefore not purely a matter of learners being able to say things correctly, but also being able to hear them accurately, knowing how to respond to what they hear appropriately, and understanding the relationship between spoken and written forms of English.

d Problems with pronunciation may cause communication breakdowns in a range of ways. Using the incorrect stress pattern may mean that the listener can't understand the intended meaning. Failure to differentiate sound distinctions in English that don't exist in the speaker's L1 (e.g. /l/, /r/) can cause words to be misunderstood. While some of these can be resolved according to the context, they can cause an interruption in successful communication. Moreover, a marked L1 accent can convey a negative impression of the speaker's fluency, especially in EFL and ESL contexts, although it is of arguably less importance in EIL/ELF contexts.

B Pronunciation exercises

1 To start this task, it may be a good idea to discuss the first activity in open class, before organizing the class into pairs or groups to continue.

A This is a receptive activity, focusing on a 'small' (i.e. segmental) and decontextualized feature of pronunciation. It is not communicative at all, since there is no interaction and nothing is being communicated. It would be difficult to make it more communicative, since the feature in question has little effect on intelligibility.

B This is another receptive activity, and focuses on the relationship between sound and spelling; there is neither context nor communication. The activity could possibly be made more meaningful (if not more communicative) if the cards showed pictures of the items, rather than the words, where possible.

C This is a productive activity focusing on the attitudinal use of intonation, and it is (minimally) contextualized and communicative.

D This is a productive activity, and the focus will vary according to the errors the students make; it is highly contextualized and communicative (although if the teacher corrects *all* errors they hear, rather than only those that threaten intelligibility, it may cease to be communicative, and just become an exercise in 'getting it right').

2 In evaluating these activities, trainees should be allowed to express their subjective opinions: some may like the game-type element of, say, (B), while others may find the constant correction in (D) off-putting. Nevertheless, the issues of *context* and *communicativeness* (highlighted in the previous task) offer criteria by which these activities can be judged more objectively. Also, activities that are *only* receptive may have limited usefulness in terms of improving learners' pronunciation. Note that activity (D) (correcting during speaking activities) is an example of *reactive* (as opposed to *pre-emptive)* teaching, and some researchers argue that it is more effective.

C Techniques for teaching pronunciation

1 The aim of this activity is to highlight that pronunciation can be referred to at many different points in a lesson, and does not only need to be covered in stand-alone activities. The examples in the final column are suggested answers – accept any plausible ideas.

10 Teaching pronunciation

Fast finishers could think of other examples of times when a teacher could use each technique in a lesson.

Technique	Aim	When a teacher might use it
Showing learners the shape of your mouth and position of your tongue when producing a specific phoneme (sound).	For learners to notice the physical changes in the mouth necessary to produce specific sounds.	As part of error correction, to help learners produce a sound in a more intelligible way. When you first introduce a new phoneme to learners who do not have it in their L1.
Displaying a word in both the written form and phonemic script, e.g. comb /kəʊm/	To show learners how the sound and spelling of a word differs.	When introducing a new vocabulary item with an unusual sound-spelling relationship, for example silent letters. As part of error correction after a speaking or writing activity.
Writing out a word in normal script, putting dots between the syllables, and underlining the stressed syllable, e.g. e·mer·gen·cy.	To show learners how many syllables a word has and which syllable carries the stress.	During a speaking activity, when a learner is having trouble producing a word intelligibly. As part of error correction after a speaking activity.
Indicating on your fingers how many words there are in a sentence, then putting your fingers together to show where there are contractions. Learners repeat the sentence with the contracted form.	To help learners to notice contractions in a sentence and encourage them to produce these contractions themselves.	After a speaking activity, as a way of helping learners to produce spoken language more fluently. When modelling a sentence to introduce a new grammar pattern, e.g. present perfect: *She's been to China.*
Substitution drill, i.e. T: *I'm going shopping. We* SS: *We're going shopping.* T: *not* SS: *We aren't going shopping.*, etc.	For learners to verbally manipulate the form of a grammar structure they have just been introduced to, including features such as contractions.	After the meaning and form focus in a grammar lesson.
Writing out a sentence from a listening transcript and highlighting features of connected speech on it.	To draw learners' attention to features of fast pronunciation of English and how the spoken form might differ from the written form.	Before a listening activity, to draw attention to potentially problematic features. After a listening activity, particularly if learners have misheard something in the audio – this can be used to focus on an individual answer.

2 Answers will vary. Encourage trainees to think about lessons they have observed as well as ones they have taught themselves.

2 – Language analysis and awareness

D Anticipating problems

Note: the language areas for this task could also be selected from the syllabus of the trainees' current coursebook. You could ask different groups to start at a different item (group 1 starts at *a*, group 2 starts at *b*, etc.), to ensure that all items are covered, even if time is short.

1 Possible problems include:
   a *can/can't*: failure to discriminate between weak and strong forms, so that *can* sounds like *can't* – this may also cause a problem when listening if learners cannot distinguish between them; use of the same vowel sound for both *can* and *can't* plus failure to articulate final *t* in *can't*, so that, again, the two words sound the same.
   b ordinal numbers: the main problem is the /θ/ sound, at the end of regular ordinals (*fourth, tenth,* etc.), especially for learners whose first language does not include this sound. Also problematic might be *consonant clusters,* as when /θ/ follows another consonant, as in *eighth, twelfth,* although, in reality, even native speakers elide (i.e. drop) the first consonant of the cluster.
   c *used to*: tendency to pronounce /s/ as /z/; failure to use weak form of *to;* inserting an extra syllable: /juːsɪd/
   d present simple questions: rhythm, particularly the use of the weak forms of *do* and *does.* Assimilation may occur with *do you:* /dʒuː/ and *don't you:* /dəʊntʃuː/ Again, these may cause problems when listening, as learners may not connect them to the written forms they know.
   e *would you mind ...-ing?* intonation, which, if flat or falling, might not convey sufficient politeness; failure to elide *would you;* the /ŋ/ sound at the end of the present participle may cause problems for some learners.
   f clothing vocabulary: vowel phonemes, particularly the difference between /ɜː/ and /ɔː/, as in *shirts/shorts,* but also the wide range of other vowels, and their different spellings (e.g. *suit, shoes*). Word stress may also cause problems in compound nouns, such as *overcoat, pullover.*

2 Assign different pairs/groups one or two of the syllabus areas to work on. Possible solutions:
   a Recognition: discriminating between *can* and *can't,* in isolation and in sentences. Production: short dialogues with both *can* and *can't.*
   b Recognition: minimal pairs exercises, e.g. contrast *thing/sing, moth/moss,* etc. Production: demonstration of the /θ/ sound (tongue between teeth); repetition in isolation and in words.
   c Recognition: discriminating between *an axe is used to chop wood; he used to live next door;,* etc. Production: drills; practice in sentences, dialogues, 'jazz chants', with emphasis on rhythm: *I used to go swimming but now I don't have time ...*
   d Recognition: asking learners to identify main stress in sentences like *What do you do?; Where do you live?* etc.; boardwork to show main stresses. Production: drills (to encourage natural rhythm and use of weak forms); 'shadowing' (a learner repeats a sentence as they hear it, aiming to imitate the original pronunciation).
   e Recognition: contrasting 'low involvement' with 'high involvement' intonation. Production: drills, dialogues, etc.; practice making requests for different situations, ranging from informal and friendly to formal and distant.

f Recognition: minimal pairs exercises to focus on contrastive vowel sounds; categorizing words according to stress. Production: sentences with high frequency of specific sounds, for repetition; games involving lists of items, e.g. *I went to the clothes store, and I bought …*

E Planning for pronunciation work

Possible ways of integrating pronunciation into the lesson include:
- Noticing pronunciation features:
  - identifying the sentence stress and intonation contours on lines of the photostory dialogue or in *WordWise 1*, or *Functions 2*
  - identifying weak forms in selected lines of the photostory dialogue or in *WordWise 1*
  - counting the number of words as learners listen to the teacher reading the expressions in *WordWise 1* (to focus on weak forms, liaisons and contractions)
- Repetition and drilling of features on the page:
  - 'shadowing' parts of the photostory dialogue (learners listen to the audio and repeat it as they hear it, aiming to reproduce the pronunciation as closely as possible)
  - drilling the different expressions in *WordWise 1* or *Functions 1*, focusing on natural rhythm and intonation
- Applying learning about pronunciation:
  - using intonation to sound as frustrated as possible in *Functions 1*
  - performing a short conversation, using the phrases for expressing frustration from *Functions 1* and getting feedback on pronunciation
  - practising reading aloud the dialogue from the photostory, deciding where to pause and how to use intonation or varied stress patterns to engage the listener and increase the sense of drama; getting feedback on this from peers or the teacher

KEY WORDS FOR TEACHERS

Remind the trainees of the need to be able to use teaching terms confidently and accurately.

REFLECTION

The aim of this section is for trainees to consider how what they have learned in this session could be applied to their own teaching, and particularly to the kinds of pronunciation problems the learners in their current TP group might have.

At this point, you may wish to draw trainees' attention to *Learner English*, edited by Michael Swan and Bernard Smith, as a source for typical pronunciation (and other) problems of learners from different L1 backgrounds.

Topic 2 – Language analysis and awareness

11 Phrases and sentences

Main focus
To learn how words cluster into phrases, and that these phrases have specific functions in the sentence.

Learning outcomes
- Trainees are familiar with basic principles of syntactic analysis.
- Trainees are aware that language analysis involves identifying phrases and their functional role in a sentence.
- Trainees understand that languages differ with regard to features such as syntax, and appreciate that this may be a cause of difficulty when learning English.

Key concepts
- meaning, concept; grammatical form
- context, function, style
- spoken and written form; pronunciation, spelling
- parts of speech
- sentence/clause elements
- similarities and differences between languages

Stage	Focus
A Warm-up	playing a game involving combining words to make sentences
B Phrases	introducing and identifying the five phrase types
C The noun phrase	investigating the elements of the noun phrase, their order and constituents
D Sentence elements	learning the basic structure of sentences and applying this in a parsing task
E Contrastive analysis	comparing and contrasting some syntactic features of three languages with English
Key words for teachers	building of specialist vocabulary to talk about teaching
Reflection	trainees reflect on the similarities and differences between English and another language

A Warm-up

This game can be played in groups of up to four, or as two teams whose members take turns to write sentences into their designated space on the board. Online it can be played in breakout rooms, with teams keeping a record of the sentences they produce. Point out that the sentences needn't make logical sense, but they must be grammatically well-formed. You might want to discuss what this means, e.g. that there must be one finite verb in the sentence (or in the main clause).

In discussing how they were able to generate sentences, the main point to bring out is that they have a knowledge of the rules of syntax, i.e. what is permitted or not in terms of the way words are grouped and sequenced. If the trainees enjoyed the game, they might want to think how it could be adapted for language learners, e.g. fewer words and a follow-up stage where errors are corrected and explained.

B Phrases

Refer learners to the 'parts of speech' activities that they did in unit 4, reminding them of the eight basic word classes. Point out that the ability to label parts of speech is of limited usefulness on its own, because it doesn't take into account the way words group together to form meaningful units.

1 You may decide to do several of these examples with the whole class until you feel they have got the idea. In which case, it might be helpful to model the thought processes involved in parsing these phrases. For example, *The Silence of the Lambs*: '*the* is a determiner and so can never be a head word. *Of the lambs* tells us what was silent and so adds information to *silence*. Silence is the head word.'

You may also want to point out that at this level of analysis, i.e. into phrases, a phrase may consist of just one word, but that a single word has the potential to be extended into a longer unit. *Clueless*, for example, is an adjective at the level of a 'parts of speech' analysis, but an adjective phrase at the phrasal level, because it can be extended to 'absolutely clueless' or 'more clueless than her best friend'. To avoid this issue, only multi-word phrases have been chosen for this task.

Finally, note that phrases can have other phrases embedded within them; this is particularly the case with prepositional phrases, where the head preposition is almost always followed by a noun phrase: *On the Waterfront*.

  2 Head = Silence; noun phrase
  3 Head = Get; verb phrase
  4 Head = Cheaper; adjective phrase
  5 Head = Nowhere; adverb phrase
  6 Head = Asians; noun phrase
  7 Head = In; prepositional phrase
  8 Head = Clockwise; adverb phrase
  9 Head = Fabulous; adjective phrase
10 Head = Look; verb phrase
11 Head = Hot; adjective phrase
12 Head = Spy; noun phrase
13 Head = Before: prepositional phrase

2 Solicit examples from the trainees and write them up. Invite other trainees to identify them.

C The noun phrase

1 It is recommended that you do a number of these with the whole class until the trainees seem comfortable with the categories. You may need to remind them that the head can consist of one word only.

2 – Language analysis and awareness

Determiner	Premodification	Head	Postmodification
The		Spy	Who Loved Me
		Murder	on the Orient Express
My	Beautiful	Laundrette	
		Airplane	
	Rosemary's	Baby	
A		Streetcar	Named Desire
The		Bridges	of Madison County
55		Days	at Peking
	Star	Trek	
Much		Ado	About Nothing

2 Determiners – as has already been mentioned – include articles and numbers, as well as possessive adjectives (*my*) and quantifiers (*much*). Premodifications are typically adjectives but also nouns (*star*), which are called noun modifiers, and the possessive form of nouns (*Rosemary's*). Postmodifications are typically prepositional phrases denoting time or place (*at Peking*) but also (and highly frequent) *of*-constructions, expressing possession or classification. Other types of post-modification include clauses, such as relative clauses (*who loved me*) and non-finite clauses (*named Desire*). Note that, in combination, all these phrasal elements add greater specificity to the head noun, so, not 'any spy', but 'the spy who came in from the cold.'

3 Learners experience problems both interpreting and constructing long, complex noun phrases: it may not be obvious what word is the head, for example. Noun phrases may also be constructed differently in the learners' L1: the 'noun + noun' (or noun modifier) construction, for example, does not exist in many languages, while the choice between noun + noun (*the baby food*), the possessive form of the noun (*the baby's food*) and the noun + of-construction (*the food of the baby*) is often subtle and difficult to explain. Similarly, the rules governing the order of adjectives before a noun (*rich crazy* or *crazy rich*?) are difficult to explain and apply.

D Sentence elements

Note: As in the previous task, it may be a good idea to do the first two or three examples with the whole class, before asking the trainees to continue in pairs or small groups.
Answers:

SUBJECT	VERB	OBJECT	ADVERBIAL	COMPLEMENT
It	Happened		One Night	
Mr Smith	Goes		to Washington	
Gentlemen	Prefer	Blondes		
The Empire	Strikes Back*			
That	's			Entertainment
The Russians	are Coming			
	Meet	Me	in St Louis	

11 Phrases and sentences

SUBJECT	VERB	OBJECT	ADVERBIAL	COMPLEMENT
Who	Framed	Roger Rabbit		
Batman	Returns			

strikes back is what is called a *phrasal verb*, consisting of a verb + particle. It would also be possible to analyse *strikes back* as VERB + ADVERBIAL

In summarizing this task, it is worth noting that *all* sentences have verbs, and *most* have subjects. (The exception is 7, where the verb is in the imperative form). You could also point out that some verbs, like *prefer* and *frame*, take objects (they are called *transitive verbs*) while others, like *happen*, *come* and *return* do not (they are called *intransitive verbs*). At this point, you might want to introduce the term **syntax,** to describe that area of grammar that deals with the way the elements of a sentence, such as its words and phrases, are sequenced.

E Contrastive analysis

> 1–2 You can adapt this task to the specific needs of the trainees by incorporating examples from the language(s) of the students they are teaching. For a useful source of information on language differences, see *Learner English* (2nd edition), edited by Michael Swan and Bernard Smith, (Cambridge University Press, 2001).
> On the evidence of the example sentences, the following syntactic features of the three languages should be noted:
> **Turkish:** Turkish uses a subject-object-verb (SOV) word order; there is no independent verb *to be*: instead suffixes are attached to the relevant adjective or noun; the equivalent of English prepositions and possessive adjectives go after the noun; there is no definite article. Of these differences, the different article systems in Turkish and English cause the most problems. Turkish learners adapt quickly to SVO word order and prepositions.
> **Arabic:** There is no present tense form of the verb *to be*; there is no indefinite article; there is no exact equivalent to the English genitive construction (*rich man's houses*); adjectives follow the noun; in the equivalent of relative clauses, an object is obligatory (*This is a letter which a famous lady sent it*). All of these differences (apart from adjective order) are transferred into English (causing *L1 interference*, or *negative transfer*).
> **Japanese:** Like Turkish, Japanese is an SOV language; Japanese employs a number of markers (or particles) to indicate, for example, the topic, subject, and object of the sentence; the equivalent of English prepositions go after the noun; subject pronouns are usually omitted: *Ate an apple*. There are no articles as such in Japanese, and plurality often goes unmarked (*zō* = elephant/elephants). These last two differences probably cause more problems than any of the others.

KEY WORDS FOR TEACHERS

Use the key words to review some of the main 'takeaways' from the session.

REFLECTION

This can be set as a homework activity, and done either individually or in pairs, if trainees share knowledge of the same language. You can allocate time in subsequent sessions for trainees to report their findings to the group.

Topic 2 – Language analysis and awareness

12 Tense and aspect

Main focus
An introduction to the way tense and aspect combine to form the verb phrase in English.

Learning outcomes
- Trainees understand the difference between (grammatical) tense and aspect.
- Trainees can distinguish between the form and meaning of eight verb forms (commonly known as tenses).
- Trainees can apply this analysis to identifying the objective of coursebook activities, and to designing a presentation.

Key concepts
- tense: present, past
- aspect: continuous, perfect
- present simple/continuous/perfect
- past simple/continuous/perfect

Stage	Focus
A Warm-up	creating sentences and identifying their verb structures
B Tense review	completing a table of verb forms, and using a coursebook text to identify their forms and common meanings
C Tense v aspect	using corpus data to identify the meanings of tense and aspect combinations
D Learner problems	correcting and explaining the errors in a learner's text
E Materials	identifying the focus of specific teaching materials
F Classroom application	applying the above analysis to the presentation of verb forms
Key words for teachers	building of specialist vocabulary to talk about teaching
Reflection	revisiting the warm-up activity to review basic concepts

A Warm-up

The aim is to generate sentences for later analysis (these sentences are revisited in the Reflection stage), while experiencing a coursebook task first-hand. If working online, it might be useful to save the sentences in digital format for later review. At this stage, it is not important that all the verb forms in the sentences are accurately identified.

12 Tense and aspect

B Tense review

1 Trainees can work individually and then compare in pairs; alternatively, project the table and elicit suggestions as to how to complete it. At this stage it is not important to make the distinction between tense and aspect. You may prefer to follow the coursebook convention and categorize all the forms as 'tenses'.

   Note that 'future tense' is not dealt with in this unit, as it is best treated as a feature of modality. Nor is voice (i.e. active and passive) included. For more information, see *A Brief Guide to the English Verb* on page 212 in the Trainee Book.

   The completed table should look like this:

	simple	continuous (aspect)	perfect (aspect)	perfect continuous (aspects)
present (tense)	they work	they are working	they have worked	they have been working
past (tense)	they worked	they were working	they had worked	they had been working

   Note that *progressive* is also used instead of *continuous* in many grammars. You may also want to point out that *work* is a regular verb, and then elicit suggestions as to how the table could be adapted to irregular verbs such as *speak, put, go*.

2 Here is the table completed for all the finite verb forms (excluding modals) in the text. (Note that there are no examples of the past perfect forms):

	simple	continuous (aspect)	perfect (aspect)	perfect continuous (aspects)
present (tense)	get, set, have, love (x2), hate, want (x3), am (sure)	am saving, am going*	have done, have wanted,	have been learning
past (tense)	learned, came, saw, faced, went, caught, felt	was working		

   *technically this is a modal phrase, but takes the form of the present continuous

   If time allows, there are a number of points that could be made about the verbs in the table: 1. The compound forms are composed of auxiliary verbs and a participle (*was working; have done*); 2. The present simple is negated using the auxiliary verb *do/does* + *not: don't want*; 3. Some of the verbs have irregular past tense (*saw, caught*) and past participle (*done*) forms; 4. Verbs not included in the table include non-finite forms (*to tell; to run; screaming*), imperatives (*[please] like …*), modals (*will, can*). These points could form the basis of a quiz or race (*Find five irregular verbs …*)

3 The completed table looks like this:
   1 present perfect
   2 past continuous
   3 past simple
   4 present simple
   5 present continuous
   6 present perfect continuous

It's important to point out that the explanations given for these 'tenses' are necessary simplifications (the task is taken from a students' book, after all) and that they omit many other uses (e.g. present continuous for future arrangements). They therefore should be treated as 'rules of thumb'.

C Tense v aspect

As already noted, most coursebooks and student grammars do not distinguish between tense and aspect. Nevertheless, an understanding of the kinds of meanings that aspect contributes to the verb phrase can help explain seemingly anomalous examples. For the purpose of this unit, *tense* can be defined as the grammatical realization of time, while *aspect* refers to the way that the state or event expressed by the verb is viewed, either as dynamic and evolving (continuous) or retrospectively connected to another point of time (perfect) or both (perfect continuous).

Point out that the task uses corpus examples, where a *corpus* is a searchable collection of naturally occurring texts, both spoken and written. Trainees can work in pairs or small groups, and should be directed to the explanations in task B3 for help.

Answers:

a and b: *works* – present simple; *is working* – present continuous. The continuous denotes an activity in progress (in this case, around the time of speaking or writing), hence possibly temporary and incomplete, which contrasts with *works*, which here describes a routine, i.e. a series of completed events.

c and d: *drove* – past simple; *was driving* – past continuous. Again, the continuous 'views' the activity as in progress, in this case in the past, where it provides the background for an event that interrupts it; *drove*, on the other hand, views a single event in its entirety.

e and f: *love* – present simple; *am loving* – present continuous. Again, continuous implies an evolving situation, consistent with the fact that the reading of the book is also 'in progress', whereas the absence of aspect views the state of 'love' in its entirety, 'from outside', as it were. Note that verbs like *love, like, hate*, as well as verbs of cognition, such as *believe, understand*, etc. are categorized as *stative* verbs (as opposed to *dynamic* verbs like *work, drive, sleep*), and hence don't usually occur in the continuous. When they do, they exploit the dynamic character of the continuous aspect in order to become more like actions: *I am understanding Chinese better each day*.

g and h: past simple – *learned*; present perfect – *has learned*. Perfect aspect (*has learned*) connects past events to the present (that is why the present perfect is a present tense), implying past learning has present relevance, and that further learning is still possible, whereas the past simple (*learned*) separates the learning from the present by identifying a specific time in the past (*as a child*).

i and j: *made* – past simple, *has made* – present perfect. Again, the perfect connects past events to the present, implying future possibility, whereas the past simple disconnects past events from the present, implying, perhaps, that Bergman is no longer alive.

k and l: *wrote* – past simple; *has written* – present perfect. Here the perfect implies that there is present evidence: what was written is still visible. The past tense (*wrote*), being disconnected from the present, has no such implication.

D Learner problems

Note that trainees are not expected to correct all the errors in the text – only those that are underlined. To save time, it may help to do the first two or three in open class.

line 2: *had* ➔ *have*: the memories exist in the present
line 3: *we've moved* ➔ *we moved*: the 'moving' took place at a definite time in the past
line 5: *doesn't looks* ➔ *doesn't look*: in the negative of present tense verbs, only the auxiliary verb (*does*) is marked for person (in this case, third person)
line 6: *come* ➔ *came*: the past tense is needed in order to situate the event in a definite past time
line 7: *I've been living* ➔ *I was living*: the 'living' took place in the past and is not connected to the present.
lines 7 and 8: *she has moved* ➔ *she had moved*: the 'moving' took place in a period prior to the moment in time established in the preceding narrative, i.e. 2006.
line 9: *I've lived* ➔ *I've been living*: while 'I've lived' is possible, 'I've been living' conveys the dynamic, possibly temporary, nature of the situation.
line 10: *you're having* ➔ *you have*: *have* as a stative verb does not usually permit the continuous aspect.

E Materials

a–b 1 present perfect for experiences at indefinite past times
2 present simple to talk about general truths, and, specifically, the negative auxiliary construction
3 present perfect, simple and continuous, to describe changing states or processes that started in the past and continue to the present

c All three activities focus on form, because in each case the form has been preselected and is explicitly modelled, but at the same time there is a focus on meaning, particularly in the case of 1 and 3, where there is a communicative exchange. 2, on the other hand, is more tightly controlled.

F Classroom application

Organize the trainees into groups, and assign one structure per group. They should devise a situational presentation for their structure, and preferably one that generates several examples of the same structure. Monitor the preparation stage, and check that the trainees have chosen the correct form of the item in question. Re-group the trainees so that they can explain their ideas to other trainees, or, alternatively, ask individuals to 'demo' their presentation to the whole class. (This may require allowing time for the preparation of simple visual aids.)

KEY WORDS FOR TEACHERS

Use the key words to review some of the main 'takeaways' from the session.

REFLECTION

Trainees can do the task in pairs, or as a homework activity, using a recommended reference grammar, or *The Brief Guide to the English Verb* on page 212 of the Trainee Book.

Topic 2 – Language analysis and awareness

13 Language functions

> **Main focus**
> To describe language in terms of its communicative functions and to apply a functional approach to teaching.
>
> **Learning outcomes**
> - Trainees understand how utterances have a communicative function, and that there is no one-to-one match between utterance and function.
> - Trainees understand how context factors affect the interpretation and production of spoken and written utterances.
> - Trainees learn how a functional approach has informed syllabus design, and they can apply these principles to the design of teaching materials.
>
> **Key concepts**
> - form v function
> - context and register (formal v informal)
> - appropriacy
> - formulaic language; functional syllabus

Stage	Focus
A Warm-up	matching utterances to contexts
B Context and function	assigning functions to utterances and relating the idea of function to context factors
C Function, style and language	introducing the notion of appropriacy, and the inclusion of functional formulae in syllabus design
D Materials for teaching functional language	studying and exploiting coursebook material for teaching functional language
E Teaching functions	trainees write dialogues that contextualize and contrast functional expressions
Key words for teachers	building of specialist vocabulary to talk about teaching
Reflection	trainees reflect on the role of appropriacy in language learning

A Warm-up

These activities are designed to introduce the idea that (a) language can be described in terms of its communicative functions; (b) function and context are interrelated; and (c) that a key factor of the context is the interpersonal relationship between speakers. Task 2 draws attention to the *linguistic* features of utterances, while the rest of the session is concerned with pragmatics – the ways that utterances are interpreted and produced in the light of their contexts.

13 Language functions

Point out that functions are usually expressed as *–ing* forms. This underscores the fact that they describe how speech acts are *performed*. It also distinguishes them from *notions,* which are more abstract concepts such as *duration, frequency, quantity,* etc.

1. 1 1–c) 2–f) 3–d) 4–a) 5–g) 6–e) 7–b)
2. 1 imperative; 2 modal verb (*will*) in main clauses, present continuous in subordinate clause; 3 present of verb *to be;* 4 present simple; 5 modal verb (*will*); 6 present simple; 7 imperative. You might want to make the point that although 1 and 7 both use the imperative, they fulfil different functions, underscoring the fact that there is no one-to-one match between the form (imperative) and the function.
3. It is not expected that trainees will be able to identify the origin of the quoted utterances; what is important is that the communicative effect of the utterances is best understood with some knowledge of the context. For reference:
    1 From the film *Casablanca* (1942), uttered by the French prefect of police to his subordinates, at the end of the film.
    2 From the film *When Harry met Sally* (1989), said by a restaurant customer to the server, on overhearing Sally's conversation with Harry.
    3 The way the fictional British spy James Bond formally introduced himself, to allies and adversaries alike.
    4 The understated way that the astronauts in the film version of a space mission in 1970 reported an onboard explosion.
    5 A theatrical phrase dating from the nineteenth century, referring to the way rehearsals often go badly.
    6 The greeting given by the explorer and journalist Henry Stanley on finally locating the explorer and missionary David Livingstone in East Africa in 1871.
    7 Attributed to the actress Mae West, addressing Cary Grant in a 1930s movie.

B Context and function

The purpose of these tasks is to demonstrate how context factors influence the production and interpretation of utterances, and that it is only by taking these factors into account that pragmatic meaning can be assigned.

1. Possible expressions (ordered from least to most formal) are: *No bikes; No cycles; Please do not ride your bike here; No cycling; Cycling (is) not allowed; Bicycles (are) prohibited; Bicycles may not be ridden here; Riding of bicycles is strictly forbidden,* etc.
    You could extend this activity by bringing other signs into the classroom (and point out how useful signage is for teaching certain language functions).
2. Factors to note include: (perceived) degree of social distance between writer (or whoever authorized the sign) and reader – a less formal style might be used within an institutional context where the 'writer' might actually know the potential reader; and the physical location of the sign, e.g. on a busy bridge v in the open countryside, which would affect the degree of risk involved, and hence the severity of the prohibition, as well as the time available to read it.
    The order of teaching would need to take account of linguistic complexity, including lexical range, and frequency of occurrence.
3. a telling the time (asking for information)
    b expressing impatience
    c teaching
    d complaining

2 – Language analysis and awareness

4 Possible contexts and functions:
 a 1 someone being followed (threatening)
   2 someone at the scene of a crime (offering)
 b 1 someone entering an airconditioned store (stating a fact)
   2 couple watching TV with the windows open (requesting)
 c 1 person pointing to a phone that a friend has left on a restaurant table (reminding)
   2 flatmates in adjoining rooms as phone rings (requesting)
 d 1 tired driver to travel companion (requesting)
   2 car rental clerk to client (asking information)

C Function, style and language

1 Possible utterances/texts might be:
 a Hi, it's Matilda at no. 26. We're having a welcome drink tomorrow around 6 pm to meet the neighbours. We'd love you to come if you're free.
 b Fancy a drink later on? / Feel like a drink after work?
 c Can I borrow your charger? I need to charge my phone.
 d Hello, X. This is Y here, your neighbour in 10A. Sorry to bother you. I wonder if you could do me a favour? I'm expecting a package tomorrow, but I won't be in, and I was wondering if you could take delivery of it?
 e I'd like to suggest that the gym installs wi-fi. / Have you considered installing wi-fi?
 f How about / Have you tried raising/lowering your monitor?

In the discussion that might ensue when checking this task, point out that the way context factors influence language choices is not a feature of English alone, but is a universal characteristic of language. The main problem that learners will have is not knowing exactly how social distance is encoded in English (compared to, say, languages like French, that have a *tu – vous* distinction). In English social distance is often signalled by the use of past tense forms, conditional constructions, and modal verbs.

2 1–d) 2–b) 3–c), f) 4–a), e)

3 Note that many coursebooks now include functional descriptors in their contents, but these may not always be labelled as such, or they might be interspersed in the grammar, thematic, or skills strands of the course, sometimes as *Everyday English* or *English in context*, etc.

D Materials for teaching functional language

1 Point out the importance of providing a context for teaching functional language, including a clear indication as to the setting and the relationship between the speakers: the picture could be used to elicit these contextual details.

2 Remind trainees that – as with any reading or listening text – it is essential that the learners understand at least the gist of the text before using it to highlight/teach specific language features. That is the point of the questions in 1B and it would be important to check the students' answers before moving to the next stage.

3 The bold font highlights the key functional language in the text and helps learners notice and extract it.

4 As in the coursebook, these items could be extracted into a table according to their functional categories.
5 As in the coursebook, the items could be reintegrated into another dialogue, or into a dialogue of the learners' own making, and then rehearsed and performed.
Here is how this is done in the coursebook: if possible, copy and project this to the class.

> C Complete the chart with expressions in **bold** from the conversation above.
>
> | Making suggestions | Accepting suggestions | Refusing suggestions |
> |---|---|---|
> | 1 _____ go out tonight? | OK, 3 _____ good. | I'm sorry, 6 _____ . |
> | 2 _____ meet at the hotel. | Good 4 _____ . | Sorry, I'm busy. |
> | | Yes, 5 _____ . | |
>
> D 🔊 2.35 Complete the conversations with words from exercise 1C. Listen and check. Then practice with a partner.
> 1 A _____ take a break.
>   B OK, sounds _____ .
> 2 A _____ have lunch?
>   B _____ , but I can't.
> 3 A Coffee?
>   B _____ idea.
>
> 102
>
> Photocopiable © Cambridge University Press & Assessment 2022   *Evolve 1*

E Teaching functions

1 Organize the class into groups of three to five. Give each group a function to work on. For example:
   - asking permission
   - making a request
   - complaining
   - apologizing and making an excuse
   - greeting

Remind trainees that they need to think of *two* different situations, where the difference is in the degree of formality. The context should be a recognisable one and easy to set up. For the demonstration, suggest that the 'teacher' uses his or her colleagues to perform the dialogues as if they were an audio or video player. In discussing the presentations, ask for suggestions as to how these could be developed into practice tasks.

2 – Language analysis and awareness

KEY WORDS FOR TEACHERS

Use the key words to review some of the main 'takeaways' from the session.

REFLECTION

Points that should emerge from this discussion are:

a An exclusive focus on language forms may mean that learners are ill-equipped for a lot of day-to-day language functions, especially those that involve interpersonal relations (such as requests, asking permission, etc.) where expressing degrees of politeness and formality may be crucial.

b Teaching only language functions may reduce the course to a succession of phrasebook-type utterances, from which it may be difficult to generalize the grammar.

c Make sure the distinction between *accuracy* and *appropriacy* is clear – the former being formal correctness, the latter being the way an utterance matches its context, especially the relationship between speakers. Most second language learners will be able to recall times when they used the wrong register (e.g. in the choice of *tu* or *vous* forms in French), or when an intended meaning – such as asking for information – was interpreted differently, e.g. as a request or a complaint.

14 Text and discourse

> **Main focus**
> To analyse ways that sentences are connected, and ways that texts achieve coherence.
>
> **Learning outcomes**
> - Trainees understand the main lexical and grammatical ways that texts are made cohesive.
> - Trainees understand the difference between cohesion and coherence, and understand how coherence is related to text organization.
> - Trainees can apply these understandings to the teaching of writing.
>
> **Key concepts**
> - text, discourse
> - cohesion, coherence
> - linking (cohesive) devices: repetition, reference, substitution, ellipsis
> - genre, text organization

Stage	Focus
A Warm-up	'chain' writing, in order to introduce notions of cohesion and coherence
B Connected text	recognizing the features of a text that determine the way it is sequenced
C Cohesion	identifying specific lexical and grammatical cohesive devices
D Coherence	contrasting incoherent and coherent text, and identifying features of text organization
E Putting it into practice	evaluating and improving learner writing
Key words for teachers	building of specialist vocabulary to talk about teaching
Reflection	recapping the main issues relating to the idea of text grammar

A Warm-up

The purpose of this section is both to demonstrate a fun writing activity and to introduce a view of language systems that function at a level 'beyond the sentence'.

1 If you are working face-to-face, ask trainees to take a blank sheet of paper and copy down the following sentence: *Once upon a time there was a farmer who dug up a big earthenware jar in his field.* They should then continue the story by adding a sentence of their own. They then pass their paper to the trainee sitting to their right, who reads what has been written and adds a further sentence. And so on, until the papers have returned to their original owners. (If the group has more than 12 trainees, you may want to cut this short).
If you are working online, you can do a similar activity using online slides. Prepare them before the session with the first line of the story and a number on each slide. Tell each trainee

2 – Language analysis and awareness

which slide to start from. They should then cycle through to the next slide to write the next sentence of the story. To avoid confusion about whose turn it is to write, it's best to give a clear signal to indicate when trainees should move to the next slide, rather than letting them move on when they are ready.

2 Ask selected trainees to read their texts aloud and invite the class to evaluate the texts and comment on them. If working online, display a selection of the texts for the trainees to read. Use their comments to establish these points:
- Language is organized at a level 'beyond the sentence', commonly referred to as discourse. One feature of connected discourse is the use of linking devices, such as referring expressions *(his, their, the former,* etc.).
- Certain text types or genres (e.g. stories or factual texts) are organized in particular ways, and knowledge of these conventions – such as the opener *Once upon a time …* – helps both in their interpretation and production.
- The connectedness of texts is called 'cohesion'; their capacity to make sense is called 'coherence'.

Note that the focus in this unit is on written texts, but that the same principles apply to spoken language, such as conversations. The types and distribution of connecting devices will differ, however, from one mode to another, and from one genre to another.

B Connected text

1–2 The purpose of this task is to raise awareness as to how texts achieve cohesion and coherence.

Show the original text:

> **Once upon a time there was a farmer who dug up a big earthenware jar in his field. 'This will make a fine jar for storing rice,' he said to himself. So he carried it home and asked his son to clean it out. But while the boy was brushing the inside of the jar, he dropped the brush inside and the jar suddenly began to fill with brushes. No matter how many were taken out, others kept on taking their place. So the man sold the brushes, and the family managed to live quite comfortably.**

Photocopiable   © Cambridge University Press & Assessment 2022

3 The following points should be made:
Ordering the sentences was possible because of (a) knowledge of the text type (or genre), i.e. a folk tale, and the way such narratives are chronologically sequenced, and (b) various lexical and grammatical linking devices (to be enumerated in the next section). Of course, if trainees are already familiar with the story, and recognize it, this will contribute to their background knowledge.

C Cohesion

1 The sentences are connected using a range of lexical and grammatical devices, as enumerated here:
Once upon a time there was a farmer who dug up a big, earthenware jar in his field. 'This[1] will make a fine jar[2] for storing rice,' he[3] said to himself[4]. So[5] he[6] carried it[7] home and asked his[8] son to clean it[9] out. But[10] while the[11] boy[12] was brushing the inside of the[13] jar[14], he[15] dropped the brush inside and the[16] jar[17] suddenly began to fill with brushes. No matter

how many[18] were taken out, others[19] kept on taking their[20] place. So[21] the man[22] sold the brushes[23], and the family[24] managed to live quite comfortably.

1. back reference using pronoun (technically, this refers to something in the speaker's context, but the reader will connect it to the previous mention)
2. lexical repetition
3. back reference using pronoun
4. back reference using pronoun
5. logical connector (result)
6. back reference using pronoun
7. back reference using pronoun
8. back reference using possessive determiner
9. back reference using pronoun
10. logical connector (contrastive conjunction)
11. definite article, implying previous mention
12. back reference using more general term
13. definite article, implying previous mention
14. lexical repetition
15. back reference using pronoun
16. definite article, implying previous mention
17. lexical repetition
18. ellipsis (*brushes*)
19. pronoun substitution (*other brushes*)
20. back reference using possessive determiner
21. logical connector (result)
22. back reference using more general term
23. lexical repetition
24. back reference to the man and his wife, using a collective noun

Note that a number of these connecting devices operate within sentences rather than across sentences, but trainees are likely to ignore this unimportant distinction. Nor is the distinction between reference and substitution worth unpacking. Other possible cohesive ties in the text are the lexical sets of agriculture (*farmer* ➔ *field* ➔ *rice*) and cleaning (*clean* ➔ *brushing/brushes*).

2. Before this activity, you may wish to ask trainees to predict how the story might continue, before reading and comparing their predictions to the actual story.
Refer trainees to the list of cohesive devices in their books which they should consult in doing this task. The following list of devices in the text is not exhaustive:
   - **Lexical:**
     - repetition of words, or words from the same word family: *brushes, jar, money, grandfather(s), shovelling*
     - use of general words to refer to something more specific that is mentioned elsewhere: *his son* ➔ *the boy* ➔ *the family; grandfather* ➔ *man*
     - use of words from the same lexical set: *coin, money, rich, gained, poor; weak, shaky, toppled; dead, buried*
   - **Grammatical:**
     - pronoun back reference: *they, them, he,* etc.
     - article back reference: *the poor man; the old man; the jar*
     - linkers: *So ... But ... however*
     Note also the back reference in the phrase *For this purpose ...*

2 – Language analysis and awareness

3 Extract A focuses on cohesive linkers, also known as discourse markers, and specifically, those that mark a contrast. Extract B focuses on pronoun reference.

D Coherence

1–2 The text obviously makes no sense, i.e. it is incoherent. It is clearly a 'collage' of sentences taken from a number of different genres: folk tale, followed by an architectural guide book, followed by a line from Shakespeare, followed by a publisher's statement of thanks, followed by a sentence from a novel, and concluding with a sentence from a folk tale again. However there are superficial features of cohesion, such as lexical repetition (*house, house; thanks, thanks*) and back reference (*the two last-named*), thereby supporting the statement that a text may be (superficially) cohesive but not coherent. You might also want to make the point that the fake text illustrates the fact that different genres have different conventions, which are recognizable even at sentence level.

E Putting it into practice

1 a *Cohesion:* the text is made cohesive by a chain of topic-related words, some of which are repeated, such as *TV, programme(s)*. There are also some linkers, like *but*.
  b *Coherence:* the use of *In the other hand* in paragraph two suggests a contrast, yet it is difficult to see what ideas are being contrasted. This threatens the overall coherence, and in fact it is difficult to see what the writer is arguing either for or against, although it is clear from the text type and the last paragraph that this *is* a letter of complaint or protest. The possible use of sarcasm (saying the opposite of what you intend), as in *clever and interesting programmes such as a Miss World Award*, doesn't help matters either.
2 The text could be improved if the writer was asked to be explicit about his/her opinion, by, for example, developing the first sentence. This might involve giving an example of *the programmes you are* showing and by saying exactly what his/her opinion is: *I think they are …* . Also, the second paragraph needs to be more clearly connected to the first, so the writer could be asked to say whether the connection is an *and, but* or *so* one, since these are the most common types of logical linkage. The writer could also make it explicit as to what *this horrible productions* (in the last paragraph) refers to. Reading other, similar, letters of protest, and identifying their overall structure, may also help.

KEY WORDS FOR TEACHERS

Use the key words to review some of the main 'takeaways' from the session.

REFLECTION

Use this task to summarize the main points in the session, i.e. that there are language systems that operate at a level beyond the individual sentence, and that these consist of *cohesive devices* that connect sentences, and features of *text organization* that structure texts in ways that fulfil the expectations of readers. Thus, when we talk about *the grammar of texts*, we are talking about these larger-than-sentence-grammar systems.

15 Presenting the meaning and form of new grammar items

Main focus
To give a variety of ways of presenting new language items.

Learning outcomes
- Trainees understand the basic principles of conveying the meaning of new items of language.
- Trainees understand the need to present new language items in context.
- Trainees understand the basic principles of highlighting the form of new items of language.

Key concepts
- conveying meaning
- contextualization
- highlighting form
- model sentence
- inductive presentation (and guided discovery)
- deductive presentation

Presenting vocabulary is dealt with in unit 7.
Checking understanding is dealt with in unit 16.
Practising new language items is dealt with in unit 17.
Teaching new language items reactively is covered in unit 19.

Stage	Focus
A Warm-up	introducing the topic
B Presenting grammar from texts	focusing on how texts can be used to contextualize new language items
C Three more presentation techniques	demonstrating presentation techniques
D Presenting new language items and highlighting form	focusing on how a teacher might highlight patterns in language for learners
E Putting it into practice	trainees develop a mini presentation
Key words for teachers	building of specialist vocabulary to talk about teaching
Reflection	trainees reflect on what they have learned

2 – Language analysis and awareness

A Warm-up

Allow the trainees a little time to think about the questions before discussing them in small groups. When they have had sufficient time, ask the groups to report back to the class.

1 There are parallels between learning grammar and other new skills. The language teacher can also tell people about grammar. Learners can be shown how grammar is used in context. Learners can read about grammar for themselves in reference works. Learners can try communicating using the language resources that they have and pick up grammar as they go along. Of course, learners may chop and change between preferred strategies.

2 It is likely that there will be a progression from having to think consciously about how to use the programme and how to apply explicit knowledge, to it becoming more automatic, with much less conscious thought required. This is a progression from so-called 'declarative knowledge' (or knowing *about*) to 'procedural knowledge' (knowing *how*). The ultimate goal of most language learning programmes is for learners to develop procedural knowledge (i.e. be able to use the language). There is an assumption that declarative knowledge of 'rules' will support this development with sufficient practice.

3 Answers may vary, but it could be argued that the processes are similar and therefore the strategies may well be similar.

B Presenting grammar from texts

1 Focus the trainees on the text and allow them to ask any questions they wish before they focus on the four questions. They can discuss these in pairs or small groups before reporting back.

   a The learners get support in working out the meaning from clues in the text. For example, in this case we know that a meeting will be 'difficult' and that the writer is busy. However, the *don't have to* example is introduced by 'good news', which may help learners recognize the lack of obligation.

   b There are questions that ensure that the learners understand the overall meaning of the text before they look at particular features of it.

   c In this example, there is a short, guided discovery activity. However, it is important that trainees realize that there are alternatives to this. For example, the teacher could select, highlight and discuss examples from the text (see Presentation 1 in task C).

   d The learners practise the language item. Although practice is dealt with in other units, this is included here so that trainees appreciate the need for learners to get opportunities to use what they learn.

2 Most of the advice is intended to be good advice, although c) should probably be crossed out. Even in this case, it could be argued that as long as the learners have spent sufficient time studying the text and are able to understand it by the point it is used for grammar study, it might not be entirely inappropriate.

The advice in f) is also misleading. Spoken texts may be used (and may be more appropriate for language features that are more common in spoken than written language). However, it is usually a good idea to provide a transcript (so a written form) as it is easier to study.

15 Presenting the meaning and form of new grammar items

C Three more presentation techniques

You may prefer to demonstrate a presentation that exploits the use of a language other than English. Obviously, at least some trainees would have to share that language. The other trainees could be given the role of observers.

Otherwise, focus the trainees on Presentation 1. The aim is to help trainees see how the learners' L1 can be used effectively. Ensure that the trainees notice that, as in task B above, the presentation follows on from the use of a text. The trainees need not worry about the precise nature of the text. They just need to realize that the model sentences come from a text that the learners have previously read.

There is a translation of the teacher's presentation at the end of the unit in the Trainee Book. The trainees could discuss the pros and cons of using an L1 to present language before completing the table.

Tell the trainees that you are going to demonstrate two short presentations at an elementary level (demonstration lessons 2 and 3, below), and explain that the trainees themselves will take the role of the students. The two demonstration lessons should follow the spirit, if not the letter, of the two scripts below.

The trainees can complete the tables after each presentation, or after both have been finished, as you prefer.

Demonstration lesson 2:

Teacher: When we want to talk about things that are not certain, we can use the verb *might*. For example, I might watch the football tonight – but I am not sure, not certain. I might watch the football. Can you repeat that? [Class repeats.] Or, Tomorrow I might go to the cinema. Repeat after me, Tomorrow I might go to the cinema. [Class repeats.]

[The teacher writes the sentences on the board, encouraging learners to contribute as they are doing so by saying things like: 'What's the next word?'.]

Teacher: Is it definite I'll watch the football? [Class answers.] These are things that are not 100% sure. We use might plus the infinitive of the verb – might watch, might go. [The teacher highlights the form on the model sentences.]

Teacher: Now write three things you might do tomorrow. Things that are not certain to happen.

Demonstration lesson 3:

Teacher: [Draws person's face on board.] OK, this is Joe. [Draws thought bubble above the face.] Joe's thinking about the future. [Draws plane in thought bubble.] He's thinking about his next holiday. What's he going to do? [Draws Eiffel Tower in thought bubble; elicits *He's going to fly to Paris.*] He's going to fly to Paris. [Teacher draws ticket in Joe's hand.] Has he got the ticket? [Students: Yes.] So, is he deciding to go to Paris now, or did he decide before? [Students: Before.] So, this is Joe's plan. Where's he going to stay? [Members of the class make suggestions, e.g. in a hotel.] Listen, He's going to stay with a friend. Everybody, repeat. [Class repeats.] He's planned this already. What's he going to do in Paris? What's he going to see? What's he going to eat? [Teacher elicits possible responses, and works on pronunciation as appropriate; some of the sentences that have been suggested are then re-elicited and written on the board. The teacher highlights the form and meaning of *going to*.]

2 – Language analysis and awareness

When all the lessons have been presented, allow the trainees to compare ideas and discuss the advantages and disadvantages of each.

Lesson 1	Lesson 2	Lesson 3
present perfect (contrasted with past simple)	modal verb: *might*	*be going to* + infinitive (for plans)
the teacher has used a text	the teacher explains	the teacher creates a situation
The use of the L1 is quick and efficient and ensures that all the learners can follow the explanation. This efficiency potentially frees up time for more communicative elements of the lesson. The teacher can contrast the ways in which the L1 and English encode the same piece of information/meaning (as the teacher does here).	It is quick, efficient (in terms of time) and this may allow more time for learners to use the language. It may fit in with many learners' expectations that a teacher will give information. In addition, it may be the only viable option when teachers respond to learners' production in a spontaneous manner (see also unit 19 Teaching language items reactively).	The learners are involved in the presentation, as they offer suggestions and contributions throughout. Some situations may be amusing or memorable for some other reason and this will aid learning.
Learners will benefit from as much exposure to English as possible and this reduces that exposure. The strategy cannot be used if the teacher and learners do not share a common language.	Learners are not cognitively involved in working out meaning or form to any great extent, and this may mean it is not particularly memorable.	Some structures may not lend themselves to such a presentation (e.g. the determiner system).

2 Focus the learners on the questions and allow them to discuss in small groups before reporting back. Ensure that they understand that they should also consider the guided discovery lesson in task B.
   i   The text-based lesson in task B and the deductive Presentation 2 (on *might*) do not rely on any (or at least minimal) input from learners, and so are most under the teacher's control.
   ii   Arguably the text-based guided discovery, task B. It does not depend on much teacher explanation. You may wish to point out that much of the teacher's work here is done before the lesson, as they find an appropriate text and plan questions. Their role in the lesson is to encourage and confirm what learners are doing. You may also wish to point out that this is an inductive presentation.
   iii   Presentation 2 on *might*. This is an example of a largely deductive presentation (although the teacher may choose to elicit some elements by asking questions).
   iv   Answers will vary.
You may wish to extend the discussion to cover any additional techniques, or variations on these techniques, that the trainees have already used, and the pros and cons of those.

15 Presenting the meaning and form of new grammar items

D Presenting new language items and highlighting form

1 Focus the trainees on the six presentation stages. Checking understanding is included here so that the trainees have a more complete record of the stages they are likely to need to go through when teaching, but it is not fully dealt with until unit 16.
   Ensure trainees understand the six stages. Encourage trainees to think about how they could make example sentences meaningful to learners (stage 1). For example, they might take them from a text that has been studied, or they might be personalized in some way.
   Of course, it is possible that stages could come in a different order. Encourage a discussion of the sequence given here, if that would be useful to your trainees.
   The trainees should then do the matching exercise.
   Answers: 1–f) 2–e) 3–a) 4–c) 5–b) 6–d)
   You may wish to focus on how the teacher (in section f) responds firstly to the communicative value of what the learners says, rather than immediately focusing on the correct form.
2 Practice would come after. It is very important that the trainees understand that practice and opportunities to use the language are essential. This is considered in unit 17, but the need to provide practice should also be highlighted here.
3 There are several ways in which a teacher could contextualize new language. For example, the teacher could use a picture, a video in which the new language is used, or a written text. There is no single best way of contextualizing new language, and using a variety of techniques is probably good for learner engagement and motivation.

E Putting it into practice

Ensure that the trainees understand the instruction – they should discuss, in groups, two alternative ways in which they could present the new language item. You may want to refer back briefly to tasks B and C at this point. Ensure that the trainees understand that they will then present the point to the class, using one of the techniques.

Split the class in groups and allocate each group a language item. These might usefully be chosen from upcoming TP points.

When the trainees have had time to prepare, they should do their mini presentations, either to the whole class or to another group. This would be a good point to review the advantages and disadvantages of each technique.

2 – Language analysis and awareness

KEY WORDS FOR TEACHERS

Remind the trainees of the need to be able to use teaching terms confidently and accurately.

REFLECTION

The trainees can work individually before discussing with a partner. Suggest to the trainees that they refer back to the list of Dos and Don'ts before they next plan a presentation of a piece of new language.

Suggested answer:

Presenting new language items	
DOs	**DON'Ts**
Check that learners have understood the meaning.	Give a lecture about grammar.
Involve learners in the process as much as possible.	Always use the same presentation technique.
Where possible, draw comparisons and contrasts between English and the learners' own language(s).	
Contextualize new language items (e.g. by using a text).	
Use clear examples.	
Highlight the form.	
Make explanations clear and concise.	
After presenting new language items, give plenty of opportunities for learners to use the language.	

16 Checking the meaning of grammar items

Main focus
To provide trainees with techniques for checking the understanding of new language items.
To review the teaching of new language items.

Learning outcomes
- Trainees are able to check understanding of new language items.
- Trainees are able to use timelines to convey and/or check meaning of appropriate new language items.
- Trainees can analyse a piece of material designed to teach a grammar point.

Key concepts
- checking understanding
- timelines

Presenting vocabulary is dealt with in unit 7.
Highlighting form is dealt with in unit 15.
Practising new language items is dealt with in unit 17.
Teaching new language items reactively is dealt with in unit 19.

Stage	Focus
A Warm-up	introducing the topic
B Checking understanding	introducing ways of checking understanding of new language items
C Timelines	introducing the use of timelines
D Analysing material	trainees analyse a piece of grammar teaching material
Key words for teachers	building of specialist vocabulary to talk about teaching
Reflection	trainees reflect on what they have learned

A Warm-up

You may wish to begin by reviewing the term 'language function' and checking that trainees understand this.

1 Allow the trainees a little time to do the matching activity individually. Alternatively, you may like to give one half of a sentence to each member of the group and ask them to mingle to find their partners (i.e. who they match with). They can briefly compare answers before discussing the questions with a partner.
Answers: 1–c)   2–d)   3–f   4–e)   5–a)   6–b)
2 a All the examples give advice.
  b Trainees may be able to make various arguments, given that some of the examples are quite neutral and so could be used in a range of contexts. Those beginning *My advice would be to* and *If I were you, I would* would both be acceptable in formal situations.

2 – Language analysis and awareness

    c *Make sure that* is restricted to relatively informal use.
    d The advice is designed to be useful. You may wish to draw attention to the idea of starting with a speaking activity (as a way of providing communicative practice and diagnosing need).
    e Matching activities can be used for a variety of things (e.g. words to definitions). Matching sentence halves can be a way of introducing examples of new language or giving very controlled practice. For example, learners could be asked to memorize their sentence half and then try to find their partner by interacting with classmates.

B Checking understanding

You may like to review what trainees remember of checking the understanding of vocabulary before moving on to this. This may help to make this task less daunting.

1. Establish that *used to + infinitive* can be used to express past states (as here) or past habits. Help trainees to see that they can only plan the successful checking of new language items, if they themselves are clear on the concept they wish to check.
2. Allow the trainees to spend some time looking at the techniques individually before discussing their ideas in pairs.
    a. Not a very useful technique. Some learners may think that they understand, when in fact they don't. Others may be embarrassed to say that they do not understand in front of the whole class.
    b. The repetition of the new item of language (*used to*) in the question makes this unreliable. It could be compared to asking 'Is a duck a duck?'.
    c. Useful – in situations where a class (and teacher) share a common language, using a quick translation exercise is an efficient method of checking understanding.
    d. Useful – this approach is further developed in the following part of this task.
3. Ensure that trainees understand that they do not need to check the meaning of the lexis. Answers will vary but example questions are given below.
    a. Are they on the plane now? (no)
       Do they already have tickets? (yes, probably)
       Is this about the present or the future? (future)
    b. Did I see Alex? (no) Did Alex leave before or after I arrived? (before)
    c. Am I Prime Minister? (no)
       Is it likely that I will be Prime Minister? (no)
       Is this about the past or present/future time? (present/future)

C Timelines

You may want to spend a little time explaining the particular conventions that you would like trainees to use.

1. Allow the trainees to work together in pairs to try to match the timelines to the pictures. Conduct feedback and clarify any points that they are unsure of. Point out how a state is represented differently to a repeated action.
   Answers: a–iv) b–iii) c–ii) d–i)

16 Checking the meaning of grammar items

2 Conventions of drawing timelines may vary but below are possible answers.

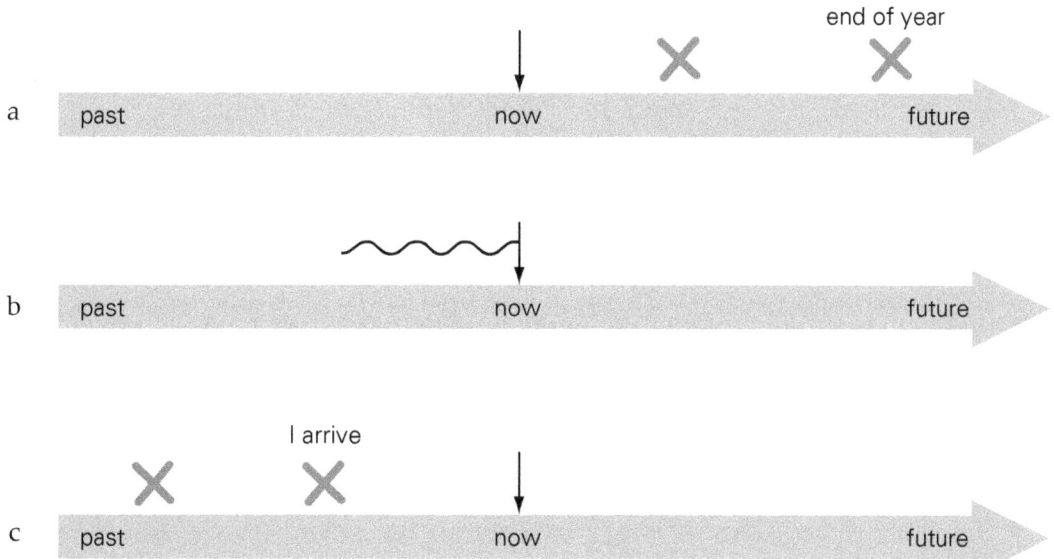

D Analysing material

1 Focus the trainees on the material and give them a few moments to look over it. Ensure they can identify each exercise and emphasize that the example sentences in exercise 1 all come from a previous reading activity – i.e. the learners would see these in context before doing this exercise.
Give learners several minutes to work individually to answer as many of the questions as they can. They can then compare their ideas in small groups before reporting back in open class.
1 The learners have seen the sentences in context and therefore how they are used as part of a text, combining with other items. The context supports an understanding of meaning.
2 The sentences have been seen already. The learners only need supply the correct form of the verb *to be* in the present simple, which at this level should be straightforward. It is desirable to ensure that the learners have the correct forms (and therefore the correct data) from which to work out rules.
3 This is a guided discovery exercise, where the materials give the learners a narrow range of choices to support the working out of the rule from the examples given.
4 Exercise 2 gives a comprehensive summary of form.
5 Exercise 3 gives controlled practice in manipulating the form.
6 Exercise 4 sets up exercise 5 by giving learners prompts to decide on things they are planning to do. This information is then used in exercise 5 to create meaningful exchanges.
7 Exercise 3 practises form. Exercise 5 involves speaking. It is personalized and there is a focus on meaning (rather than form).
8 Learners could be encouraged to extend the short exchanges with additional questions.

2 – Language analysis and awareness

9 The teacher will monitor the pair work during the activity and may offer some correction to individuals. After the activity, it is likely they will encourage some reporting back and sharing of information before giving feedback to the class on how the new language was used.

10 Answers will vary. However, it is worth pointing out that both meaning and form are covered and there is some opportunity to communicate (albeit briefly at the end of the sequence). Encourage trainees to suggest any adaptations that they think would improve the material for the learners that they are teaching in TP. This will lead into activity 2.

2 This subsection aims to help trainees see why they may wish to adapt coursebook material.

1 Although inductive approaches tend to be used in a lot of classroom material, deductive approaches can save time – time that might be more usefully spent in allowing the learners the space to try to use the language. Some learners may feel more comfortable with the teacher telling them information, rather than being asked to work out rules for themselves and being more actively involved in processing the information.

2 Translation can be a useful learning activity. In this case, the learners will see that their own language (Spanish) has an equivalent pattern to the *going to* + infinitive structure in English. This is likely to give them confidence in how to use the English version.

3 The need to fit a lot of information onto a page of a coursebook can sometimes make them look quite cluttered. It is likely that the teacher has typed out this information for learners who have difficulty with reading, perhaps caused by dyslexia, for example.

4 The most likely explanation for this is that the teacher wants to give the learners the opportunity to talk about the things that are important to them. This is an attempt to personalize the activity.

5 Coursebooks often assume quite a lot of knowledge of metalanguage (language that is used to describe language). This is probably a legacy of the view that language is learned through study, rather than through being used. It is a good idea for teachers to at least check that their learners do indeed possess the knowledge of terminology that is assumed by the materials writers.

KEY WORDS FOR TEACHERS

Remind the trainees of the need to be able to use teaching terms confidently and accurately.

REFLECTION

Set a time limit and tell the learners that they should work collaboratively in pairs to gain as many stars as they can in that time. They can select questions from any box and answer questions in any order. When the learners have finished, ask them to report back on the questions they answered and allow them to decide how many stars they believed they succeeded in gaining.

After the activity, you may wish to point out that this activity is a form of differentiating material, and in a class would allow learners to work at a level at which they felt comfortable.

One-star Questions

a The trainees might say 'past simple negative' or *did* + *not* + base form. You could accept either and elicit the other version.

b iii) is not useful as it does not check that learners have understood the concept. They could answer without appreciating that this is an unlikely/hypothetical situation, for example.

c The first language might be used to explain the form and/or meaning. It could be used to check understanding. The first language could be used to deepen understanding of a new item through comparison and contrast to English. Translation could be used as a means of practice.

Three-star Questions

a i This focuses on differentiation. The teacher could use a more deductive approach and tell the learners more about the language. They could split the two parts of Section 1 and ensure learners had used the correct form of *be* in each case before completing the rule. The teacher could use the learners' first language.

ii The teacher could allow the learners the chance to try to communicate about their plans before pre-teaching the new language item. If learners can do this successfully, some of the controlled practice might not be necessary.

b i Trainees should underline *'ve lived*.

ii Questions suggested may vary but things like: *Did they live in the house in the past?* (yes) *Do they live there now?* (yes) Are they likely to live there in the future? (yes – at least there is nothing about the grammar to suggest otherwise)

iii Trainees should indicate something started in the past, continuing to the present and in all likelihood into the future.

Five-star Questions

Answers will vary. You may like to stress the need to provide plenty of varied practice. This will be the focus of the next unit.

Topic 2 – Language analysis and awareness

17 Practising new language items

Main focus
Ways in which controlled (or restricted) practice can be provided when teaching new language items.

Learning outcomes
- Trainees can provide practice of the meaning and form of new language items in controlled (or restricted) contexts.
- Trainees can select, adapt and sequence activities, according to the needs of a group.

Key concepts
- repetition; choral and individual drills
- accuracy and fluency
- personalization
- interactive and communicative practice

Stage	Focus
A Warm-up	a discussion activity in which trainees discuss their experience of practice
B Controlled oral practice	introducing the rationale and mechanics of drilling
C Controlled written practice	introducing common types of controlled written practice
D Interactive and communicative practice	introducing the principles of interactive and communicative practice
E Putting it together	trainees integrate their knowledge about presenting and practising language
Key words for teachers	building of specialist vocabulary to talk about teaching
Reflection	trainees demonstrate what they have learned by discussing questions

A Warm-up

If you prefer, you could start the session with books closed and discuss different learning experiences and their parallels with language learning.

Ask the trainees to read the two short texts and encourage them to discuss the parallels with language learning in small groups. Remind them to discuss their own experiences.

The tennis example highlights practising parts of something in isolation and repeatedly before attempting to integrate the new skill into existing skills.

The cooking example takes a far more 'deep end' approach – with the learner experimenting, benefiting from guidance (including both positive and negative feedback), but essentially learning in a more holistic sense.

The quote highlights that controlled practice is a controversial topic in language education. While some see it as being of very limited value, others (such as DeKeyser) see language learning as being similar to learning any other skill.

B Controlled oral practice

This task can be done with books closed if you prefer, and with you modelling the initial drilling exercise (choral to individual) and then the backchaining example.

1 The questions can be discussed in open class or in small groups.
   a Repetition may, to some extent, aid memory and help commit chunks of language in working memory. It gives the teacher the chance to monitor the accuracy of production, including stress, rhythm and intonation. Repetition may also meet the expectations of language learners.
   b This sort of repetition is rarely communicative and it can become quite tedious if overdone – a mere parroting of sounds. Repetition is no guarantee of storage in long-term memory, or that the new item of language will be used accurately once the learner attempts to integrate it with other language items.
   c The received wisdom would be that this gives learners the chance to 'get their tongues round' the new item before any individual is put on the spot. It can build confidence.
   d No – it is unlikely to be required if the spoken form of the item is easy for learners to say, or if the item is needed primarily for reading or writing.
   e No – and particularly with large classes this would become quite tedious and would risk a drop in learner engagement. This means that the teacher needs to take care not to always select the same members of the class.
2 Backchaining is often used when the teacher wants to focus on weak forms, and other features of connected speech. It's often used with longer stretches of language which learners might be having trouble remembering, for example a sentence or a multisyllabic word: the sentence is broken into meaningful phrases as far as possible. Some learners might also consider it a slightly more fun alternative to traditional drilling.
3 The trainees work in pairs to practise a backchaining drill. The model sentences could be replaced with something more relevant to the trainees, such as a language item that will be part of an upcoming teaching session.

C Controlled written practice

1 The activities become increasingly challenging. In (a) the actual words are supplied in the correct form. In (b) the verbs are supplied but the correct forms have to be inserted and in (c) the learner has to think of an appropriate verb (there are several possibilities in each case) and then put it into the correct form. This sort of exercise can be easily manipulated to suit the learning needs of a class, or indeed, individuals within a class. This is important when teachers need to differentiate material to meet the needs of individuals.
2 The activities are different from drills in that: (fairly obviously) they are written and not spoken; they don't involve repetition; they require the learners to make choices and display knowledge about the form and/or meaning of the target language items. The advantages of using written exercises are: learners can work at their own pace and/or in pairs; it is easier for the teacher to monitor each learner's progress; it is perhaps easier for learners to focus on the formal features of the new language items because they have time to think. The obvious conclusion is that both oral and written practice will have a place in most contexts.

2 – Language analysis and awareness

D Interactive and communicative practice

Again, you may like to briefly demonstrate some of the activities in this task. Trainees may have a better idea of the 'mechanics' of an activity from having experienced it than from having read a description of it, and will also find it more engaging.

It is important to establish the difference between an activity that is simply interactive, i.e. one where learners interact and/or take turns, and one that is communicative, i.e. one in which the outcome of the activity depends on the learners listening to one another and processing what they hear. In the latter, learners will need to negotiate and repair communication breakdowns, and adapt their own contributions in accordance with their partner's: there is an element of unpredictability.

	Dialogue practice	Circle drill	Find someone who …	Write five sentences
There is built-in repetition: the activity gives learners opportunities to use the new language item on several occasions.	✓	✓	✓	✓
The language is contextualized.	✓			
Learners interact and/or take turns.	✓	✓	✓	✓
Learners communicate – they must both speak and listen to what is said.			✓	✓
The language is personalized.		✓	✓	✓
The activity is fun and playful.*		✓	✓	✓

*This is obviously subjective to an extent.

Point out that dialogue practice might be personalized, as it depends on what is in the text. There is arguably an opportunity to personalize this example in a limited way (at stage 2). Some of these activities may suit particular groups of learners more than others. For example, circle drills are often used with young learners. As always, teachers need to make thoughtful choices about what activities they think will work in any given context.

2 Trainees should share their ideas in groups before reporting back. You may wish to include the following points.
   a repetition: the acquisition of a new skill usually involves some element of repetition – why should language be different?
   b context: this helps reinforce the meaning of the new item, and shows how it might be used in real life
   c interaction: most authentic language use is interactive in some way; learners can work together and maximize learning and practice opportunities
   d communication: the ability to negotiate and repair communication breakdown, and to adapt one's message according to the ongoing nature of the discourse, is crucial for effective real-life communication
   e personalization: language practice is likely to be more interesting and hence more memorable if it is personalized
   f fun: activities are often more motivating if there is a fun element

3 Encourage the trainees to look back over all the activities that they have seen in this unit (or elsewhere) and adapt two that could be used for the structure given. They may suggest a sequencing strategy of easier to more difficult, or more controlled to less controlled.

17 Practising new language items

E Putting it together

The aim of this task is to give trainees an opportunity to see how this unit links to presenting new language items, and also to provide an outline plan for teaching new items of language that they could adapt to aid the planning of their own lessons.

Trainees can work in small groups to piece the plan together. You may like to stress that this is one option for presenting new items of language, and that there are other ways in which it could be approached.

Of course, arguments could be made for alternative sequences. Trainees should justify the choices they make.

Stage	Activity
Building context	The class talks about what things they enjoyed doing when they were children.
Model sentence	Teacher says, *David used to play football.*
Highlight meaning	The teacher draws a timeline on the board, showing a period in the past with several crosses within it.
Checking understanding	Teacher asks, *Did he play football in the past?* (Yes) *Does he play football now?* (No)
Highlight spoken form	The teacher repeats the model sentence with natural linking, stress and intonation. The class repeats.
Highlight written form	The teacher writes the model sentence on the board. Draws a box round *used to* and writes *base form* over *play*.
Summarize 'rule'	Teacher says, *used to + infinitive can be used to talk about things we regularly did in the past, but don't do now.*
Practice 1	Learners choose an activity they enjoyed as children and then walk round the class asking if other people used to do the same thing.
Report back	The teacher asks some individuals how many people shared their interest and corrects errors if they are made, as well as praising good examples of language use.
Practice 2	The learners discuss their memories of their first school in small groups.
Report back	The teacher asks some individuals what they talked about. Afterwards, she highlights good uses of language and writes some errors she heard on the board and asks learners to correct them.

Answers: 1–e) 2–h) 3–a) 4–j) 5–b) 6–c) 7–f) 8–i) 9–d) 10–g)

2 – Language analysis and awareness

> **KEY WORDS FOR TEACHERS**

Remind the trainees of the need to be able to use teaching terms confidently and accurately.

> **REFLECTION**

Allow the learners to think individually for a few moments about the questions and then encourage them to share their ideas in small groups. You may like to highlight the following points.

1 Knowing a rule – in the sense of being able to put it into words (i.e. have declarative knowledge of the rule) – is different to being able to operate it under time pressure, which typically applies when speaking, for example. This calls for procedural knowledge – an ability to apply it without conscious thought. Skill theory suggests that practice will help transform declarative knowledge into procedural knowledge. Practice of new language items should help to make the use of those items more automatic and therefore make language production more fluent.

2 As these activities are partly targeted at promoting accuracy, then in most cases teachers would probably want to correct learners as they go along. Also, by correcting learners from time to time, the teacher is gently reminding the learners that they should pay at least some attention to form.

3 The activities in this unit have all been fairly controlled. Learners will also need to practise with fluency-focused activities. (See unit 22 Focus on speaking skills.)

4 Not necessarily. It is often assumed that there is a progression from 'controlled' to 'freer' activities within a lesson, but this need not always be the case. However, the notion of 'controlled' is not unproblematic in itself, because activities may be controlled either in the sense that the teacher controls who says what, and when they should say it, or in the sense that there is tight control over the language used in the activity. Drills, for example, are controlled in both senses, but a Find Someone Who ... activity is only controlled in the latter sense. There is no reason why the teacher shouldn't sometimes challenge the learners early on with an activity which is relatively free, and then go back to something more restricted if it is necessary. Activities need to be sequenced in accordance with the needs and preferences of the group. The key thing is for teachers to be able to provide a lot of varied practice activities.

18 Providing feedback on learner production

Main focus
Ways of providing feedback to learners on spoken language.

Learning outcomes
- Trainees understand the main considerations in providing feedback.
- Trainees understand a variety of techniques for providing feedback.

Key concepts
- errors, mistakes
- correction: teacher, peer, self-
- reformulation
- immediate/delayed correction

Giving feedback on written work is dealt with in unit 23.

Stage	Focus
A Warm-up	introducing various views of feedback
B Types of error	introducing trainees to types of error
C When to intervene	introducing some of the principal considerations in deciding when it is appropriate to give feedback
D Correction strategies	introducing correction strategies
E Putting it into practice	the trainer demonstrates some correction techniques and then trainees practise error correction
Key words for teachers	building of specialist vocabulary to talk about teaching
Reflection	trainees reflect on what they have learned as they create sentences from prompts

Note: The term 'error' is used throughout this unit. The literature on error often draws a distinction between mistakes, which are not systematic, and 'errors', which are systematic, i.e. they are evidence of the learner's developing language system, or 'interlanguage'. In theory, a learner can self-correct a mistake because they know the correct form – they simply got it wrong on one occasion, perhaps through inattention and the demands of 'on-line' processing. However, a learner might not be able to self-correct an error, since it results from a gap in their knowledge. In practice, it is difficult, if not impossible, for the teacher to decide if a non-standard form is systematic or non-systematic, hence the distinction is ignored in this unit.

Throughout the unit we encourage trainees to take a positive view of non-standard forms – seeing them as an inevitable part of language learning and as providing opportunities for language development.

2 – Language analysis and awareness

A Warm-up

1 Allow the trainees some time to discuss the different teachers' views in small groups before reporting back to the whole class.
Avoiding error is very difficult if learners are given any freedom to create the messages they want to with the language. Most people would argue that learners should be encouraged to become 'risk-takers' and that this will inevitably lead to some errors, which is largely Mariagrazia's position. Over-correction may lead to a loss of confidence (Paula) but it is worth pointing out to trainees that the majority of learners expect their teacher to correct them, and are far more likely to complain if they are never corrected than if they are corrected a lot. It should, of course, be done in a sensitive and encouraging way. Tomas and Carol both point out the need to praise learners, and Carol highlights the need to focus on the process, or effort, as well as the results. Not all correction need come from the teacher – learners may be able to correct themselves or each other (Marco).

2 Allow trainees to briefly reflect on their own experience of receiving feedback in language lessons.

B Types of error

We suggest that you collect some errors made by learners in TP sessions before you do this unit. Collecting these errors could be part of an observation task for trainees and then they could be analysed in part 2 of this task.

1 This should be a quick exercise. The aim is simply to demonstrate that not all errors are grammar errors. In fact, errors in vocabulary and prosodic features of pronunciation may lead to more breakdowns in communication than many grammar errors. Of course, this activity does not cover all possible categories of error.
Allow the trainees some time to complete part 1 of this individually before checking with a partner and then confirming those answers in open class.
Answers:
1–f) – present perfect would be more appropriate
2–e) – too informal for the given context
3–d) – *injured* or *hurt* rather than *damaged* (which is not generally used to describe physical injury).
4–b)
5–a)
6–c)

2 Answers will vary. You may wish to have a note of some errors that have been made by learners in TP classes and feed them in at this point.

C When to intervene

Allow the trainees some time to discuss the situations in pairs before they report back. Arguments could be made for alternative strategies because there is no easy formula to follow on when and how to give feedback. It will depend on many variables, such as the context, goals, personalities, group dynamic, level, previous history of correction, and so on. However, some suggestions follow.

1 None of the errors (a, b, d) appear to interfere with communication, so there seems no necessity to interrupt the flow of the lesson with immediate correction in any of these cases. However, higher level learners are often fluent and need to work on becoming more accurate, and so some delayed correction may be appropriate. You might like to point out that at lower levels a teacher may choose to correct less often, in the interests of encouraging learners to 'keep talking'. Depending on the class, contribution c) seems worthy of praise, either immediately or after the activity.

2 a It would probably be appropriate to ignore this error as the communication is unaffected and the most important thing is that the new student feels welcome and remains keen to participate.
   b The vocabulary, particularly of the collocation of *endangered* and *species*, makes this worthy of praise, probably immediately as it takes place in open class.
   c This requires immediate feedback because communication breaks down (it is unclear what the job is) and cannot go forward until it is repaired. The teacher is likely to use a question to establish the intended meaning.

3 a This can be ignored because the message is clear and the teacher probably just wants to move the lesson on from the checking of correct answers. It is possible that the teacher could use delayed correction.
   b Feedback needs to be given immediately because the answer does not appear to relate directly to the question and so communication has probably broken down.

D Correction strategies

1 Ensure the trainees understand the strategies. These could be demonstrated.
Give the trainees some time to look at the responses in pairs before conducting a group discussion and highlighting the key points.
If you are short of time, you may like to divide the class into pairs and ask each pair just to look at one or two strategies, before they report back.

Strategy	Advantages	Disadvantages
Teacher prompts using terminology, e.g. 'grammar', 'tense', 'pronunciation', etc.	Easy to use and prompts the learner to self-correct. Indicates the type of error that the learner should be looking for.	Learners need to be familiar with the terminology used.
Note: The value of encouraging self-correction before peer- or teacher- correction could be discussed at this point.		
Teacher repeats the utterance to the point of the error. e.g. *Yesterday you ...*	Quick and easy. Prompts self-correction. Gives guidance as to where exactly the problem is.	Teacher needs to use appropriate intonation, or gesture, to ensure that the learner understands that this is a correction procedure and not part of the communication.

2 – Language analysis and awareness

Strategy	Advantages	Disadvantages
Finger correction	Gives a very clear indication of where the problem is. Quite flexible – can be used to indicate the need to put a word in, take a word out, or run words together (*I'm*, etc.) Again, prompts self-correction.	Only works with short utterances. Takes practice for most teachers to become confident.
Teacher uses questions to establish the meaning, e.g. *Do you mean you go every day?*	A good way to discover the learner's intended message and 'repairs' the communication after a breakdown. It mirrors authentic communication. It is necessary if the meaning is genuinely unclear. Even the implication of a lack of clarity may help the learner consider the formulation used.	Questions need to be clear and easy to answer to avoid further confusing the learner.
Reformulation (recast), e.g. *You went to the beach.*	Quick and easy. Doesn't break the flow of communication.	Learners may not realize that they are being corrected and it may therefore have little impact.
Delayed correction	Does not interfere with the flow of the communication. The teacher has time to 'prepare' what to say, rather than having to do it immediately.	Correction may have less impact if 'served cold'. A learner may not recognize that they were the person to make the error and so may be less likely to benefit.

2 Ask trainees to reflect on the correction strategies they have seen, either in teaching practice or in their observed classes. If you have access to video footage of classes in progress, these can be a useful way of showing different correction strategies in action, and of evaluating their effectiveness.

E Putting it into practice

1 Ask the trainees to shut their books so that they do not try to complete the table as you go along. Give out the grey cards to a selection of trainees. Tell the trainees that they should say **exactly** what is on the card – i.e. they do not produce a 'correct' version.
Correct the errors in any way in which you feel comfortable – it would be useful to demonstrate a range of techniques, including some from the previous task.

18 Providing feedback on learner production

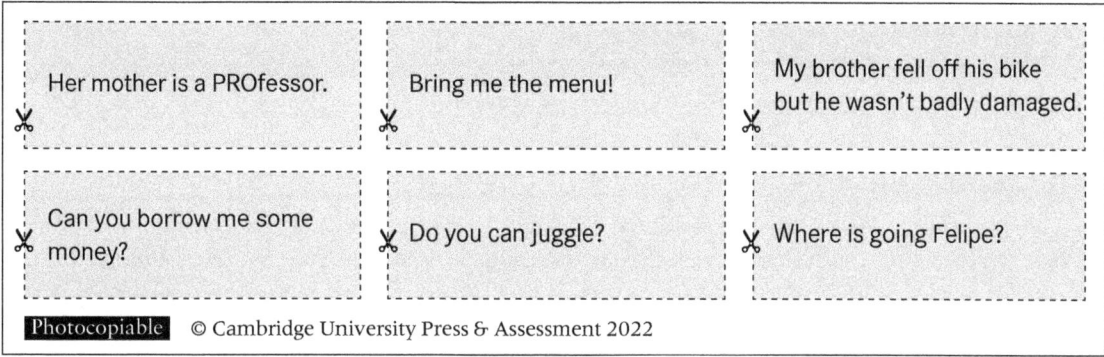

| Her mother is a PROfessor. | Bring me the menu! | My brother fell off his bike but he wasn't badly damaged. |
| Can you borrow me some money? | Do you can juggle? | Where is going Felipe? |

Photocopiable © Cambridge University Press & Assessment 2022

2 Ask the trainees to open their books and allow them to work in groups to complete the table.
3 The aim here is to reinforce the message that there is no single correct way to give feedback in any instance. Accept any plausible suggestions.
4 Ensure that the trainees understand the instruction in their books. Give each group a set of cards.

After the trainees have had time to practise, collect in the cards, nominate a trainee, read out one of the cards and let the trainee correct you.

He likes CIGars.	He has lots of friends. He gets on well with his pears.	(Said with very flat ('bored') intonation) I can't wait for the next session.
(in a cafe and to a member of the staff) I want coffee.	She no likes me anymore.	Helen is wedding her partner next week.
Do we must leave now?	I leaving here on Friday.	Sam and Alex is married for two years.
He stopped to smoke three years ago.	She has sister.	I had gone to cinema yesterday.
I was late because I stopped talking to a friend.	She likes her job. She works for the same company for years.	I going to New York at the weekend.

Photocopiable © Cambridge University Press & Assessment 2022

2 – Language analysis and awareness

KEY WORDS FOR TEACHERS
Remind the trainees of the need to be able to use teaching terms confidently and accurately.

REFLECTION

1 Give the trainees some time to write their sentences. If there is time, they can compare in pairs before reporting back. Many variations are possible, but potential answers are below.

You may like to encourage the trainees to reflect on the activity as a writing exercise and consider its potential use in their teaching.

   2 Most learners probably expect to receive feedback and correction in lessons.
   3 Correction should be done quickly.
   4 Correction should be done clearly.
   5 Errors need to be corrected immediately if they interfere with meaning.
   6 Sometimes delayed correction is useful because it does not stop the flow of communication.
   7 There are no fixed rules on when or how to give feedback.
   8 Praise should not be overused, because it needs to sound sincere.
   9 Sometimes teachers should praise effort, as well as results.
   10 Feedback should always be provided in a supportive manner.

2 Encourage the trainees to discuss which sentences they believe to provide the most useful advice. This is likely to depend on their own views of correction. None are intended as bad advice.

3 Focus the trainees on the quote. It is included here to provide evidence that giving feedback is an essential part of language teaching, and when done well can be a driving force of language development. Here, errors are seen as inviting opportunities for further learning by highlighting the gap between current knowledge and potential knowledge.

19 Teaching language items reactively

> **Main focus**
> To learn the basic principles of teaching reactively.
>
> **Learning outcomes**
> - Trainees understand the main considerations in planning and executing a reactive lesson.
> - Trainees understand the advantages and disadvantages of reactive teaching.
>
> **Key concepts**
> - reaction (as opposed to pre-selection)
> - monitoring
> - providing feedback

Stage	Focus
A Warm-up	introducing some basic principles of teaching reactively
B Planning a reactive lesson	trainees understand the essential shape of a reactive lesson
C Selecting what to teach	trainees practise selecting content and how they would use it
D Concerns of teachers	reflecting on common issues experienced by teachers
Key words for teachers	building of specialist vocabulary to talk about teaching
Reflection	trainees answer questions about reactive teaching to support their reflection

A Warm-up

1 Elicit from the trainees what 'teaching reactively' might mean. The definition of *reactively* can be used if necessary. We have chosen not to link explicitly this term to Task-based Learning, Dogme, or any other specific language teaching approach because we did not want trainees to see this as something very different to what they have already learned. In fact, they use many of the skills (setting up an activity, monitoring, providing feedback, for example) that they have already been practising. There is more on Task-based Learning specifically in unit 27.

2 Allow the trainees some time to mark the sentences as they wish. After the discussions, invite the trainees to report back and comment on the statements as necessary. Ensure that any that were marked with a question mark are addressed.

Teaching reactively means putting learners first. Many people would agree with this because teaching takes place in direct reaction to the needs of the learners at a point in time. The syllabus (what gets taught) is dictated by the learners rather than any external agenda.

Teaching reactively means never using a coursebook. Teachers are able to use coursebooks and teach reactively. Although coursebooks are generally built around a syllabus of preselected items, there are often opportunities for teachers to teach reactively. For example, a speaking and listening activity might be exploited in this way. Also, teachers might teach reactively in part because they want to introduce variety and a different type of lesson to those the learners usually receive.

Teaching reactively means never planning lessons. This is not true. The teacher has to plan how communication activities will be prepared and set up, which learners should work together, and so on. They also need to plan how to recycle content from one lesson into other lessons.

Teaching reactively starts with a focus on meaning. This is true. The learners start by trying to communicate the meanings they wish to express using whatever language resources they have (potentially including L1). The teacher then helps them shape and develop that language by focusing on how those meanings were expressed.

Teaching reactively is only for experienced teachers. Experienced teachers may feel more confident in dealing with language issues as they arise in the lesson. However, the skills of managing an activity, monitoring and giving feedback are important in all lessons and so trainees need not feel overwhelmed. They can also start with quite short activities to build their own confidence.

Teaching reactively involves setting up an activity, monitoring and giving feedback. This is the case, and is included to help trainees see that they already have many of the skills needed.

B Planning a reactive lesson

The purpose of the task is to help trainees understand simple sequences in planning.

1 a Answers:
    2 The learners work in small groups to complete the activity.
    4 The learners report back what they discussed.
    3 The teacher monitors the groups carefully – listening and writing down examples of good language use and also areas of possible improvement.
    5 The teacher praises and highlights good uses of language and elicits, or shows, how the learners' use of language could be improved.
    1 The teacher sets up a group speaking activity.
   b The teacher is very likely to ask learners to report back on their discussions. This may be done, for example, by nominating a spokesperson from each group. This is important because it highlights the importance of communication, and effectively communicating a message. The teacher should show interest in the ideas expressed by, for example, positive backchanneling, asking follow-up questions, giving praise and encouragement, and inviting further comment.

2 The correct sequence is:
   - set up and encourage communication
   - monitor and support learners
   - give feedback

3 The term 'scaffolding' is introduced here. It is a term derived from sociocultural learning theory but is often used in a variety of ways. It refers to the support that a teacher (or any other more skilled person) might provide to allow a learner to complete a task (spoken or written) more successfully than they would be able to on their own.
   The teacher might, among other things:
   - provide necessary vocabulary (as a learner tries to communicate)
   - use prompts
   - ask questions
   - reformulate language used by learners into more standard forms
   - provide positive feedback and encouragement

19 Teaching language items reactively

4 Research evidence suggests that repeating this kind of communicative activity can lead to gains in accuracy, fluency and complexity of learner output. It is unlikely that trainees will volunteer this information, but they are likely to say that learners should perform better the second time. You could elicit the particular areas that are likely to be better – accuracy, fluency, complexity. Repetition of the activity gives the learners a chance to use the new items of language that the teacher has covered in feedback. You may wish to point out that changing the groupings of the learners, or making some other small adjustment, will help to retain motivation to do the activity, because it will not be exactly the same.

C Selecting what to teach

This task gives the opportunity to develop the trainees' language awareness, asking them to identify errors in language and suggest explanations without preparation – a skill all teachers need to acquire.

1 Explain the activity to the trainees. Remind trainees that they should focus on highlighting form (e.g. by using the board) and also meaning. They could elicit information from learners (e.g. by asking for suggestions about how an error should be corrected). In the case of 'good' examples, they should check everyone has understood, and encourage learners to try to use the item themselves. Feedback should be clear and concise.

There is one error (The victim he goes to the police now) where the meaning is hard to recover, and so it can only be 'corrected' through asking questions to find out what the intended meaning was. Teachers often prioritize such errors that cause a communication breakdown over those where the meaning remains clear.

You may like to demonstrate one example and then have another one or two examples done in open class before the trainees work in groups. In your own demonstration, you may wish to provide a very short bit of practice to draw attention to this possibility. It could be something very simple that the trainees could later use themselves, such as saying 'now write a sentence using … '.

When the groups have had time to go through the items, ask them to report back and comment on their suggestions as necessary.

2 Give the trainees some time to focus on the extract, and then work in groups to develop a table similar to the one in the activity above.

Good points	Things to correct/improve
Kah Yee, what do you think? (good to manage the conversation/discourse and include others)	✗ I am agree ✗ (agree is used as a verb in English)
	✗ the cooker ✗ (the cook/chef)
victim (good vocabulary)	✗ the cook isn't working that night ✗ (wasn't working)
what we know for sure (good chunk of language)	✗ what you said? ✗ (What did you say?)
	✗ that is importance ✗ (adjective – important)
	– the reason is for the money (*motive* often used in the context of crime)
	– I think the cook is not the person we need (I don't think the cook is …)

2 – Language analysis and awareness

3 Reassure the trainees that they do not need to use a lot of metalanguage to offer correction, although, of course, they may choose to if they think the learners will understand it. Remind them that explanations should be brief and in some cases either eliciting or giving the correct form will be sufficient.

Monitor the groups as they work and afterwards offer feedback using the same pattern as the trainees have been practising – highlighting good examples and discussing/'correcting' where the interactions were less convincing.

D Giving advice: concerns of teachers

The trainees should discuss their ideas in small groups before reporting back. You may wish to highlight some of the following points.

Teacher 1: 'I can't always hear what the students are saying, and I feel I have let the students down if I don't comment on anything they said.'

The teacher could experiment with where they position themselves when monitoring. They could use slightly bigger groups so that learners have to speak a little louder to talk to the whole group. The teacher could focus particularly on the reporting back phases of activities and select examples to comment on from there to supplement what they heard in the group work.

If your trainees have difficulties similar to this, you could set up some practice in the session. For example, have two trainees do a short, paired discussion and have a third monitor, experimenting with where they position themselves, before swapping roles. Alternatively, you could make monitoring the focus of an observation task.

Teacher 2: 'I would like to teach by responding to what students say, but I am worried that I won't be able to explain their mistakes if I don't prepare before the lesson.'

This is a natural anxiety. However, a teacher has helped a learner if they can give them a better / more appropriate form to express their meaning. They could always offer to research the language point and clarify it in more detail the following lesson. This has the advantage of also building in some recycling of new language.

Teacher 3: 'I tried this with a class of 20 students and it was a bit chaotic. Most of the students chatted in their own language.'

This can be a problem in some classes. A task with a clear outcome might help, especially where there is a focus on 'getting it right' (e.g. a report to the whole class, or creating a written text). The teacher could also allow some preparation in L1 but then ask for the reporting to be in L2. For large classes, the teacher could split the group, with some doing the task and others 'shadowing' their performance without speaking, before switching roles. The teacher could introduce reactive lessons gradually, with short activities, so that learners get used to the expectations.

Teacher 4: 'I have seen this type of teaching work really well. But at my school there's a fixed syllabus and we are expected to work from that.'

The teacher could deliver the syllabus but build in some reactive teaching to what they already do. For example, they could take a communicative activity that would traditionally come at the end of a sequence such as PPP, and switch the order of the stages around so that this becomes the start. The teacher can support the production and give feedback.

Teacher 5: 'I think my students expect a fairly traditional grammar lesson. I'm worried that they will think that they are not learning anything.'

Learners' expectations are an important consideration. Teachers need to ensure that learners appreciate that they are learning new material by, for example, creating a retrospective syllabus of points that have been covered and also by reviewing them regularly. The teacher can also provide more traditional lessons, of course.

Teacher 6: 'What about practice? How can I give the students any practice when I teach them something new?'

The teacher could develop a small bank of practice activities that will work with any language point and then use them as required. For example, the learners listen and repeat, the learners do a short dictogloss activity, or write sentences using the language item (see unit 17).

Alternatively, the teacher could provide a brief practice activity that is specific to the language point the following day.

Teacher 7: 'I worry that the cycle of communication followed by correction can become repetitive.'

This is a potential problem, but it could probably be levelled against any lesson format that was repeated time after time. Reactive teaching can be embedded within a lesson of another type or within a sequence of lessons. You could also point out that the teacher's feedback should not be solely about correction, but also highlighting good uses of language. The teacher should also show interest in the content of what the learners express.

KEY WORDS FOR TEACHERS

Remind the trainees of the need to be able to use teaching terms confidently and accurately.

REFLECTION

1. Does every lesson need to have a pre-selected grammar point?
   Not all lessons have a pre-selected grammar point, as the trainees are already aware (for example, a reading or listening lesson may not have a grammar point within it). It is possible to work from the meanings that the learners wish to express to the forms they use to achieve that.
2. What would you say to someone who said: 'I don't like reactive teaching. Students need to learn grammar.'?
   The main point to be made is that learners will still learn grammar. In fact, there is likely to be quite a strong focus on accuracy when the teacher gives feedback. It is simply that grammar points will emerge according to need, as opposed to being predetermined before the lesson.
3. Can you summarize how teaching reactively is different to other ways of presenting new language?
   Answers will vary, but most traditional approaches to teaching start with a language item and then ask 'what can be expressed with it?'. Teaching reactively starts with what learners want to communicate, and then aims to provide them with the forms needed to do that successfully.

2 – Language analysis and awareness

4 Can you think of any circumstances where teaching reactively might be particularly appropriate?
It is likely to be in circumstances where the teacher has some control of the syllabus, or at least is free to depart from it some of the time. It will suit contexts where there is an emphasis on developing the ability to communicate rather than where learners are, for example, preparing for a formal exam, based on grammar.

5 Have you tried teaching reactively? Would you like to?
Answers will vary. However, hopefully trainees might be excited about experimenting with a new lesson format and realize that they already have many of the skills needed to do it successfully. The extent to which it can be implemented on a CELTA course may vary. There is a need for trainees to demonstrate that they can write (and then meet) a clear aim in a systems lesson. This is an important skill. However, trainees may also be able to experiment with writing communicatively focused aims (see unit 26) and this may allow for reactive teaching.

20 Focus on listening skills

Main focus
To learn the basic principles of developing the listening skill, and to apply these to the design of a skills-based lesson.

Learning outcomes
- Trainees understand different purposes and ways of listening.
- Trainees understand how top-down and bottom-up factors influence comprehension.
- Trainees can apply these understandings to the development of the listening skill.

Key concepts
- interactive/non-interactive listening
- transactional listening, listening for pleasure
- listening for gist, intensive listening
- top-down v bottom-up processing
- pre-listening, while-listening and post-listening tasks

Stage	Focus
A Warm-up	reflecting on real life listening and categorizing listening events
B Comprehension	distinguishing between top-down (knowledge-based) and bottom-up (language-based) factors in understanding
C Listening texts and tasks	matching text and task
D A listening lesson	identifying the aims and sequencing principles of the stages of a listening lesson
E Classroom application	applying these principles to the design of a listening lesson
Key words for teachers	building of specialist vocabulary to talk about teaching
Reflection	reflecting on some of the problems faced by students and teacher in classroom listening activities

A Warm-up

1 Start the activity by giving some examples of your own – including examples that involved both speaking and listening.
2 Point out that each listening experience may involve more than one item from the list (a–f). In the discussion, the following points should be highlighted:
   - Listening can range from being very interactive to wholly non-interactive.
   - Listening can be face-to-face, or 'disembodied', as when listening to a podcast or on the phone; it can also be multimodal, i.e. reinforced with images, as when watching a film, or with text, as when the film is subtitled.

3 – Language skills: listening, reading, speaking and writing

- The purposes of listening can vary, from the purely transactional (as when information is being conveyed) to 'listening for pleasure', as when listening to songs, or when watching a film.
- Listening can be intensive, where every word counts, or it can involve simply listening to the gist.

2 All of these situations present possible difficulties, exacerbated by the fact that the language is not the listener's first language. Factors that could make listening difficult include:
- the lack of visual reinforcement, as when listening to a podcast or a recording (although sometimes visual reinforcement can itself be distracting)
- the inability to interact, in order to sort out difficulties, as when listening to a recording
- the inability to control the rate of live input, by pausing or replaying it, as is possible when a text is recorded
- the pressure in real-time interaction, whether face-to-face or online, to speak, which might interfere with listening
- poor acoustics, as in many classrooms or online
- the mode, e.g. whether listening to monologue, where information may be densely packed, or listening in a less formal, conversational mode, where information is less densely distributed

B Comprehension

1 Read the following two texts to the trainees, at a natural speed, with natural pausing. Avoid supplying any paralinguistic support, e.g. the use of gesture, in order to clarify understanding. Allow the trainees to discuss their level of understanding. If requested, read the texts again.

Text a[1]:

Before they start, conditions are less than ideal and security is at risk. But the problem is soon resolved as each of their adjacent arms repeatedly describes the same short arc, the one in time with the other. In this way the impediment is removed, thus avoiding the need to stop and perform the operation by hand. The process continues until such time as a change in conditions renders it unnecessary.

Text b[1]:

We sat down at the table in the corner and the forby took our order. To start with, Therese ordered gumble, and I had a green dibblet. For the main course, Therese went for the pan-fried lunk with a fibitch sauce, while I opted for the house speciality, a shoulder of roast chorton. We rounded off the meal with a delicious homemade ice-cream and a steaming cup of black jimmery.

Read these second versions of the texts (the differences are in italics):

Text a[2]:

Windscreen wipers

Before they start, conditions are less than ideal and security is at risk. But the problem is soon resolved as each of their adjacent arms repeatedly describes the same short arc, the one in time with the other. In this way the impediment is removed, thus avoiding the need to stop and perform the operation by hand. The process continues until such time as a change in conditions renders it unnecessary.

20 Focus on listening skills

Text b(2):
We sat down at the table in the corner and the *waiter* took our order. To start with, Therese ordered *soup,* and I had a green *salad.* For the main course, Therese went for the pan-fried *sole* with a *dill* sauce, while I opted for the house speciality, a shoulder of roast *lamb.* We rounded off the meal with a delicious homemade ice-cream and a steaming cup of black *coffee.*

2 In discussing the task, the following points should be noted:
1) and 2) Comprehension depends on a number of factors, and is not simply a case of 'understanding every word'. In text a (in its first version), trainees will have understood all the words, but will probably have been unsure as to what the text was about. They lacked the necessary (extralinguistic) background information, such as an awareness of the context, to make sense of the words. In other words, they lacked 'top-down knowledge'.
In text b (in its first version), they were unfamiliar with a number of the words (since these were invented): in other words, they lacked some 'bottom-up knowledge.' But they had a clear idea of the situation, and therefore could supply some of the missing (linguistic) information. Comprehension, then, results from the interaction of top-down and bottom-up levels of knowledge.
This is true for both listening and reading. (Reading is dealt with in unit 21.)

3 The implications are that in order to maximize comprehension, it helps:
- to establish the general situation, the speakers, topic, context, etc. of the text (i.e. so as to activate top-down knowledge)
- to provide help with individual words (i.e. bottom-up knowledge), e.g. in the form of pre-teaching, or allowing dictionary use

When choosing or designing listening texts, these factors can be balanced against one another, in order to achieve an appropriate level of difficulty.

C Listening texts and tasks

1 Appropriate tasks for each of these text types might include:
1 a news broadcast: *a, c* and *g*
2 an exercise routine: *b, f,* and *l*
3 the directions to a local landmark: *d, g*
4 the description of a missing person: *f, j*
5 an embarrassing personal anecdote: *a, b*
6 a shopping dialogue (sales assistant and customer): *a*
7 a pop song: *a, f, h, i, k*
8 recorded travel information: *a, e, g*
9 a weather forecast: *a, d, e, h*

2 Criteria for choosing a task include:
- Does the task replicate an authentic (i.e. real-life) response to the material? For example, when listening to directions, we often take notes and/or draw a rough map.
- Does the task reflect the way the information is organized? For example, information that is in a particular sequence (as in a story) is best extracted by means of a sequencing task; on the other hand, information which is organized into categories (such as travel information) is best extracted by means of a grid or table.

Note that the most generally applicable task type is *a* (answering *wh-questions):* most listening texts lend themselves to this treatment. On the other hand, the least applicable task types

3 – Language skills: listening, reading, speaking and writing

are *i* and *k*, (writing the exact words or filling in gaps), since these do not usually reflect real-life listening tasks. However, they can be useful – in the classroom – in order to focus on specific language features in a text and to develop bottom-up processing, but may be best used *after* tasks that require less intensive listening.

D A listening lesson

1. Activity 1: (*pre-listening*): activating interest and background knowledge; could also provide an opportunity for pre-teaching vocabulary.

    Activity 2a (*while-listening*): gist listening; gaining overall familiarity with content.

    Activity 2b: (*while-listening*): more intensive listening for specific information.

    Activity 2c: (*post-listening*): response to content of text; opportunity to re-use items from text.

    Activity 3a: (*post-listening*): exploiting the text for a focus on grammar.

2. 1 Ideas for adaptation might include: pre-teaching more vocabulary; breaking the listening text into sections and summarizing the content of each section; providing learners with a transcript of the text after the initial listening.
   2 No major adaptations would need to ensure that the activities work in an online setting, although individual students may have problems hearing the recording if their internet connections are poor. To pre-empt this, the learners could be sent a link to the recording so as to be able to listen in advance as often as they need. Depending on the size of the group, and the platform being used, the discussion tasks might be more easily managed in 'open class' rather than breakout room mode.
   3 It may be worth pointing out that there is no single 'correct' order, but that the ordering of stages will follow a logic dictated in part by the content of the text, the level of the class, and the purpose of the activity. Nevertheless, a basic 'default' order might be: d, e, g, b, c, f, a. You may want to point out that stages c (reading the transcript) and a (a focus on language) are optional, and may detract from the purely skill-focused nature of the lesson. (For more on using texts for language presentations, see unit 15.)
   4 The rationale for this order is:
      d Activating interest and background (top-down) knowledge helps understanding.
      e Pre-teaching vocabulary (bottom-up knowledge) helps understanding.
      g Setting task provides a motivation to listen; more general tasks precede more specific tasks.
      b More specific tasks, requiring more intensive listening, follow more extensive tasks.
      c Following the transcript helps resolve residual problems of understanding, and forms links between aural signal and written words.
      f Assuming that students now understand the text, it can be used to promote discussion; this is also a further check of understanding.
      a Text is used as a source of language focus, but only after it has been thoroughly understood.

E Classroom application

1. Point out that this three-way division is a convenient way of classifying listening (and reading) tasks. Pre-listening: *d,e*; while-listening: *g, b, c*; post-listening: *f, a*.

2 Trainees work in small groups, and should be prepared to present their tasks to the class. It is expected that their task sequences reflect the principles outlined above.

(Note: as an alternative, set the trainees a recorded text from the current coursebook they are using; they can then compare their treatment of the recording with the way it is dealt with in the coursebook. Different groups can also work with different texts).

KEY WORDS FOR TEACHERS

Use the key words to review some of the main 'takeaways' from the session.

REFLECTION

Points that could be made include:

Q1: Speaking *involves* listening, so for students who want to learn to speak, listening would seem to be essential; also, there are some grounds to believe that 'understanding messages' is a prerequisite for language acquisition.

Q2: There are acceptable alternatives, but they don't necessarily involve reading aloud: for example, simply talking to the students ('live listening'), and/or using online video sites as a source for listening material. Such video sites often have an option for displaying subtitles and also may allow for control of the pace of delivery. This can help particularly if learners access them for homework and autonomous study.

Q3: Tasks that divert attention away from processing the text at the word level can help, e.g. matching, sequencing, selecting, etc. tasks. Learners' need to 'understand every word' can be satisfied towards the end of a task sequence, by giving them the transcript, which is often included in coursebooks.

Q4: Songs can be used like any other listening text, but many do not lend themselves to in-depth scrutiny. The best are probably those that have some narrative element, and/or that include the repeated use of (useful) formulaic language. A diet solely of songs would probably not be a good idea, but their occasional use is likely to motivate many students, especially if they are songs they have themselves chosen.

Q5: Coursebook texts may sound unnatural because in order to control their level of difficulty and speed of delivery, or to build into them specific language items, they have often been scripted and then recorded, rather than recorded spontaneously. Teachers can make their own unscripted, or semi-scripted, recordings, using colleagues or friends, but there is often a price to pay in terms of acoustic quality. Another source of more natural-sounding speech is authentic recorded material, such as TV and radio interviews, films, and soap operas.

Q6: One way of helping learners become 'strategic listeners' in interactive talk is to teach them some expressions with which they can control the input, such as *Do you mean ... ?, Did you say ... ?, I'm sorry, I didn't understand ...*, etc. Practice interacting with each other, and with the teacher, obviously helps.

Topic 3 – Language skills: reading, listening, speaking and writing

21 Focus on reading skills

Main focus
To learn the basic principles of developing the reading skill, and to apply these to the design of a skills-based lesson.

Learning outcomes
- Trainees are aware of different purposes and strategies for reading.
- Trainees understand how comprehension is achieved in reading.
- Trainees apply these principles to the design of lessons aimed at developing the reading skill.

Key concepts
- reading for information/gist/pleasure; intensive reading
- skimming, scanning
- top-down v bottom-up knowledge
- linguistic v extralinguistic clues
- pre-reading, while-reading, and post-reading tasks

Stage	Focus
A Warm-up	introducing the topic through discussion questions
B Reading purposes and strategies	highlighting different reasons for, and ways of, reading texts
C Reading in a second language	experiencing reading in another language
D Coursebook reading texts and tasks	identifying the rationale behind coursebook reading tasks
E A reading lesson	ordering the stages of a reading lesson
Key words for teachers	building of specialist vocabulary to talk about teaching
Reflection	reviewing the issues discussed in this unit

A Warm-up

The following points could be made, in discussing these questions:
a This might just work if (a) the spelling-to-sound relationships in English were more regular than they are; (b) the student was already familiar with the spoken form and meaning of the words being sounded out; and (c) understanding the words in a text constituted understanding the text as a whole (but see the next point).
b Vocabulary is very important, but a knowledge of all the words does not guarantee comprehension, since other kinds of knowledge (such as grammar knowledge, and background knowledge of the topic) are also implicated.
c Reading aloud, on the part of the students, does not ensure understanding – indeed, it may actually interfere with understanding – and can be very tedious for anyone listening. Moreover, it is not a skill that has wide application in the real world. It is therefore best avoided, unless the students are already familiar with the text (e.g. if they have written it themselves) and they are rehearsing it for performance.

d Simplifying texts can make them more accessible to learners, but a diet of only simplified texts may not be the best preparation for 'real-life' reading.
e Reading *is* a good way of improving vocabulary, although more for receptive than for productive purposes. Moreover, classroom reading is seldom sufficient to trigger incidental vocabulary learning: it needs to be supplemented by a great deal of out-of-class reading.
f This is largely true, but the successful *transfer* of reading skills from one language to another depends on the reader having a core of language knowledge (e.g. vocabulary and grammar).

B Reading purposes and strategies

The completed chart should look like this: (Note that more than one way of reading may be possible, as the reader alternates between different modes, according to his or her purpose.)

Text type	Reason for reading		Way of reading		
	primarily for pleasure	primarily for information	close (intensive) reading	skimming for gist	scanning for specific information
instructions for playing a board game		✓	✓		
a memo from your boss		✓	✓	✓	
a weather forecast		✓			✓
the news report of a sports event		✓		✓	✓
a short story	✓		✓	✓	
a research paper published in a scholarly journal		✓	✓	✓	✓

Note the following points:
- Reading purposes vary according to text type, and basically, they divide between *reading for information* and *reading for pleasure*.
- Readers read some texts very closely (such as instructions) while other texts they may simply *skim*, in order to get the main *gist* (as, for example, in reading the report of a sports event, where they may be less interested in the detail than in the main facts). Readers may also *scan* a text, searching for a specific piece of information, as when they are reading a weather forecast. In actual fact, readers will probably apply several different strategies to the one text. Their purpose for reading the text, e.g. the need for specific information as opposed to getting the gist of a story, will determine the strategies they employ.
- The main point to note here is that different text types will require different kinds of classroom tasks. For example, it would be inappropriate to ask learners to read an instruction manual just for gist, or to read a poem for specific information.

3 – Language skills: listening, reading, speaking and writing

C Reading in a second language

1 Before you start this activity, check if anyone is familiar with Esperanto. If they are, ask them to imagine how an English speaker with no knowledge of Esperanto would process this text. Trainees should read the text individually and silently, and attempt to answer the questions in parts 1a and 1b. If you feel the text may be too difficult, even for the relatively simple task, supply them with these word glosses:

malaperis: disappeared

feriis: were on vacation

aperis: appeared

   a Answers:
      1 a news item (of the human-interest type)
      2 a cat that crossed Canada to get home
      3 Tonto = the cat; Betty and Andreo = its owners
      4 happily – the cat is welcomed home
   b The questions translate as:
      1 What is the name of the cat? (Tonto)
      2 How many kilometres did the cat travel? (4,000)
      3 How many weeks did he need? (three)
      4 Where did Betty find her cat? (in her garden)

For your information (although this does not need to be shared with trainees) here is a translation of the text:

A cat that had travelled 4,000 kilometres returned to its owners, who believed it was dead. The cat, Tonto, disappeared when its owners, who live in Hamilton, Ontario, were vacationing in Vancouver. On the day they had to return home, they did not find the cat. Andreo and Betty Overden had no choice but to leave Tonto to his fate. Miraculously Tonto began the 4,000-mile journey through Canada. He needed only 3 weeks to get home. 'I couldn't believe my eyes,' Betty says, when the cat showed up one morning in her garden in Hamilton. 'Tonto was sitting there, hungry and dirty, but really happy to see us again!'

2 Trainees can then compare their answers to activity C1 in pairs.
   1 Even with limited knowledge of the language of the text, the reader can use a range of clues to decode the gist of it as well as identifying some specific facts. These clues include:
      • layout, type face, etc. which triggers background knowledge of this kind of text type (news report), including the way that news information is typically organized, i.e. main facts first, then background information
      • the picture and map, which provide information about the topic as well as a graphic summary of the gist
      • words that are similar to English or other language words (e.g. *kato, kilometrojn, ĝardeno*) as well as other *cross-linguistic* information, such as numbers and place names
   2 Answers to this self-rating task may vary considerably, but the point is to demonstrate (a) that comprehension is a somewhat subjective construct and (b) that a degree of comprehension is achievable even when a language may be largely unfamiliar (assuming familiarity with the script).
   3 This suggests that learners do not need to know all the words in a text in order to be able to gain some understanding of its content, and that understanding is the result of the

interaction of a number of factors, including non-verbal (extralinguistic) and 'top-down' ones, e.g. graphics, familiarity with similar texts, and linguistic (bottom-up) ones, including familiar words. This in turn supports the case for using authentic (ungraded) texts with learners, even at relatively low levels, so long as the reading tasks are matched appropriately. Trainees may also point out that they were able to find the answers to the questions in Esperanto, in 1b, without necessarily knowing what the questions meant; this may have implications for the way teachers check understanding (see below).

4 Teachers can help learners understand texts by setting tasks that exploit their different kinds of knowledge. For example, the students can be asked to use their knowledge of text types and/or any *extralinguistic* information (such as pictures) and/or their background knowledge of the topic to make predictions as to the content of the text, in advance of reading it. They can also be asked to *skim* the text initially, using the words that they recognize, to give them a general idea of the gist, before a closer, more intensive reading. Vocabulary that may be unfamiliar, but which is judged necessary for task completion, can be pre-taught. Finally, using questions in the target language may not always be the most reliable way of checking understanding, since learners may not understand the questions.

D Coursebook reading texts and tasks

1 a The purpose of these tasks can be summarized as:
   1 Using discussion questions to trigger background knowledge of, and interest in, the topic of the text, and any related vocabulary that learners already know.
   2 a Pre-teaching key vocabulary in order to make the text easier to understand. (Tasks 1 and 2a are *pre-reading tasks*.)
   2 b A general gist reading task, to give the students a purpose for reading, without encouraging them to read (and try to remember) every detail. (This is a *while-reading task*.)
   3 a More detailed questions, to provide a purpose for a more intensive re-reading of the text. (This is another *while-reading task*.)
   3 b These questions invite learners to demonstrate their understanding of the text by responding to it, while at the same time using the text as a bridge to further speaking activities. (This is a *post-reading task*.)
  b The highlighted sections of the text share the same grammatical feature: they are all relative clauses. This points to a further way the text is exploited at the post-reading stage – it is used as a context for teaching or practising selected linguistic features.
2 a The features of the text that might help understanding include: its *title* and the *illustration* (which allow the reader to predict the content of the text); topic familiarity, at least with other ball games, which helps make sense of potentially ambiguous words like *court, rings, pads*; and the logical organization of the text into paragraphs, each with its own topic. Factors that might inhibit understanding include the use of rare or specialized vocabulary (*ritual, sacred, enactment; rectangular, sloping, diameter*, etc.), and the use of some 'higher level' grammar structures such as the passive (*was played, were divided*, etc.) and modal constructions (*would have weighed, must have made ...*).

3 – Language skills: listening, reading, speaking and writing

  b Possible *pre-reading tasks* might include:
  - using the picture and/or title to activate background knowledge and to brainstorm vocabulary (e.g. associated with ball games)
  - pre-teaching unfamiliar vocabulary

  Possible *while-reading tasks* might include:
  - answering gist questions, e.g. *What was the aim of the game? What was its significance? Or: How similar/different was this game to modern basketball?*
  - using the information to draw a ball court, or to choose the picture that best represents the game in action
  - answering more detailed questions, such as true/false, or multiple choice

  At this point, it may be useful to remind trainees that the purpose of these tasks is not to *test* the learners' understanding of the text. Rather, it is to *lead* them to an understanding of the text, by, for example, helping them organize the content of the text. For this reason, it is important that the tasks are done collaboratively, with the learners working in pairs or small groups.

  Post-reading tasks might include:
  - discussing the topic, e.g. what they found interesting, surprising about the text
  - focusing on language features such as *modality*, by, for example, underlying all the *modal verbs* and other expressions of probability/possibility
  - writing a description of modern-day football or basketball, from the point of view of a writer 1000 years from now

E A reading lesson

1 The most logical order is probably: c, h, f, d, a, b, e, g. Note that stages (b) and (g) are designed to exploit the language 'spin-off' from the text, and may not always be relevant to the purposes for which a text has been chosen, nor essential to a more exclusively skills-focused lesson.

2 For this task, it may be appropriate to use the coursebook that the trainees are using in their teaching practice. You may wish to assign particular sequences to look at. Encourage trainees to think of ways of extending the task sequence by, for example, adding stages that are mentioned in activity E1.

KEY WORDS FOR TEACHERS

Use the key words to review some of the main 'takeaways' from the session.

REFLECTION

These questions could be assigned to different groups, e.g. questions *a–d* to one group, questions *e–g* to another. The groups can then re-form and compare their responses, before a general, open-class discussion.

Points that could be made here include:
a This extralinguistic information can help activate background knowledge, which in turn assists comprehension by compensating for lack of linguistic knowledge.
b Authentic materials may be more motivating for learners, even if challenging, and they are arguably better preparation for 'real-life' reading. They may also retain textual and extralinguistic features that assist comprehension, and that are often lost in simplified or specially written materials.
c A task provides the learners with a purpose for reading the text, and (depending on the choice of task) it can help divert the students away from the temptation to focus on decoding the meaning of every word.
d If a text is of a type that is typically *scanned* (such as a take-away food menu), a task that 'matches' this text type would be a scanning one. On the other hand, if a text is of a type that is typically read intensively, such as a set of instructions, an appropriate task would be one which requires the students to process it in a similar, intensive, way. It is a good idea to match the tasks with the text, since such a matching is more likely to prompt learners to transfer their first language reading skills into their second language. Moreover, it provides realistic preparation for real-life reading.
e In this way, the focus is moved away from *testing* reading to developing reading skills, i.e. *teaching* reading. Allowing students to share how they 'processed' the text provides opportunities for mutually improving their reading skills, and also takes the pressure off having to 'get the answers right' in the public forum.
f Students tend to over-rely on dictionaries and translation apps unless trained in how to use them constructively. An alternative is to try to work out the meaning of unfamiliar words from context, or to provide a 'gloss' of words that are likely to be unfamiliar at the end of the text.
g The ability to recall the details of a text is a reliable gauge of understanding, but understanding is not dependent on memorizing details. Most kinds of texts, in fact, are read for immediate understanding, not for later recall. Moreover, answering questions from memory is associated more with testing than with skills development.

Topic 3 – Language skills: reading, listening, speaking and writing

22 Focus on speaking skills

Main focus
To learn the basic principles of developing the speaking skill, and to apply these to the design of a skills-based lesson.

Learning outcomes
- Trainees understand the main considerations in dealing with a speaking skills lesson.
- Trainees understand the uses of a variety of speaking activities.

Key concepts
- communication
- information gap
- outcome
- monitoring

Stage	Focus
A Warm-up	a speaking activity about speaking
B Speaking activities	introducing a range of common speaking activities
C Giving advice: concerns of learners	reflecting on common issues experienced by learners
D Giving advice: concerns of teachers	reflecting on common issues experienced by teachers
Key words for teachers	building of specialist vocabulary to talk about teaching
Reflection	trainees apply what they have learned to analysing and planning a speaking activity

A Warm-up

Focus the trainees on the questions in their books and give a few moments for them to prepare what they want to say.

Questions 3 and 4 are an opportunity to highlight some key issues in speaking. When speaking we need to use vocabulary knowledge, grammar knowledge, and discourse knowledge (of how texts are constructed, for example, how conversations are opened, or topics are changed, or how conversations are brought to a close). In addition (as indicated in the quote) we need pragmatic knowledge of when it is appropriate to speak, and the degree of formality and politeness that is expected, and this may vary with culture. When speaking with others, we will need to listen and tailor contributions to what we have understood. All of this often happens extremely quickly, with little planning time. Where there is planning time (for example, when we give a presentation) speaking performance may be associated with greater expectations of accuracy (as compared to when there is very limited planning time).

B Speaking activities

1 The aim of the first part is to ensure that trainees appreciate that there is more to teaching speaking than learners using speaking to display grammar knowledge. This should not be confused with a belief that grammar is not important in communication – it plainly is – but not all speaking activities focus on communication. 2 and 3 seem to be based on communication and 1 and 4 focus on using speaking to develop grammar awareness. However, the discussion of grammar may develop a communicative emphasis, particularly if opinions vary and are discussed.

2 The trainees have already done one of the activities as the warm-up. They do not need to do the others themselves, but you may want to spend a few minutes ensuring that they understand the mechanics of each activity and how it works.

3 Ensure that the trainees understand the questions. It may be useful to give some examples of different class types (question 3b), for example, ESP, CLIL and exam classes.
Trainees can work in groups of three or four to discuss the questions and then ask them to report back.

Discussion
a Learners will find it hard to discuss without a fair amount of vocabulary and grammar knowledge, meaning that it more likely to be used from B1 level upwards.
b Yes, there is no reason why a discussion would not be appropriate for several different class types. For larger classes, the teacher will need to give additional attention to how to organize and monitor the groups.
c There is no clear outcome, unless an instruction saying that agreement should be reached is included.
d Yes

Role play
a Yes, role plays can be designed for a range of levels.
b Yes, but see caveats on class size above.
c This will depend on the design of the role play, but an outcome can be designed into the material. In the example given, the Headteacher could be required to decide on guidelines for the use of mobile phones in lessons, for instance.
d Yes.

Conversation
a Yes, but the learners need some linguistic resources to be able to participate, so probably from elementary upwards. At higher levels, learners may find this quite easy and so the teacher would need to work hard on shaping the language and improving it for the learners to see the usefulness of the activity. This is particularly true if learners are in a context where they get to use English outside the classroom anyway.
b Yes, but classes with very clear goals (such as exam classes or EAP classes) may feel that time could be better spent, so the teacher needs to work hard on helping learners improve through feedback and so on.
c No, like most conversations, there is no specific outcome.
d Yes, though turn-taking may be a little more challenging in an online lesson than a face-to-face one.

3 – Language skills: listening, reading, speaking and writing

Information gap
Information gap activities are a fundamental tenet of Communicative Language Teaching and there are a wide range of activities that would include some kind of information gap. The answer is 'yes' to all four questions.

Surveys and presentations
a Yes, depending on the demands of the presentation.
b Yes.
c Yes (the presentation).
d It can easily be done in a classroom. In an online environment it may depend on the software available, but if the survey includes a lot of respondents (i.e. each student has to speak to many other students), it may be difficult to set up.

4 Focus the trainees on the three questions and ensure that they understand them.
 a Which activities encourage learners to share personal information and opinions?
   Discussions and surveys will almost certainly do this, as will the activity described as 'Conversation' here. Information gaps can be designed so that they have an 'opinion gap' element, and in these cases there is the exchange of opinions.
 b Which activities could be set up so that the grammar and vocabulary required by the learners are predictable?
   To some extent, the vocabulary required can be determined for most activities, assuming that the material used dictates the topic of the task. Activities can be designed to make certain grammatical structures more likely. For example, if a role play includes a witness to a crime that they saw yesterday, it is likely the past tense will be required. However, it is also likely that there will be a degree of unpredictability in many activities. This is particularly true of the Conversation activity.
 c What would the teacher's role be before, during and after these activities?
   The teacher needs to select an appropriate activity and estimate how long it will likely take learners to complete. They need to set it up, ensuring instructions are clear. They should monitor carefully and support learners where necessary. They should organize a reporting-back phase and respond to what the learners said, and also offer feedback on how ideas were expressed.

C Giving advice: concerns of learners

If you are short of time, tasks C and D could be done as a jigsaw, with some trainees looking at task C and others D, before sharing ideas.

1 A teacher could nominate learners to speak, rather than always accepting those that volunteer; they could use more pair and group work so that more people speak; they could give a little preparation time so that everyone is ready to speak when asked.

2 To some extent this is natural, particularly if learners have not had many chances to use English. The teacher must ensure that the classroom is a safe and supportive environment, where people are encouraged and there is an atmosphere of trust. The teacher can also use the classroom to 'rehearse' the sort of situations that learners will encounter outside the classroom. The learner might also use strategies that may decrease their anxiety, such as anticipating and preparing for occasions they need to use English.

3 If the learners in a group can already communicate what they need to without undue hesitation, it is important that class time is devoted to further improvement. This may be through error correction, for example, or by focusing on appropriacy and developing a range of ways in which an idea can be expressed. In this way the learners will see the value in the activities.

4 This learner could make recordings of themselves speaking and then play the recording back, checking for accuracy and ways of improving. They could look to join groups on social media which use English for conversation exchange. They could set up 'let's use English' meetings with classmates outside of lessons.

D Giving advice: concerns of teachers

1 The teacher could use group work rather than pair work where possible, as the learners will be pushed to speak more loudly. The teacher could monitor more obtrusively than usual, and so ensuring that they can hear. The teacher could focus particularly on language used during the reporting-back phase of the lesson.

2 There is no simple solution, but teachers should probably start with the assumption that learners will work effectively, even without the 'global monitoring' associated with a physical classroom. The teacher could try keeping activities quite short to start with, so that learners are less likely to lose focus, and also ensure that learners understand the purpose of the activity and what they are expected to achieve. Teachers could also move between rooms quite quickly to try to pick up on difficulties. They should ensure that learners know how to ask for help and get the teacher's attention, should they need it. Also, they could ask for feedback on the usefulness of breakout room activities, to see if the learners find them useful even without the sort of monitoring that is possible in physical classrooms.

3 Where learners share a common first language, this is inevitable to some extent. The teacher can encourage the learners to use English wherever possible and explain the benefits that this will have. In addition, they could relatively reduce the time spent working in pairs and groups and place more emphasis on reporting back in open class. They might also choose to see the use of L1 as a natural resource that learners will use to plan and achieve tasks, but then push the learners to reproduce their discussion, or parts of their discussion, in English, using formulae such as 'That's good – how do you say it in English?'.

4 While speaking might be used to practise a particular language point, it does not have to be the case. The learners can benefit simply from having opportunities to communicate in English, particularly if the teacher's feedback is well judged.

3 – Language skills: listening, reading, speaking and writing

KEY WORDS FOR TEACHERS

Remind the trainees of the need to be able to use teaching terms confidently and accurately.

REFLECTION

Ensure that the trainees choose an appropriate activity from the coursebooks they are using. Focus the trainees on the four questions.

1 Answers will vary.
2 Trainees could suggest using more groups – the more groups there, are the more chance that more people will be speaking at any one time. Preparation time and giving learners a chance to think of ideas before speaking is likely to lead to more production. Learners could repeat the activity with different partners.
3 Answers will vary, but it may be worth encouraging trainees to think about possible adaptations (for example, if the class is weak, it may be a good idea to build in more preparation, such as teaching appropriate vocabulary).
4 See B4c, above.

23 Focus on writing skills

Main focus
To learn the basic principles of developing the writing skill, and to apply these to the design of a skills-based lesson.

Learning outcomes
- Trainees understand ways of developing the writing skill in a classroom context.
- Trainees understand the principle of writing as a process.
- Trainees can respond to written work in a variety of ways.

Key concepts
- communication, readership
- text type
- product v process writing
- drafting
- corrective feedback

Stage	Focus
A Warm-up	introducing some practical considerations and background issues in teaching writing
B Writing activities	introducing some writing activities
C Stages in writing	focusing on the idea of writing as a process
D Providing feedback on written work	introducing ways of responding to writing
E Analysing material	analysing the purpose of stages in a writing lesson
Key words for teachers	building of specialist vocabulary to talk about teaching
Reflection	trainees reflect on what they have learned by doing a short writing task

A Warm-up

You may want to elicit the views of some of the trainees before starting this activity. They could talk about their experiences of dealing with writing in TP, or of learning to write in other languages.

Allow the trainees to work in small groups to discuss their responses before reporting back. You may wish to highlight some of the following points:

Tracy: It is a common view that writing can be done almost exclusively outside the class. However, there are several stages to a writing lesson that can be done usefully in class – thinking of ideas, discussing and organizing ideas, collaborative writing, working on editing skills and so on. Moreover, if writing is done in lessons, learners can benefit from 'real time' immediate feedback. It may also be that if writing is seldom done in class, learners believe it is not really very important and so dedicate little time to practice.

3 – Language skills: listening, reading, speaking and writing

Korali: This view – that writing in class is essentially used in class to practise new language items – is quite common. This use of writing contrasts with using writing for communicative purposes, which is also necessary in lessons. Typically, learners are under less time pressure when they write than when they speak. This allows them time to think of 'rules', correct mistakes and think of alternative ways of expressing themselves if they are unsure, all of which can lead to greater accuracy.

Chris: The provision of a model text, accompanied by some analysis of it, is a common and effective way of familiarizing learners with the text types they need to be able to write. However, this focus on the 'products' of writing has been criticized on the grounds that it ignores the processes – such as writing multiple drafts – by which a text gets created (see task C below).

Laura: Some learners may already be aware of the tools that are available to them, but it is a good idea for teachers to make sure that everyone knows how they can use software to support their work. The use of machine translation may be more controversial, but it is likely to only become more widely used and sophisticated in the future, so its use could be considered an important skill to learn.

David: David is probably right to pick out only some of the errors. If a learner gets a piece of work back which is covered in corrections, it can be demotivating. It is also a good idea to respond, not just to the form of the message (including its errors) but also to its content, as this reinforces the idea that writing is a means of communication, not just a way of practising grammar and spelling.

Quyen: This can be a very useful strategy, not least because it creates a readership for the writing learners do. However, it is also true that learners can be doubtful of these benefits, and so the benefits need to be explained. Peer feedback promotes interaction between learners and thus a sense of class community. It also encourages learners to think critically about writing and what makes a piece of writing 'good'.

B Writing activities

1 You may prefer to demonstrate one activity, for example the interactive writing (c).
Afterwards analyse the activity, drawing attention to the sorts of issues raised in the table.
The trainees could then discuss the other activities.
Ensure that the trainees understand the questions at the top of each column before starting.
An activity has a **communicative purpose** if it requires writers to communicate meanings in order to affect the thoughts or behaviours of their reader(s).
A **text** is a coherent and cohesive piece of language, which typically extends beyond a single sentence.
In column four ('Is the activity similar to what learners might do outside the language classroom?') you may wish to introduce the term 'authentic task'.

23 Focus on writing skills

Analysis of activity types					
Activity type	Is there a communicative purpose?	Do the learners produce texts?	Is the activity similar to what learners might do outside the language classroom?	Does the writer know who the reader will be?	What level could it be used for?
a Multiple choice gap-fill	no	no	no	no	all levels
b Reproducing a model	no – unless the rubric creates this opportunity	yes	yes – assuming the model is reasonably real-life-like	no – unless the rubric creates this	most levels depending on model text
c Interactive writing	yes	yes	yes	yes	all levels
d Writing an essay	no – unless the rubric creates this	yes	no*	no – unless the rubric creates this	intermediate and upwards
e Dialogue writing + items	no	yes	no	no	elementary upwards

* It may be argued that the answer could also be 'yes', particularly if a learner is in education and following a programme in which English is the medium of instruction.

2 Allow the trainees to work in pairs to discuss their answers before reporting back.
   a Various answers are possible, but the key thing is that other people should read what is written and react to it. For example, learners could work in groups of three and read each other's work. Each learner could say which of the other two films they would most like to see.
   b Learners could be asked to write a short review, rather than six standalone sentences.
   c The task could be designed to make it a little more life-like. A review would be the easiest option, and there could be more information about the type of review. For example: 'You have just read a blog post about movies and the writer has encouraged their readers to submit a review of their favourite film in less than 50 words.'
   d Learners could read each other's work. Work could be displayed on a noticeboard in a physical classroom, or shared and displayed digitally in an online classroom.

3 – Language skills: listening, reading, speaking and writing

C Stages in writing

1 Explain the activity to the trainees. Allow them to work individually for a minute or two before comparing with each other in pairs and then agreeing an appropriate order with you. You could point out that these stages may overlap to some extent.
   1 e Consult books and talk to colleagues to get ideas.
   2 d Organize ideas.
   3 c Write a rough draft.
   4 b Read and make changes and corrections.
   5 a Write a final copy.
2 Writing in the classroom needs to be treated as a process, with attention being given to each stage. For example, time needs to be dedicated to the collection of ideas; this might be done through brainstorming in class, or, at higher levels, asking learners to do some research before the writing activity. Organization may be addressed through the study of model texts and studying the genres that the learners will need to work in outside the classroom. Time should be set aside for responding to feedback (either from peers or the teacher).

D Providing feedback on written work

As an alternative to the procedure here, you could collect some samples of writing from learners in TP classes and photocopy them for trainees to correct.

You may like to lead into this activity by asking trainees about their recollections of how teachers marked their work at school, particularly anything written in a foreign language.

1 Ask the trainees to look at the three samples of types of marking and allow them to discuss their ideas in pairs briefly. If you need to, prompt the trainees to think about which method(s) involve the learners and also ask them to consider how much guidance the learners get. The final method (using the code) both involves learners and gives guidance, and is very much part of a 'process view' of writing (as it encourages editing and rewriting). On the downside, it can be very time-consuming for both teachers and learners – not least, because the teacher needs to check that corrections have been made appropriately.
2 The approach to error correction may be different at different levels, because at low levels it may be overwhelming to be asked to correct a series of errors. Also at low levels, the teacher may also prefer to focus on what the learners have successfully communicated rather than too many errors.
3 The key to the code is below, but you may wish to stress to the trainees that this is only an example – they could alter it to suit themselves and their learners. It's important that the learners have a copy of the code and that they know what each item means. It is also worth pointing out that classifying errors is exceptionally complicated and there is some overlap here. All 'tense' errors are also 'grammar' errors, for example.

   ww = wrong word
   sp = spelling
   wo = word order
   G = grammar
   T = tense
   P = punctuation
   un = unnecessary word
   + = add a word, or part of a word

E Analysing material

You may want to discuss how the writing activity is given a context and a purpose by setting up the situation through a previous listening activity, in which Ahmed talks to a friend about the most appropriate homestay family for him to stay with when he visits Australia. The email (part of 2a and b) is from Ahmed to the family he chose.

If you are short on time, you could provide the purposes and ask trainees to match them to the exercise numbers.

1 The overall purpose of 2a and b is to introduce the genre of an email of introduction in this context (which the students later write in 4d). In particular, 2b focuses on the organization of the text.
2 The overall purpose of 3a, b and c is to introduce a language focus (vocabulary that can be used for linking ideas). This could be seen as a way of giving students at this level (A2) additional support for when they come to write.
3 The overall purpose of 4a, b and c is to give learners the opportunity to plan their writing – trainees should be able to see that this is part of a process approach to writing. 4b is also an opportunity to practise speaking and listening, so the authors are integrating skills to some extent.
4 4d is the actual writing stage of the lesson, where learners produce their email. Notice how much support they get (again linked to the level of the material – A2) as there is a checklist of things to include.
5 The purpose of 4e is to provide a readership for the emails produced. Learners are encouraged to use the checklist to ensure that the email they read has included the key points that were suggested. In other words, learners are supported in reading and giving feedback, and this encourages them to give feedback to their peers on content (as well as language forms).
6 Answers will vary but trainees should show awareness of their learners' abilities, needs and interests.
7 Questions 7 and 8 encourage trainees to consider how they might adapt and differentiate material to suit different learners in their group. The trainees can be supported in this by thinking about how they have themselves adapted material in their lessons to make it more or less challenging, even if that was only for the whole group. To make the material more challenging, stronger learners might be asked to include an additional item that is not given in the checklist. (For example, ask the family a question.)
8 Learners could be given a partially written email, so that they write only the missing sections, or they could be given sentence stems throughout the email, which they then complete.

3 – Language skills: listening, reading, speaking and writing

KEY WORDS FOR TEACHERS

Remind the trainees of the need to be able to use teaching terms confidently and accurately.

REFLECTION

Allow the trainees a little time to write their sentences, before comparing them with a partner and then sharing some with the class.

The aim is to review the key parts of this unit. If trainees do not include the following ideas, you can feed them in as you see fit:

Writing is both a way of communicating and used in the classroom as a learning aid and a way of practising language. Writing can be done collaboratively, and tasks often work best when it is clear who will read the piece of writing – either another member of the class or a fictitious recipient. Different text genres have different characteristics (some of which can be taught fairly easily) and learners can be supported in their writing by analysing model texts. Teachers can usefully spend time focusing on the different stages of producing text – the process – as well as the final product.

24 Teaching basic literacy

Main focus
To understand typical literacy needs and explore a range of activities to help develop literacy skills.

Learning outcomes
- Trainees understand the principal ways of developing basic reading and writing skills.
- Trainees consider the teaching implications of working with different types of learners who need support with basic literacy.

Key concepts
- literacy, illiteracy
- reading, writing, spelling
- first language (L1), second language (L2)

Developing reading skills is dealt with in unit 21.
Developing writing skills is dealt with in unit 23.

Stage	Focus
A Warm-up	defining literacy
B L1 and L2 literacy	introducing typical profiles of learners who may have literacy needs
C Lessons from learners	practical tips on conducting reading and writing classes with learners with literacy needs
D Reading activities	introducing a range of reading activities, appropriate for learners with literacy needs
E Writing activities	introducing a range of writing activities, appropriate for learners with literacy needs
Key words for teachers	building of specialist vocabulary to talk about teaching
Reflection	trainees review key points in teaching learners with literacy needs

Note: This is an introduction to basic literacy, in terms of reading and writing. Literacy covers a wide range of different areas, including but not limited to digital literacy, media literacy and visual literacy. They are beyond the scope of this session, though you may want to point out to trainees that many literacies can be developed in an English language classroom. It is also worth mentioning that reading and writing literacy does not only need to be a survival skill – it can go much deeper than that.

3 – Language skills: listening, reading, speaking and writing

A Warm-up

You could start this task by asking the trainees themselves to define literacy. They can then read the text. Note that literacy, as defined here, is more than simply the ability to read and write; it entails knowing how to function actively in the target culture, as a reader and writer of that culture's texts. As such, the concept of literacy is particularly relevant to ESL (English as a second language) learners.

1 Trainees should be able to come up with a variety of text types, many of which will be bureaucratic in nature, e.g. applying for asylum seeker status, reading a housing contract, filling in a medical history form, etc.

2 The main difference between 'doing reading and writing' and teaching what is sometimes called 'functional literacy' (the fact of being literate in areas needed in the user's daily life) is the nature and purpose of the texts, and the fact that some ESL learners may lack basic literacy in their first language.

B L1 and L2 literacy

You may choose to have each group of trainees discuss one of the learners, then share their answers in groups.

1 Aasmah is literate in her first language, but not in English. Halima is neither literate in her first language nor in English. Huseyin is literate in his first languages and, to a certain extent in English, but lacks functional literacy.

2 The important point to make is that learners who have problems with literacy could have speaking and listening skills at any level from beginner to advanced. Therefore it is difficult to speak of an overall level for these learners, because their abilities in each skill are so uneven.

3 Reading and writing are often used to create contexts, give practice, create records of new language items and so on. Without literacy in English, it will be much harder for Aasmah and Halima to pick up on this new language.

4 Aasmah and Huseyin are literate in their own languages and this may help them in becoming literate in English. They may be familiar with certain text types and their organization (although this can vary with culture). They will be familiar with the sort of information available in a dictionary and may be able to use a bilingual dictionary. They will know how to hold a pen, and probably how to use a keyboard, as well as perhaps knowing how to exploit spell checkers and so on. On the other hand, it's worth pointing out that they may not be familiar with Roman script and its conventions, such as capitalization, punctuation and so on.

5 Huseyin needs to be able to read and write connected text, and often texts that are of a rather formal register; the ability to write isolated sentences does not necessarily prepare him for his specific needs.

6 He needs to be familiar with the specific genres that he will encounter, and the way that the register of these genres is sensitive to such context factors as the relationship between writers and readers.

24 Teaching basic literacy

C Lessons from learners

1 This task gives some practical tips on the needs of learners. Allow the trainees to think individually before comparing with each other and then confirming ideas in open class. If time is short, you can allocate different 'case studies' to different pairs or groups of trainees. The first five case studies are connected to reading, and the remaining five to writing.

Karim: At low levels of reading ability it is generally considered good practice to use large fonts and to put little on the page.

Soula: Teachers need to stay patient and be very encouraging.

Li Na: Learners need 'bottom-up' strategies (letter/sound relations) but this can be integrated with a 'top-down' approach, at least for some words, particularly those that are very frequent and familiar. It could be pointed out that context (including co-text) may be one thing that helps in the decoding process, and this may make simple sentences and texts relatively easier than some individual words presented in isolation.

Shireen: Teachers need to teach reading skills based on language that is already known to the learners orally.

Vashti: Different fonts or styles of handwriting, as well as the use of capital letters, bold or italic, can change the shape of a letter or word and make it seem unfamiliar to a learner, even if they would recognize it in other circumstances. Trainees may better understand this if you encourage them to notice the range of shapes for the letter 'a' or the word 'to' in this table in the trainee book. Teachers need to point this out to learners, and be aware of it when creating materials or asking learners to read each other's work.

Ali: Fatigue is a factor. Writing activities need to be short at this level and learners will need breaks.

Samia: Learners who have literacy needs are unlikely to be able to copy things from the board quickly and efficiently. Teachers may need to consider putting more on handouts or sending summaries to learners after lessons, so that learners get a written record of the key points. Learners with literacy needs may be reluctant to speak up for fear of losing face or causing problems to classmates or teachers, or have self-esteem or embarrassment issues connected to their literacy.

Daryan: Some learners, particularly those who are not literate in their own language, will need help with things that may seem obvious to a teacher and can therefore be overlooked. This may include help with developing fine motor skills.

Mei Yan: Even copying can be difficult for learners with literacy needs, because there is a limit to what can be stored in 'working memory' – causing delays as they need to constantly look for the next part.

Shan: Learners may not see the value of developing handwriting skills, and/or may rely on technology to do their reading or writing for them. Teachers need to consider to what extent handwriting may be useful for their learners, and therefore how much time to spend on it in class. They should probably also spend time on teaching learners the skills to make better use of the technology tools they have access to, as well as showing learners how they can use these tools to help them, for example by looking at a text as it is read to them.

3 – Language skills: listening, reading, speaking and writing

> **Trainer tip**
>
> If you are running this session online, you could create a table of the learner names in a collaborative document for feedback. Trainees could then add comments to the document simultaneously, building up a single set of useful tips which they can refer back to later.
>
> As an optional follow-up activity, you may wish to draw trainees' attention to the range of different fonts used in the table. Focus on the letter 'a' and ask them to notice how many different ways it is rendered. Highlight that learners need to be able to recognize multiple different shapes for a single letter, both in lower case and upper case.

2   The aim of this activity is to show the trainees that the issues discussed so far can be relevant to any classroom, not just adult ESL/ESOL classrooms.
Possible answers:
YL: Karim (anxiety), Soula (patience/encouragement needed), Shireen (using known language), Vashti (fonts/handwriting), Ali (tiring), Daryan (fine motor skills)
Special Education Needs (SEN): Karim (anxiety), Soula (patience/encouragement needed), Vashti (fonts/handwriting), Ali (tiring), Samia (time to copy, self-esteem), Mei Yan (limitations on working memory), Shan (reliance on technology)

D Reading activities

The main point of this task is to give the trainees a set of reading activities that would be appropriate at very low levels of reading ability. You may like to spend some time ensuring that they understand how each activity works, perhaps demonstrating some of them.
Trainees could work in pairs before reporting back their ideas.

word level	sentence level	text level
a) Reading bingo	f) Describing pictures	b) Find and underline
c) Odd one out	h) Sentence halves	e) Ordering
d) Matching		g) Next word

E Writing activities

Again, the main point of this task is to give the trainees a set of writing activities that would be appropriate at very low levels of writing proficiency. You may like to spend some time ensuring that they understand how each activity works, perhaps demonstrating some of them.
a) and f) both practise spelling
b) and e) both practise the mechanical formation of letters
c) and d) both practise sentence-level writing

24 Teaching basic literacy

KEY WORDS FOR TEACHERS
Remind the trainees of the need to be able to use teaching terms confidently and accurately.

REFLECTION
In a face-to-face input session, you may prefer to reproduce the diagram on large pieces of paper and have the trainees make a poster. Among the points that the trainees could make are the following:

Reading	Reading and writing	Writing
• Use large fonts. • Don't put too much on a page. • Practise reading single words, sentences and short texts. • Be aware of how words change their shape depending on the style of writing.	• Be patient. • Work with 'known' language. • Remember that learners get tired very quickly. • Introduce learners to particular genres, for example job applications. • Use model texts. • Help learners to make the best use of technology tools at their disposal.	• Allow lots of time. • Practise forming letters, spelling, and handwriting. • Ask learners to produce sentences and short texts.

Topic 3 – Language skills: reading, listening, speaking and writing

25 Integrating skills

Main focus
To review procedures aimed at developing skills, and see how different skills can be combined within a single activity or activity sequence.

Learning outcomes
- Trainees understand the main considerations in dealing with integrated skills lessons.
- Trainees are able to analyse integrated skills activities.
- Trainees consolidate their understanding of procedures used in skills-based lessons.

Key concepts
- communication
- combining skills
- receptive v productive

Note: *Integrate* and *combine* are used interchangeably through this unit.

Stage	Focus
A Warm-up	trainees experience and reflect on a short integrated skills activity
B Combining skills	trainees consider how the same skill may be treated differently in different contexts
C How teachers combine skills	trainees are given some practical ideas on how to combine skills in lessons
D Putting it into practice	trainees consider how they can provide practice of different skills using a single text
Key words for teachers	building of specialist vocabulary to talk about teaching
Reflection	trainees reflect on the teaching of skills by doing a quiz

A Warm-up

1 Choose one of the following activities, A or B. (Clearly, the running dictation will not work if you are teaching online.) The text is the same for both activities and the questions in the Trainee Book are suitable for either activity, although answers will vary slightly.

A: Running dictation

This activity can be set up without the trainees opening their books.

You need one copy of the text below for each pair of trainees. Stick the copies around the room. One person in each pair should walk quickly, or even run, to the text, read a chunk, go back to their partner and dictate it. The listener should write down what they hear and the 'runner' should go back for the next part. The winners are the first pair to finish. As pairs finish, take a copy of the text off the wall and ask them to compare what they have written with the original. Pairs who finish early can consider the question at the end of the text.

> You get a text message, you read it and you text back. You read an interesting news story and you tell someone about it. You go to a lecture and you take notes. If you hear some gossip, you might pass it on. So, outside the classroom, language skills are not always used in isolation. They tend to be combined. Think back to the last lesson you taught. Were any skills combined?

Photocopiable   © Cambridge University Press & Assessment 2022

B: Mutual dictation

Divide the class into pairs – A and B. A should look at page 180 in the Trainee Book and B should look at page 182. Trainees take it in turns to read a chunk of text for their partner to write. They should not show their texts to their partners. Pairs who finish early can consider the question at the end of the text.

2 Allow the trainees a little time to gather their ideas before reporting back in open class.
   a–b Running dictation: The 'runner' will predominantly practise reading and speaking.
       The writer will predominantly practise writing and listening.
       Mutual dictation: Both roles involve all four skills.
   c Answers will vary.
   d Answers will vary but both activities are quite flexible.
   e The running dictation activity is restricted to a physical classroom. The mutual dictation activity will work in either environment, although there may be a limit on the number of breakout rooms that can be created and effectively monitored.
   f Genuine communication depends on skills being combined – this is what happens outside the classroom – and so there is a strong argument that they should also be combined inside the classroom.

3 – Language skills: listening, reading, speaking and writing

B Combining skills

The trainees could do this activity in small groups. They may be able to make arguments for the inclusion of additional skills, such as writing in a) if the journalist makes notes, or the answers to a journalist's questions are written.

		Listening	Speaking	Reading	Writing
a	Learners do a 15-minute role play in pairs. Half the class are journalists, who interview the other half of the class, who are environmental campaigners.	✓	✓		
b	Learners work briefly in small groups to discuss ideas to put into a piece of writing on animal rights. They then do a piece of writing in the style of a blog post on the subject.	✓	✓		✓
c	Learners read a text about language teaching methodologies and answer multiple-choice questions. They discuss their answers in small groups before reporting back to the teacher.	✓	✓	✓	
d	Learners read a short description of a podcast. They then listen to the podcast and answer some true/false questions.	✓		✓	
e	Learners work in pairs to write a review of a restaurant they like.	✓	✓		✓
f	Learners make notes as they listen to a short, pre-recorded lecture.	✓			✓

2 The aim of this activity is to demonstrate to trainees that a particular skill will not always have the same degree of prominence in all lessons. This will have implications for teaching. One or two examples should suffice to make the point, but you may wish to add others. Examples: a teacher may want to correct errors when speaking is the main focus, but when learners are speaking to compare answers to a listening comprehension exercise the teacher may choose to ignore all errors other than those that affect understanding.
If reading is the main focus of an activity, then the teacher may wish to set several reading tasks on the same text and, indeed, to select a text that will challenge learners. But if reading

is used as a prompt for writing, the teacher may prefer to choose a text which is relatively easy to understand and set only a single comprehension task, so that the lesson can move forwards to the writing.

3 Explain the activity to the trainees. Allow them to work together before reporting back in open class. An alternative focus for this task could be the trainees' own lessons in TP: ask them to reflect on a lesson they have taught recently, and to identify the different skills it involved. Were there opportunities for yet more integration? This task would work best if trainees were organized into their TP groups.

C How teachers combine skills

1 Allow the trainees to work individually before comparing their answers. When they have finished, you may like to ask them which skills (speaking, listening, reading and writing) they used to complete the activity. If they compare answers, it will be all four.
   a model text
   b to discuss
   c communicative
   d nodding and asking
   e give feedback
   f the transcript
   g read a text
   h speaking and listening
2 Encourage trainees to engage with the ideas above and critically assess whether they would be useful in their teaching going forward.

D Putting it into practice

This text has been chosen so that trainees are reminded of different approaches that may be used in the teaching of language. However, you may wish to choose a text that is more topical, or one that is more relevant to the trainees' own classes.

There are various ways the text could be exploited, and you may like to give an example or two at the start so that trainees are clear on what is expected of them. Ensure that trainees understand that they can use different activities to practise different combinations of skills.

The text could be read aloud to the class as if it were part of a podcast, or dictated, or in the form of a dictogloss (listening).

The learners could read it themselves (reading).

They could discuss it, saying whether the approach sounds plausible to them, and what the implications might be for teaching (speaking and listening).

They could brainstorm the questions that they would like to ask a CLIL expert (speaking and writing).

They could role play an interview, with one role being a student who had experienced CLIL (speaking and listening).

They could discuss any additional skills (over and above those of a language teacher) that a CLIL teacher would need (speaking and listening).

They could be given further reading about CLIL, or be asked to research CLIL, and then write about its strengths and weaknesses (reading and writing).

3 – Language skills: listening, reading, speaking and writing

> **KEY WORDS FOR TEACHERS**

Remind the trainees of the need to be able to use teaching terms confidently and accurately.

> **REFLECTION**

Explain how to play the game. You may have to act as a 'referee' if there is a disputed answer. Summarize the answers after the groups have finished. Some questions refer to material covered in other units on skills, rather than solely material in this unit.

1. reading and listening
2. writing and speaking
3. A text that has not been produced with language teaching as its purpose. Typical examples include newspapers, magazines and TV/film trailers.
4. Usually not. Teachers are often encouraged to help their learners move away from thinking they must understand every word of a text. Understanding every word might be unrealistic for many learners, even at quite high levels. Understanding the overall message is much more important. Of course, there may be instances where every word is important (e.g. on a medicine bottle: 'Take three tablets a day') but generally this is not the case.
5. Various answers are possible. For example, some learners could be provided with a glossary, or a summary of key points. If learners suffer from dyslexia, the teacher may need to provide the text in a different, or bigger, font.
6. Trainees could talk about things such as brainstorming ideas, collaborating on a first draft, editing the first draft (by finding errors and so on), and producing a final draft, perhaps for homework.
7. Whenever learners speak, it is usually the case that someone will be listening.
8. Various answers are possible, but some suggestions would be that trainees could read a model answer or read input data (such as a letter that they have to respond to). They could discuss the content of what to write (speaking/listening) and so on.
9. Again, there are many possibilities, which include: writing a letter or email of complaint, and discussing their own holiday experiences.
10. The text should be interesting to the learners. The text should also be of an appropriate length and complexity.

26 Lesson planning: defining aims

> **Main focus**
> To distinguish and describe different kinds of lesson aims.
>
> **Learning outcomes**
> - Trainees understand the differences between types of aims.
> - Trainees are able to analyse material and identify appropriate aims.
> - Trainees can apply their understanding, allowing them to write appropriate lesson and stage aims.
>
> **Key concepts**
> - linguistic aims, communicative aims, skills aims and developmental aims
> - main aims, subsidiary aims
>
> Note: The term *aim* is adopted in this unit (rather than *objective* or *learning outcome*) because it seems dominant in the ELT profession.

Stage	Focus
A Warm-up	trainees consider the importance and purpose of defining lesson aims
B Types of aim	comparing different types of lesson aim
C Material and aims	trainees identify the aims of pieces of material and practise wording accompanying aims
Key words for teachers	building of specialist vocabulary to talk about teaching
Reflection	trainees reflect on what they have learned by giving advice to others

A Warm-up

1 Check that the trainees understand the terms used. Give them a few moments to choose the ones that they want to, and then compare their choices with a partner.
  a *trainers (and directors of studies) require them.* While this is true, it is not an end in itself, and it is important that trainees do not see defining aims as solely an imposition.
  b *they make planning easier.* This is a strong argument for defining an aim for a lesson. If teachers know what they are trying to achieve it should be easier to select material and so on. It should also be easier to make decisions during the lesson in a principled way (which activities to extend, which to leave out, for example). However, there are also many other factors that become apparent during a lesson that influence such decisions – previous knowledge, levels of interest, and so on.
  c *they make lesson plans look more professional.* It is the content of the aims that is important, rather than the inclusion of any aim, regardless of what it says.

4 – Planning and resources for different teaching contexts

   d *they frame the criteria by which the lesson will be judged.* This is relevant to the immediate course, where trainees will be asked to justify their lesson planning decisions; in their future practice, having a clearly defined lesson aim will make self-evaluation easier.
   e *learners need to know the focus of the lesson.* This may be useful for many learners, as it will help them to set goals (and may therefore positively impact on motivation) and also to reflect on progress. Of course, knowing the aim of the lesson is no guarantee that learners will successfully learn.
   f *they set a goal that can be used to test the learners' achievement.* This is a valid reason, especially when aims are framed in the form: *By the end of the lesson, learners will be able to … .* However, it is a moot point as to the extent that aims, particularly linguistic aims, should be designed to ensure all learners will achieve them (for example, through using formulae such as *will be more likely to understand …*). And of course, an ability to do something can be realized at a range of levels – so making it hard to define precisely. That said, the goal-setting function of an aim does at least give some definition as to the area in which learners would be expected to develop.
2 This activity is designed to encourage trainees to make planning decisions that actually meet the needs of their learners. Focus the trainees on the quote and the question. Amongst other things, it is likely that expert teachers think about the goals of their learners, their interests, their level, and how they have responded to similar activities in the past.

B Types of aim

1 Trainees can work in pairs or small groups. The point of this task is to show that one lesson can share a number of interrelated aims, depending on the viewpoint that is taken. In this particular case, all the aims, apart from (c) (expressing future plans …) seem compatible, since it's easy to imagine a lesson that focuses on the present perfect *and* talking about experience *and* informal conversation, etc.
2 Answers:
   communicative aim = b, c
   linguistic aim = a
   professional developmental aim = e
   skills aim = d
3 Trainees can continue working in their same groupings. The wording that best matches the teacher's lesson description is (e). The problems of the other wordings are:
   a too vague
   b this doesn't appear to be the main aim (there is no explicit presentation as such)
   c too general (e.g. what text type will they write?), and not the main aim
   d this is a potted description of what will happen, but is not an aim as such
   f too vague (e.g. what words will they learn?), and not the main aim

   You can use the above task to introduce the concept of a *main aim*, e.g. (e) and a *subsidiary*, or *secondary, aim*, e.g. (b).
4 Answers:
   a A: The main aim is the contrast of the verb forms. In the process of achieving this, the learners are going to do some reading practice.
      B: The main aim is to teach vocabulary (verbs that collocate with *money*); the subsidiary aim is to write a financial plan.

26 Lesson planning: defining aims

b   A: By the end of the lesson, the learners will better understand the difference between the present perfect simple and continuous. They will also have read and understood a short text. (As the text is used to contextualize language items, it is likely that the teacher would not need to make the reading aim any more detailed.)
B: By the end of the lesson, the learners will be able to use verbs that collocate with *money*. They will also have written a short financial plan.
c   A: linguistic (structural/grammatical)
B: linguistic (vocabulary/lexical)

C Material and aims

Introduce the material and allow trainees to look through it for a few moments. They could consider if they think the material would be appropriate for the learners they are currently teaching.

If you prefer, switch the material for something more relevant to the group.

1–2 Point out that the objectives for *American Think* (top right of the first page reproduced) might be misleading because they cover the entire unit, not just these two pages.

American Think Level 2
Main aim: By the end of the lesson the learners will have developed their ability to listen and read for detailed information. (skills-focused)
Subsidiary aim: The learners will be better able to have an informal discussion about the use of social media.

English Unlimited Elementary
Main aim: By the end of the lesson the learners will have practised using the verb *to be* in the present affirmative, interrogative and negative forms. (linguistic – structural/grammatical)
Subsidiary aim: The learners will practise speaking about people through short, guided dialogues.

3 The goal of this section is to help trainees see that material can be adapted to suit the needs of their class, and also that one piece of material could be used to meet several different aims, depending on the focus of the activity.

A potential subsidiary aim might be: *The learners will learn words to do with the internet and social media.*

The aim may be achieved by highlighting any relevant words in the text (*a post, to post, a comment, to comment, cyberbullying,* for example). Learners might be given a gloss or a translation and be asked to find the words in the text. The teacher could also teach additional relevant words not in the text (e.g. *to block, to ghost, to follow*) that could be used in the final speaking activity.

4 – Planning and resources for different teaching contexts

> **KEY WORDS FOR TEACHERS**
>
> Remind the trainees of the need to be able to use teaching terms confidently and accurately.
>
> **REFLECTION**
>
> The trainees should report back in open class, having discussed the questions in groups. You may like to highlight:
>
> Andrzej: This is hard to answer definitively and you may like to prompt trainees to think of what other information they might need. One obvious point may be the level of the class – was it a challenge for the learners to speak in English? What did the teacher do with the language produced – was there any feedback? The probability is that if the lesson was supposed to practise reading, then the teacher should have ensured there was time for it.
>
> Sophie: Variety of pace can be important. There is no reason why some of the controlled practice could not have been done after the game when perhaps, having made mistakes, the learners would more easily perceive the need for it.
>
> Samira: Trainees need to be careful not to include too many new language items in a single presentation phase, so that there is plenty of time for learners to practise using the new language.
>
> Jane: Adapting the material (in this case by adding an additional activity) is a good thing to do as long as it 'adds value' for the learners. You could relate this back to the quote at the beginning of the unit, which highlights that expert teachers start by thinking about learners, including their needs. Of course, it is not always necessary for teachers to adapt material – sometimes the material might work perfectly well without adaptation.

27 Lesson planning: lesson design and staging

Main focus
Designing and staging lessons.

Learning outcomes
- Trainees understand the principles of planning a balanced lesson.
- Trainees can apply these principles in order to structure a plan for a lesson on language systems.
- Trainees have a basic understanding of task-based learning.

Key concepts
- Presentation, Practice, Production
- Task-based learning
- interaction patterns

Stage	Focus
A Warm-up	introducing the topic of lesson design and staging
B A common lesson format: PPP	trainees focus on PPP format for designing lessons
C A common lesson format: Task-based learning	trainees focus on TBL format for designing lessons
D Giving advice	considering options in lesson design
Key words for teachers	building of specialist vocabulary to talk about teaching
Reflection	trainees reflect on what they have learned by completing sentence stems

A Warm-up

1–2 Allow the trainees some time to finish their chosen sentences. If you have time, allow them to mingle to find a partner who completed the same sentence and to compare their endings. Get them to report back in open class. The following are suggestions:
a film – has a structure of beginning, middle and end. The beginning has to create interest and the end give a sense of closure. Parts may be predictable, but other parts may provide twists and surprises.
a football match – has pace (although this will vary at different stages of the match) and energy. Trainees may compare the roles of teachers and coaches, or teachers and referees.
a meal – (in three courses) again has a beginning, middle and end structure and closure at the end. It could also be argued that a meal is a combination of ingredients that complement each other.
a symphony – has a predictable structure, a variety of pace and a theme or themes that run through it.

4 – Planning and resources for different teaching contexts

B A common lesson format: PPP

You may prefer to use a plan for a lesson that the trainees have seen. This could come from an observation task, for example.

1–2 Allow the trainees to work in pairs or small groups before comparing their ideas with each other and you. A suggested answer is below, although alternatives could be justified.

Having established the order of the stages, you could ask the trainees to provide a very brief rationale for each.

Stage	Time	Interaction	Activity
1	0–5	T–Ss Ss–T Ss–Ss	The teacher asks learners about their favourite stories when they were young. Learners volunteer stories and/or work in pairs to tell their favourite stories.
2	6–10	Ss–text	The teacher gives out a short story and asks learners to underline examples of the past simple in blue and underline examples of the past continuous in red.
3	11–18	T–Ss Ss–T	The teacher confirms and/or clarifies the form with examples on the board, and then gives out a series of rules of use of the verb forms. Learners decide which rules go with which verb form and pick out examples from the text.
4	19–20	T–Ss Ss–T	The teacher asks questions to check understanding. Learners respond.
5	21–28	Individual	Learners complete sentences, deciding whether the past simple or continuous is more appropriate.
6	29–35	Ss–Ss	The teacher divides the class into three groups. Each group makes up a story.
7	36–45	Ss–Ss	The teacher forms new groups, comprising one person from each of the other groups. The learners tell each other their stories.

3 Most teachers would check after stages 2, 3 and 5. You could use this opportunity to reinforce any key messages about lesson planning that you feel your trainees need reinforcing, such as the need to plan specific checking questions in advance (stage 4).

4 Allow trainees some time to think about the questions before comparing with each other and reporting back. Suggested answers:
   1 Stages 1–4
   2 Via a text (in this case, a story)
   3 Stage 5
   4 The learners focus on the new language items only and in this case, there are specific, 'correct' answers.
   5 Stages 6 and 7
   6 Comment on the content of what was said, and also provide some feedback on how the learners used language.

27 Lesson planning: lesson design and staging

C A common lesson format: Task-based learning

1 Focus the trainees on the lesson description. Allow them some time to consider the questions in pairs before reporting back.
   a The trainees draw up a list of guests for a dinner party and report back their ideas. It could be argued that the reporting back is part of the post-task sequence.
   b The teacher builds interest and explains the task.
   c The teacher offers feedback on the language used to accomplish the task.
2 a Again, allow some time for trainees to discuss. There are two obvious points at which the recording could be used. One is after the main task, as a way of prompting the learners to notice differences between their own language use and that of more proficient others. It could also be used prior to the task as a model for the learners.
   b Research suggests that task repetition is likely to lead to gains in accuracy, fluency and also the complexity of language used. It might also give learners the opportunity to try out new bits of language that were highlighted at the feedback stage.
2 Trainees should work in groups to plan the lessons. You may want to provide more detail on the things they should consider. If preferred, you could provide questions such as:
   - How will you build interest in the task?
   - How will you explain the task?
   - Do you need to prepare any materials before the lesson? (For example, a teacher might provide some information sheets about the work of different charities.)
   - How long will the learners have to complete the task?
   - How will the teacher support the learners during the task?
   - How will the reporting back be organized?
   - What will happen after the reporting-back stage?

D Giving advice

1 There are many advantages to presenting language using texts, but any technique, if overused, may become a little dull. The teacher could try varying the approach a little. For example, after the learners have read the text, they could move to a discussion activity that would allow them an opportunity to use the new language item, before it has been formally presented.
2 This can be a common problem. The production phase, which is often the most useful for many learners, is the one that gets cut short because it is the last. Teachers could try moving the production phase to an initial position and then repeating it towards the end of the lesson, if there is time. Alternatively, they can experiment with ways of making their presentation techniques quicker (perhaps through using a deductive approach and/or the learners' L1). Teachers could also experiment with reducing the practice phase of the lesson and setting controlled exercises as a homework task to consolidate what has been taught. Conceivably, such controlled practice could be used as a diagnostic tool, or preparation, for an upcoming lesson.
3 It is important to respect learners' needs and expectations. Communication activities could be introduced gradually – very short to start with and building up to longer activities if the learners respond well. The teacher can ensure that the learners get detailed feedback (including both positive feedback and correction) on their language use so that there are clear learning outcomes. These can be reemphasized at the end of the lesson in a summary of what has been learned.

4 – Planning and resources for different teaching contexts

4 Tasks need not be long or require very sophisticated language (e.g. a simple ranking activity). The teacher could also try to anticipate language needs (vocabulary items and even grammar structures) and build them in to a pre-task activity. Some may argue that such pre-teaching moves the lesson away from a pure form of TBL, but if it makes the communication focus more achievable it may have some merits.

5 The teacher could perhaps build a small bank of activities that would work with almost any language item. For example:
- Listen and repeat.
- Write five sentences about yourself, using …
- Grammar dictation/dictogloss

At the planning stage, the teacher might also try to predict two or three potential language items that might be generated and plan ways to practise them.

KEY WORDS FOR TEACHERS

Remind the trainees of the need to be able to use teaching terms confidently and accurately.

REFLECTION

1 Give the trainees a little time to think before discussing in small groups and reporting back. They should be able to see that both will provide an opportunity for learners to communicate. Both will teach new items of language. A traditional PPP lesson format will put the language focus before the communication stage. However, teachers could experiment with changing the sequence of the three Ps or building in an additional Production stage before the language focus. A TBL format will typically have the language focus after the communication stage. Where tasks are repeated, learners have the chance to put into practice what was covered in the language focus.

2 Allow the trainees time to complete the sentences individually before comparing and reporting back. Answers will vary, but some suggestions are below.
   1 Learners' needs and interests should be considered when *planning a lesson / considering the design and staging of a lesson*.
   2 A good lesson usually includes a variety of *activity types* or *of interaction patterns*.
   3 There is more than one way that teachers can *present new items of language*.
   4 Communication phases of lessons can be placed *before or after a language focus*.
   5 The language focus of a lesson can be placed *before or after a communication phase*.
   6 Most lessons should include both communication and *a language focus*.

28 Lesson planning: planning beyond the single lesson

Main focus
To develop the ability to plan beyond the single lesson.

Learning outcomes
- Trainees understand the principles of selecting and sequencing lessons according to the needs of a group.
- Trainees are able to analyse schemes of work and see strengths and weaknesses.
- Trainees are able to produce their own medium-term plan.

Key concepts
- variety, balance, linkage
- sequencing
- review and recycling
- language-focused v skills-focused lessons

Stage	Focus
A Warm-up	introducing the topic of planning beyond the single lesson
B Schemes of work	establishing the types of lesson that may be included in a scheme of work
C Sequencing lessons	analysing a scheme of work and commenting on its strengths and weaknesses
D A lesson sequencing puzzle	planning a logical sequence for a group of lessons
Key words for teachers	building of specialist vocabulary to talk about teaching
Reflection	trainees reflect on what they have learned by planning a sequence of lessons

A Warm-up

1 The trainees work in small groups to discuss the complaints and how they could have been avoided. It is likely that all the problems could have been avoided with better planning.
   Emiliano – over a period of a course it is usually necessary to build in a variety of material so that lessons do not become overly predictable and eventually boring.
   Eriko – language learning does not proceed in a linear way, always going forward. Teachers also need to build in time to practise and revise (to recycle) previously covered material, in order to give the learners the best chance of being successful. If the class has access to a virtual learning environment, the teacher might post revision activities in some cases.

4 – Planning and resources for different teaching contexts

Sophie – learners often have a good idea of why they are learning language and what they want to learn. Teachers can find out this information (for example, by simply discussing this with their learners or by using a simple needs analysis) and use it to inform their planning.

Thomas – where two or more teachers share responsibility for a class, it is obviously important that they liaise closely so that lessons fit together appropriately.

Suriya – the teacher could help Suriya simply by telling the class what things they will be doing. For example, the teacher could post a plan for the next ten lessons on the virtual learning environment, or put a hard copy on a classroom noticeboard.

2 This is designed to help trainees appreciate the need to link lessons. Focus the trainees on the quote and the prompt. Amongst other things, coherence will be achieved by referring back to previous lessons and recycling material (such as new grammar and vocabulary items). Coherence may also be created by having a consistent topic across lessons (such as a group of lessons that all relate to the topic of 'work'). In some contexts, an English language course may be just one strand of the curriculum (such as in a state school, or learners having additional EAP classes while at university). In these cases the teachers will need to liaise with the teachers of the other curriculum strands, to ensure that lessons are relevant and relate to other aspects of the curriculum.

B Schemes of work

1 Give the trainees some time to discuss the different types of lesson that they have either given or seen, before asking them to report back. They might include:
- grammar
- vocabulary
- pronunciation
- functional English (sometimes covered under headings such as 'social English' in course materials)
- reading skills
- listening skills
- speaking skills
- writing skills
- review
- exam preparation

2 Responses will vary. Trainees may want to consider how the focus may shift at different stages of lessons, making it hard to generalize. However, they may well suggest that 'systems' lessons, such as those with a grammar or vocabulary focus tend to have a teacher-fronted focus, at least for part of the time, and that in some classes there is more 'urgency', while in others the pace is more relaxed. The diversity of lesson types will have implications in terms of longer-term planning, as it will provide a means for incorporating variety into the scheme of work.

3 Again, there can be no definitive answers as all classes have varying needs and expectations, but suggestions follow.
A There is likely to be a need for quite a lot of reviewing (as the learners have long gaps between lessons). As this is an evening class, you may expect the teacher to build in a lot of fairly relaxed activities. The class will probably be quite learner-centred, as it is likely that the teacher will want to maximize the opportunities for the learners to practise using English (they are studying in their own country).

B One may expect to find an emphasis on productive skills (on the basis that the learners are in an English-speaking context and should therefore get plenty of reading, and particularly listening, opportunities outside the classroom). There may be a need for quite a lot of functional/social English (ordering food, asking for directions, and so on).

C IELTS has no specific grammar paper but tests all four language skills, so this may encourage teachers to choose a more skills-based approach. There are likely to be a number of practice tests and as the stakes are quite high for this class, there is likely to be quite an intensive 'hard-working' atmosphere.

D More than in any other case, the teacher should be able to respond to the needs of the learner. It is likely that the skills required by the learner will be targeted and also the genres of language they need to produce or decode – so, for example, there may be a lesson sequence on giving presentations. There is likely to be quite an intensive 'hard-working' atmosphere. The class is unlikely to become teacher-fronted for any length of time.

E Typically early lessons in this context focus on skills work. Receptive skills work may well be apportioned more time, given the level of the learners. Classes may be quite teacher-centred, again, largely because of the level. There will be a need for a lot of functional/social English and also a lot of review work. (See also unit 24 Teaching literacy.)

C Sequencing lessons

Allow the trainees to work in groups to discuss the plan and the answers to the questions. The main point for them to see from this activity is that the lessons are more or less randomly placed. With a little more thought, a plan could be developed with a more logical sequence.

This task aims to prepare trainees for the planning phase in task D. There is no need for the trainees to analyse each day in detail. As soon as they have understood the main points (see above), you can move on.

Before they start, ensure the trainees understand that each lesson has a main focus (which is given), but that this does not preclude other things happening in the lesson: a grammar lesson may well include some speaking, listening, reading or writing, for example. However, for this activity they should concentrate on the main focus, rather than thinking about how individual lessons may be structured.

1 In terms of quantity in the week, there is probably a reasonable balance between grammar and skills work. It could be argued that there is insufficient vocabulary work (just one lesson) but the teacher could balance this out over other weeks. The problem is in the sequencing, rather than the amount of work in each area over the week.

2 No – Monday has two grammar lessons, while Wednesday has none. Wednesday has three skills lessons but the middle one seems unrelated to the other two. The lessons on Friday contain no obvious links.

3 There is a group of lessons centring around work (Listening – working in a call centre, Speaking – Role play: job interviews, Reading – How to do well in a job interview and Speaking – jobs). How to do well in a job interview may link with the grammar lesson on *should* and *must*, which will also link with the lesson on giving advice. The lesson on the present perfect might link to the lesson on writing a news story.

This plan does not exploit these links to the best effect and trainees should be able to see some obvious improvements. For example, the work on *must* and *should* may combine with the reading text on how to do well in a job interview, and this would naturally lead onto a role play of job interviews.

4 – Planning and resources for different teaching contexts

D A lesson sequencing puzzle

Divide the trainees into small groups. In a face-to-face class, cut the lessons up to make cards and give one set of cards to each group. For an online group, share a blank grid for trainees to type into. There are four additional cards, which are designed to widen the number of choices that trainees must make. Obviously, there is no single correct answer. However, a possible answer is included below. You may wish to photocopy this and use it in the feedback process, with trainees comparing their answer to the one given.

If you are short of time, you could tell trainees which lesson should start each day. Alternatively ask the trainees just to plan two or three days.

Quiz based on work from this week	Vocabulary – collocations with *make*	Functional language – asking for advice	Reading/ Listening – jigsaw text: husbands and wives	Pronunciation – intonation in questions
Vocabulary – linking words	Speaking and writing – preparing a news story	Listening – a day in the life of an agony aunt	Grammar revision – present perfect simple	Listening – video: a television news bulletin
Pronunciation – /p/ or /b/?	Writing – writing a narrative	Grammar – second conditional	Functional language – asking for directions	Listening – working in a call centre
Speaking – jobs	Speaking/ Vocabulary – money	Vocabulary – describing emotions	Writing – a letter of application	Grammar – uses of *should* and *must*
	Speaking – role play: job interviews	Speaking – phobias	Listening – gap-filling a song	Reading – how to do well in a job interview

	Monday	Tuesday	Wednesday	Thursday	Friday
9–9.50	Listening – working in a call centre	Grammar – uses of *should* and *must*	Functional language – asking for advice	Reading/ Listening – jigsaw text: husbands and wives	Speaking/ Vocabulary – money
10–10.50	Vocabulary – linking words	Reading – how to do well in a job interview	Listening – a day in the life of an agony aunt	Grammar revision – present perfect simple	Listening – video: a television news bulletin
11–11.50	Speaking – jobs	Pronunciation – intonation in questions	Vocabulary – describing emotions	Vocabulary – collocations with *make*	Speaking and writing – preparing a news story
12–12.50	Writing – a letter of application	Speaking – role play: job interviews	Speaking – phobias	Listening – gap-filling a song	Quiz based on work from this week

Photocopiable   © Cambridge University Press & Assessment 2022

28 Lesson planning: planning beyond the single lesson

> **KEY WORDS FOR TEACHERS**
>
> Remind the trainees of the need to be able to use teaching terms confidently and accurately.
>
> **REFLECTION**
>
> On many CELTA courses, trainees take responsibility for planning their last lessons, with only minimal guidance. You could use this as an opportunity for trainees to plan their final lessons. If so, you will need to ensure that trainees understand the requirements of your centre (length of lessons and so on). It is probably a good idea to get a TP group to outline the main focus of all the lessons the group will teach and to identify the material to be used. You can then check that their ideas are appropriate, before allocating lessons to individual trainees to prepare on their own.

Topic 4 – Planning and resources for different teaching contexts

29 The online classroom v the face-to-face classroom

Main focus
To learn about differences between teaching in online and face-to-face classrooms.

Learning outcomes
- Trainees understand key differences between teaching in online and face-to-face classrooms.
- Trainees can reflect on how planning may need to change, depending on what kind of classroom they are teaching in.

Key concepts
- online teaching
- classroom teaching
- synchronous learning/teaching
- asynchronous learning/teaching

Stage	Focus
A Warm-up	trainees picture different types of classroom (online and face-to-face) and consider what students and teachers do in those lessons
B Different classroom, different activities?	trainees consider which activities might work best in online and face-to-face classrooms
C Possible opportunities and challenges	trainees think about opportunities and challenges of different types of classrooms, and how to exploit or work around them
D Adapting a lesson	trainees reflect on how the same lesson might be approached in a different context
Key words for teachers	building of specialist vocabulary to talk about teaching
Reflection	trainees identify which techniques they can already apply to different classroom contexts and one priority area to work on

Caveats: Online teaching in this session refers to synchronous teaching. It assumes the use of a platform that integrates video, audio, a chat box, the ability to share and annotate screens, and the ability to move learners into breakout rooms to work in pairs or groups.

This session is probably best done at a later stage in the course, when trainees can draw on a range of activities and techniques they have previously learned. If possible, you may wish to run this session online if you've been conducting a face-to-face course.

29 The online classroom v the face-to-face classroom

A Warm-up

This activity is best set up without trainees opening their books.

1 Talk trainees through the guided visualization. Then allow them some time to draw their lesson. Ask them not to show anybody else at this point.
2 Put trainees into pairs to find similarities and differences between their pictures. Give them a couple of minutes to do this.
3 Ask for a show of hands: who drew a face-to-face classroom? Who drew an online classroom? Get trainees to imagine the alternative type of classroom and consider what their answers to activity 1 would be now. Give them one to two minutes to do this before they share answers with a partner. If possible, pair with someone who drew the other type of classroom.

B Different classroom, different activities?

1 Trainees work in pairs or groups. Be prepared to explain or demonstrate any of the ideas in the list that the trainees don't understand.
2 Put two pairs together to form small groups. Trainees share the ideas they added to the list. If they disagree, encourage them to justify why activities would work better in one type of classroom or the other. Suggested reasons are given below.

Online	Example: switch your camera off, change something around you, switch it on and ask learners to spot the difference(s) – *this exploits the fact that cameras can be switched on and off easily, and makes use of the speaker's surroundings*
	b learners write short written responses to a question for everybody to see – *this works well in a chat box, where responses can be read instantly without having to move around*
	g scavenger hunt, e.g. find something old/red/useful – *every learner has a different environment to draw from, e.g. their home or office, rather than only the classroom*
	h interviewing guests from outside the class – *the range of guests who can be invited into an online classroom is potentially much wider than a face-to-face classroom, as there are no constraints of geography*
Face-to-face	Example: gallery activities, e.g. reading excerpts from a text around the room – *physically moving around to read different parts of a text or different questions is logistically easier in a face-to-face classroom; online learners may get confused if they have lots of different files open*
	d running dictation – *this requires learners to be in the same physical space*
	e class surveys – *learners have the freedom to move around the room and speak to anybody for any length of time*
	i board race – *the race element of this activity can be more effective in a face-to-face classroom, as you don't need to factor in internet/typing speeds*

4 – Planning and resources for different teaching contexts

Both	Example: pair and group work – *in a face-to-face classroom, learners can easily turn to classmates to work together; online, pairs or groups can be created if your platform allows this*
	f pronunciation drills – *listen and repeat is possible in both classrooms; face-to-face it may be easier to hear everyone at the same time, but online learners can probably see the movements of your mouth more easily*
	a collaborative writing – *face-to-face, learners can work on the same piece of paper or at the same computer; both online and face-to-face, learners can work in a single document from different devices, for example using Google Docs or Microsoft Word Online*
	c error correction through the use of gestures – *supporting error correction through gestures adds an extra element beyond the purely visual of writing on a whiteboard or audio of saying an error; providing there is a video feed in the online classroom, this support can be exploited equally well in both types of classroom*

C Possible opportunities and challenges

1 Divide trainees into two groups: Group A: online classrooms; Group B: face-to-face classrooms. If any trainees have prior teaching experience, aim to mix those who have worked primarily in face-to-face or online classrooms, so that trainees can draw on this experience.
Elicit one example of possible answers for each type of classroom, for example:

A Online classrooms
Advantage: In pair and group work, learners can't hear their classmates. Learners benefit because it's easier to concentrate. Shyer students may be more willing to speak because nobody else can hear them.
Challenge: Learners type at very different speeds. When sharing answers in the chat box, ask learners to write their answer, but only press enter to send it when the teacher tells them, so slower typists don't feel pressured.

B Face-to-face classrooms
Advantage: The furniture in the classroom can often be moved around. Teachers can exploit this by creating a suitable environment for a role play, for example create a restaurant by moving two chairs around a table, or a plane by putting chairs out in rows.
Challenge: Teachers often have a blind spot: a particular area of the classroom which they pay a lot less attention to, for example the row of students closest to them, or four students on the right of a horseshoe. Encourage students to sit in different seats in each lesson. When monitoring, or giving instructions to the whole group, focus on the students in your blind spot first.

Give groups time to brainstorm other ideas. Ensure that they are also thinking about how learners benefit from and teachers can exploit opportunities, and how to work around challenges.

2 Pair one trainee from group A with one from group B. Give them time to compare their ideas and suggest additional ones.
To summarize their ideas, you could create a collaborative document for trainees to write into, or ask them to share ideas in open class. Accept any ideas which are suitable.

D Adapting a lesson

Elicit one sample answer for each of the questions, then give trainees time to discuss their answers before reporting back in open class.

There is a little overlap with task C regarding predicting challenges and opportunities of different classroom types. However, in this stage these predictions are focused on a specific lesson, rather than in general, so they provide the opportunity for some recycling.

KEY WORDS FOR TEACHERS

Remind the trainees of the need to be able to use teaching terms confidently and accurately.

REFLECTION

Allow the trainees a little time to complete their sentences. They can share them in pairs or small groups. Encourage them to focus on both strengths and areas to work on, and to consider what they can learn from and with each other, e.g. by observing their colleagues or by brainstorming activity ideas together.

To wrap up the session, remind trainees that online and face-to-face classrooms is just one example of alternative contexts they may encounter after the course. Considering the opportunities (affordances) and challenges of different types of classroom can help them to think creatively and be prepared for a wide range of working environments.

Topic 4 – Planning and resources for different teaching contexts

30 Choosing and using teaching resources

Main focus
To raise awareness about the range of resources available and how these can be best exploited.

Learning outcomes
- Trainees know how to select and evaluate coursebooks and other resources.
- Trainees are aware of the need to adapt and supplement materials where appropriate.

Key concepts
- coursebooks, workbooks, etc.
- supplementary materials
- criteria for materials evaluation
- selecting, adapting and supplementing materials

Stage	Focus
A Warm-up	trainees consider their own opinions of language learning materials
B Criteria for evaluating materials	trainees design criteria for selecting and evaluating materials
C Sources of materials and resources	trainees identify possible sources of materials and evaluate one set of materials
D Adapting materials	trainees adapt materials to their current TP group
Key words for teachers	building of specialist vocabulary to talk about teaching
Reflection	trainees reflect on key issues related to choosing and using teaching resources

A Warm-up

The aim of this activity is to highlight that different people are likely to have different instinctive reactions to resources, and that these may be coloured by whether we are teaching or learning from those resources. This is in contrast to task B, where the aim is to be more principled and objective about evaluating materials.

Ask trainees to identify a few examples of resources they have used as a language teacher or learner, for example coursebooks, photocopiable, resource books, apps, blogs, etc. Allow them a few minutes to complete the table alone, before comparing it to a partner.

B Criteria for evaluating materials

1. You may wish to point out the contrast between the subjective nature of what trainees identified in task A and the more objective nature of task B, highlighting that it can be useful to identify clear criteria for good materials for the context. These criteria can then help the teacher to assess the potential effectiveness of materials, and what changes might need to be made.

Divide the trainees into four groups. Allocate one section of the table to each group. Encourage them to frame their points as questions, as this should make evaluation easier in task C. The key words below show some of the topics which trainees' questions may cover. If a group is having trouble thinking of their own ideas, you may wish to feed in some of these key words. There is no obligation to cover every area, though this could be a good opportunity to challenge some of the stronger trainees.

1 Suitability for learners   English level, L1/L2, interests, cultural background, educational background, professional background, identity (gender, race, religion, etc.), expectations of teacher/student roles, activity preferences
2 Suitability for teachers   cultural background, teaching experience, knowledge of methodology, knowledge of English (descriptively and instinctively), confidence, ability to adapt and supplement materials, teaching style
3 Suitability for the context   mode of delivery (face-to-face, online, self-study, teacher-mediated study, etc.), classroom environment, syllabus, aims of the course, assessment requirements, class size, additional resources available, technology available
4 Suitability of language and skills focus   choice of grammar/vocabulary/functions, receptive/productive language work, balance of language work and skills work, range of text types, metalanguage used, contexts used for introducing language, approach to teaching grammar, clarity, accuracy and ease of use of language references (e.g. grammar reference, vocabulary bank)

2   Pair trainees up with somebody from the same TP group. Allow time for them to select six to eight questions from the list in B1. Highlight that a short list like this can be used as a starting point for evaluation, and they can return to other questions in more depth later, if necessary. Tell trainees that they will use this list later in the session.

C   Sources of materials and resources

1   You may need to clarify some of the items in the list, for example *graded readers* and *a phonemic chart*. Allow time for trainees to discuss their answers.
2   To add some variety, you could conduct this activity as a board race on a face-to-face course. To conduct a similar activity on an online course, divide trainees into groups in breakout rooms. Create a table in a shared document, with one column per group. Give groups a time limit to add as many items as they can to the table. The only limit is trainees' imagination!

4 – Planning and resources for different teaching contexts

Further examples might include:

- paper flashcards
- posters
- mini whiteboards
- brochures
- leaflets
- newspapers
- radio programmes
- TV shows
- film trailers
- game instructions
- book covers
- Cuisenaire rods
- Lego ®
- puppets
- bags

3 Put trainees into the same pairs as activity B2. Give each pair different materials, for example a coursebook, a resource book, a book of grammar activities, a website, a song, and a news article. Allow time for trainees to use their short list of questions from activity B2 to evaluate the suitability of these materials for their current TP group.
Fast finishers can discuss whether the questions they selected were the most appropriate for the learners and materials, or whether other questions might have been more useful.

D Adapting materials

1 The key words are designed to serve as a guide for trainees as to the range of different ways in which materials can be adapted.
Answers: 1–c) 2–d) 3–b) 4–a)
2 Put trainees in the same pairs as activities B2 and C3. Set a time limit to allow a reasonable time to think about how to adapt or use a range of materials and resources. Encourage them to cover a range of areas from D1, and to be as specific as possible, i.e. saying exactly how many questions they would trim from an activity, or which interaction patterns they would change.
You may wish to push stronger trainees to differentiate activities for their learners, for example by showing how they could use the same activity but add challenge or support to help specific learners in the group.
3 Group the students by putting two pairs together, preferably from different TP groups. Allow time for them to report on their decisions related to evaluating and adapting materials for their current TP group. For trainees who have already switched TP groups during the course, encourage them to evaluate the other pairs' decisions in light of their own knowledge of the group.

30 Choosing and using teaching resources

> **KEY WORDS FOR TEACHERS**

Remind the trainees of the need to be able to use teaching terms confidently and accurately.

> **REFLECTION**

1 The questions chosen will probably reflect different priorities:
   a young learners: age, language level and educational level (pre-primary, primary, secondary), as well as development of other non-linguistic skills, such as teamwork or fine motor skills
   b university students: assessment may be more important; the alignment of text types and language taught to the students' subject and future professional needs could be focused on
   c a company executive who you teach one-to-one: language and skills needs may be more clearly defined than for a general English learner; professional background and roles could be considered, as well as differing interaction in a one-to-one lesson compared to a group lesson
2 Answers will vary, but some of the following aspects related to using coursebooks may be discussed.

	Possible ways it might have helped	Possible problems
For learners	• They provide a reference which learners can look at after the lesson. • There are often extra activities not covered in lessons which learners can use in their own time. • As learners move through a book, they may get a sense of progress in their learning.	• Topics may not be interesting or relevant to the learners. • They may feel there is too much of a focus on grammar, and not enough on other areas. • The pace of progress through the coursebook may be too fast or too slow for some learners.
For teachers	• Coursebooks can reduce preparation time, as learners already have the resources they need. • They provide a clear structure for the course, making it easier for teachers to select what to teach next. • The majority of coursebooks come with other components which can support the teacher in planning, as well as in adapting and supplementing materials. These may also contribute to a teacher's professional development.	• Teachers may feel their creativity is stifled if they are required to use a coursebook, especially if they were not involved in choosing it. • If the coursebook is not a good fit for the learners, for example with regards to level, topics or age, it can create extra work for teachers as they need to adapt the materials. • It can be demotivating to use materials which the learners or the teacher don't like, and this can lead to a reduction in positive wellbeing over time.

4 – Planning and resources for different teaching contexts

3 You may wish to introduce the term 'authentic materials' at this point, as it has only been referred to in 'Key words for teachers' so far. Answers will vary, but some of the following points may come up in the discussion.

	Possible things that work well	Possible challenges
For learners	• Content can be personalized to learners' interests. • Culturally appropriate materials can be selected. • Learners can be exposed to real examples of genres they need to be familiar with.	• Too much culture-specific information can make materials difficult to understand. • Learners may not feel a sense of progress if authentic materials are used all the time. • They may feel demotivated if they feel the language is too hard for them.
For teachers	• Learners are likely to be more engaged and motivated in lessons, potentially making it easier to teach them. • Teachers can exercise their creativity when exploiting the materials. • Teachers can experiment with different methods, approaches and activities in a way that might not be possible when using coursebooks.	• Finding authentic materials can be something of a rabbit hole if teachers are not disciplined – it's easy to lose time to find the 'perfect' song/article/etc. • It can be challenging to choose the most appropriate activities to exploit the materials. • Teachers may feel demotivated if learners do not respond in the way they expect, for example if a lesson they have spent a long time preparing falls flat.

31 Teaching with limited resources

> **Main focus**
> A review of some design principles and practical applications for making the most out of teaching situations where resources are scarce.
>
> **Learning outcomes**
> - Trainees appreciate that successful teaching does not require a great many resources, and that a low-resource teaching context is not necessarily an impoverished one.
> - Trainees are able to exploit whatever resources are available, including the material, cognitive, experiential and affective contributions of the learners.
> - Trainees are familiar with some basic activity types that circumvent the need for copious resources, while still being able to achieve curricular goals.
>
> **Key concepts**
> - learner-centredness
> - resourcefulness

Stage	Focus
A Warm-up	evaluating the usefulness of different resources
B Teaching in difficult circumstances	experiencing a dictogloss activity on the subject of teaching in difficult circumstances
C Low resource activities	experiencing and evaluating classroom activities that exploit whatever is physically in the room
D Learner-generated material	using what the learners bring to the class, in terms of knowledge, experience, etc.
Key words for teachers	building of specialist vocabulary to talk about teaching
Reflection	planning activities using the ideas in this session

A Warm-up

Note that, although this unit applies to teaching situations that lack resources, the principles behind the selection and use of materials apply equally to situations that are better-resourced. The important point to get across is that lack of resources should be considered less as a deficit than as an opportunity, and that 'being resourceful' is a better predictor of teaching ability than 'having resources'.

Set the scene: trainees have opted to teach in a totally under-resourced region, and they are packing to leave. What would they take? Allow them to create their individual lists of six items, and then negotiate in groups a definitive list, giving reasons. If time allows, elicit an agreed list for the whole class.

You might also want to point out that this activity can be replicated in the classroom: e.g. items you would pack for a vacation, items you would buy for a new kitchen, etc.

4 – Planning and resources for different teaching contexts

To lead into this activity, you could do the describe-and-draw task described in C1, describing a desert island (two palm trees, a hut, a volcano …).

B Teaching in difficult circumstances

1 Demonstrate this dictogloss activity in the following way:
   1 Tell the class they are going to hear a short text which you will read aloud. (You may want to write up the proper names on the board in advance: *New Guinea, Rabaul, Madang*). Tell them that, while they listen, they should not write nor speak, but, once you have finished reading and at a cue from you, they will individually try to write down as much as they can recall. (Some advocates of this activity encourage the learners to note down key words as they listen, but there is a risk that this will turn the activity into a very fast dictation.)
   2 Read the text clearly and at a natural pace. Signal to the trainees when they should write.
   3 Monitor the writing stage: if it seems that the trainees need to hear the text a second time, stop them and reread it.
   4 Once they have reconstructed as much of the text as possible individually, ask them to work in pairs or groups of three to create a consensus version of the text.
   5 Read the text one more time, allowing the trainees to make any running changes.
   6 If the means are available, project the original text so that they can compare it with their versions.

   Text:[1]

   'When I was a youngster I was recruited to start up, alone, an Australian government primary school deep in the rainforest of New Guinea. After a training course in Rabaul I received my teaching certificate, along with a big box stuffed with teaching notes, black paint to make a blackboard, and chalk. On the way out to my first school, three days' walk from Madang, we were crossing a ravine on a rope-bridge when a carrier lost his footing – the box plummeted into the river and smashed against the rocks, never to be seen again. The day I arrived at the school site, the wet season started, and the rivers flooded behind me. There were a hundred children waiting for me, and I had nothing whatever to teach them with and no way of getting anything in or out for the next four months.'

2 Point out that this is a true story. Ask trainees to imagine what Wade might have done in this situation. Elicit ideas, and then read how the text continues:
   'That was when, as a brand-new teacher, I started developing teaching without textbooks. I asked the children to show me what they wanted to know about, and gradually introduced English through their responses. … We did our math and science in the bush by estimating how many kernels we could get from an ear of corn. We checked with the villagers where and how far apart we should plant them, and how big an area we would need to clear … When I finally saw a copy of the primary school syllabus I was surprised to find that we had covered just about every item listed. So I put the syllabus away, and continued as I had been doing.'

You may want to make the point that – even if you cannot take your learners into the 'bush', or even outdoors – the principle that learning English can be integrated with (a) other aspects of the curriculum and (b) familiarity with the local context is an important one in terms of making the English class both relevant and 'materials-light'.

---

[1] adapted from Wade, E.J. 1992. *Teaching without textbooks: Accelerative learning in the language classroom.* Carlton, Victoria: CIS Educational. p.x.

1 The stages of the dictogloss technique include listening, individual and then group reconstruction from memory, and finally comparison with the original text. Perhaps point out that this text is longer than might be used with learners, the optimum size being around 50–75 words.
2 Any pre-selected grammar item can be embedded into the text, either once or more often, on the principle that, even if learners are not familiar with the item, there is sufficient context for them to infer its meaning. It can then be highlighted in the final comparison stage.
3 The technique can easily be adapted to a wide range of levels and contexts.
4 Its potential strengths are that:
   - it offers a technology-light way of distributing a text
   - it encourages holistic language processing
   - as it requires collaboration and negotiation, it offers opportunities for peer instruction
   - it provides a means of 'feeding in' pre-selected language items
   - it is easily adapted to a variety of contexts

Note also that the same principle – of text-reconstruction from memory – can be implemented using a written text, which the learners are briefly exposed to before it is hidden.

C Low-resource activities

Choose three of the following activities to demonstrate with the trainees, who act 'as students'. If time is short, it may be enough to initiate the activity without working it through its different stages. Withhold giving the activity a name, since trainees will be asked to do this, as a way of seeing to what extent they understand its basic nature.
Note that some of the activities are easier to adapt to online classes than others.

Guess what? The teacher says: 'You have to ask yes/no questions to guess the mystery object that I have on me, with me, am carrying, wearing, etc. Who's going to start?' You can use this demonstration stage to elicit, model and write up typical guessing questions, such as: *Can you ... with it? Is it made of plastic/metal/paper/etc.? Is it bigger/smaller than ... ? Is it used for ...-ing? Is it used to ... with?*, etc. Once students have guessed your mystery object, show it to them and invite them to ask 'normal' questions about it: *How long have you had it? Was it expensive?* Use this stage to 'tell the story' of the object. Then put students into pairs or groups of three and they do the same sequence, i.e. asking questions to guess the object, and then telling the 'story' of the object. This activity is easily adapted to online teaching.

What's different? Tell the class to look closely around them, and try to remember the details of the layout of the room and the things in it. Then ask two or three students to leave the room for a minute. While they are outside, ask the others to quickly make five changes to the room – e.g. moving a picture on the wall, opening a window, etc. Ask the students who are outside to return and to ask questions to find out what has changed. You can supply a model (or models) for the questions on the board. For example, *have you opened the window? Has someone opened the window? Has the window been opened?* When all the changes have been identified, another group of students have a turn to go out. In an online classroom, the activity can be adapted by switching off the webcam and making three changes to your immediate environment. Trainees try to guess what you might have changed (insist on full sentences!) and then switch the webcam back on, and they tell you what you have changed. They can then replicate the activity in small groups in breakout rooms.

4 – Planning and resources for different teaching contexts

Describe and draw: Before the class, the teacher prepares a dozen or so drawings to show the class. These need to include variations of the design she has chosen as the basis of the activity. The teacher first 'dictates' a hidden picture – e.g. a combination of different geometrical shapes, the interior of a room, a desert island – that the learners draw. The original is then revealed for comparison purposes. Learners do the same in pairs. (Up to this point, the activity can easily be adapted to online classes). The class is then divided into two teams, and the board is divided in two by a line down the middle. Each team has a representative at the board, each with a piece of chalk or a board marker. The teacher ensures that the two team representatives at the board cannot see the previously prepared designs, and then selects one and shows it to the two teams. Each team attempts to describe the design to its representative at the board, and the first team to do this successfully, so that the design is replicated on the board, is the winner of that round. The teacher then selects another design and the game continues. The game can also be played with simple pictures of, for example, landscapes or room interiors.

Who's that? The teacher asks students to access a photo on their phone that shows a number of their friends and/or relatives, and uses one student's photo to model questions and answers about it. Students then stand in two concentric circles, the outer circle facing in, the inner circle facing out, forming pairs. They show their photos, asking and answering questions, before the outer circle moves around one, at a cue from the teacher, and the activity continues. (If not all students have either phones or photos, only those who do can form one of the circles, the others simply asking the questions.) Include a report stage, where individuals tell the class something interesting they have learned about another student. This activity can be adapted to online classes, where learners can post photos into a shared online space, and then answer questions about them.

Paper conversation: learners have a 'conversation' with their classmates, but instead of speaking, they write the conversation onto a shared sheet of paper. Demonstrate this with one student, using the board. This activity can be replicated using a chat window, or a mobile texting app.

1 Allow trainees to complete the relevant section of the table after each activity, so as not to make too many demands on their memory. You may want to do some of the items in the table with the class as a group, before putting them into pairs. Essential features to focus on at the reporting stage are the way the activities address a number of skills (or could be made to, with the addition of a writing stage, for example) and are highly interactive, as well as being very productive, generating language items that can then be the focus of a grammar or vocabulary presentation.

D Learner-generated material

1 Ask trainees to read the three activities and match them with the 'field' that they activate, i.e. learners' experience, knowledge, opinion, preferences, abilities, needs. If time is short, assign one activity per group and ask them to report to the whole class.
   1 'One of us can … ' – abilities
   2 'Five finger exercise' – experience
   3 'Class poll' – opinions

2   1   Each activity can be adapted to target different domains as well as specific grammatical or functional areas. For example, the *can* in the 'One of us' activity can be substitute with 'has/have -ed' to focus on experience; the 'Five finger exercise' could focus on hopes and predictions, using prompts such as *work*, *travel*, *family*, *health* and *the world*. The 'Class poll' can be used to find out learners' (language learning) needs, or their experiences.
    2   It is important to show how the language that is generated from these activities can be extracted and highlighted, using the board, for example, and practised, using substitutions and personalized examples. (For more ideas, see unit 19 Teaching language items reactively.)

KEY WORDS FOR TEACHERS

Use the key words to review some of the main 'takeaways' from the session.

REFLECTION

1   Trainees could be organized into their TP groups to discuss this question.
2   Many of the activities in this unit 'bring the outside world' into the classroom, since they encourage personalization by the learners of the lesson content. The feasibility of taking the learners into the real world in the way that E.J. Wade did in Papua New Guinea (what is sometimes called 'wilding' the language learning experience) will depend on the local and institutional context, but digital technologies now allow a much easier flow of communication between the classroom and the outside world.

Topic 4 – Planning and resources for different teaching contexts

32 Using educational technology

Main focus
To introduce trainees to key issues related to the use of educational technology with learners.

Learning outcomes
- Trainees gain an awareness of a wide range of different factors which might influence their choice of whether to use a given technology tool with learners.
- Trainees learn one possible way to evaluate technology tools, and consider how these tools might be used with learners.
- Trainees are introduced to a range of different technology tools.

Key concepts
- educational technology
- synchronous learning/teaching
- asynchronous learning/teaching

Stage	Focus
A Warm-up	trainees reflect on how they have seen technology used during the course so far
B Factors influencing the use of educational technology	trainees consider criteria for selecting which technology tools to use
C Opinions about technology and education	a discussion of various statements connected to the use of educational technology
D Putting it into practice	trainees evaluate one technology tool of their choice and consider how it might be used in their lessons
Key words for teachers	building of specialist vocabulary to talk about teaching
Reflection	trainees reflect on key points to remember from the session

A Warm-up

Put trainees into pairs or small groups to discuss this activity. Encourage them to consider a range of examples covering different technology tools and contexts if possible, for example not only restricted to input sessions or online lessons (if they have had the chance to observe both online and face-to-face lessons at this stage of the course).

For the reporting back stage, you could start to create a summary of points for teachers to remember. This would be a good opportunity to demonstrate an answer collection tool, or to compile a collaborative document which trainees could refer to after the session.

B Factors influencing the use of educational technology

Emphasize that there is no correct answer to this activity, although the first point (learning benefits) should always be a priority. Ask trainees to justify their answers.

When reporting back after the activity, you may choose to share these factors as a poll to demonstrate another technology tool and get an overview of the whole group's responses.

Highlight that by choosing a few areas to prioritize, it can help trainees to quickly assess new tools they come across. They can go into more depth and consider more factors, if they are satisfied with their findings from their priority areas and have time for a more in-depth analysis.

C Opinions about technology and education

If you are short on time, you may choose to skip this stage or reduce the number of statements which trainees discuss.

Give trainees time to consider the opinions individually before discussing them in pairs or small groups. They may discuss some of the following:

- The age of a learner does not necessarily determine how comfortable they are with technology. Rather, their previous exposure to and training in technology determines this. Teachers are sometimes surprised to discover that younger learners may lack skills such as how to use search engines efficiently or how to use keyboard shortcuts to copy and paste, while older learners may use technology all the time in their jobs and feel very comfortable with it.
- While technology is undoubtedly a part of our everyday lives, it should be used mindfully in lessons, with due consideration to the benefits learners will get from specific tools and learning particular skills related to technology. Teachers should always ask what added value a given tool brings before deciding to use it.
- It's important for teachers to consider aspects of online safety and data protection when choosing which tools to use, especially with potentially vulnerable students. Parental consent should be sought if under-18s need to create an account to use a website. Learners also need to know which of their data will potentially be shared if they use a technology tool in lessons.
- There is an argument that data literacy and critical thinking are key components of all modern-day teaching, not limited to information technology lessons. When considering the technology we bring into our lessons, we also need to consider who created the websites and the content on them and who benefits from our use of them. We may wish to discuss this with learners, or to choose alternative tools or reduce our use of technology if we are not prepared to do this.
- Using online games for the sake of it can be a gimmick, but it is also possible for learners to gain a lot from the principled use of technology tools. This is especially true if learners choose to go back to the tools in their own time and continue to use them. Online games can be a great way to promote learner autonomy and encourage learners to extend their learning beyond the classroom.
- When we first come across a new app, website or piece of hardware which we like, it can be tempting to try to find ways of including it in our lessons. However, it is important to make sure we consider the goals of the lesson, and our learners' preferences, rather than emphasizing any desire we might have to experiment with technology in our classroom. Pedagogy should always be prioritized over technology.

4 – Planning and resources for different teaching contexts

D Putting it into practice

1. You may need to have a list of possible tools for trainees to choose from for this stage. Tools might include apps, websites, or hardware. Encourage pairs to choose different tools so that a range is covered across the whole group. You may also want to have an example evaluation prepared for a tool which you find beneficial. Include information about how the tool benefits the learning process specifically, as well as referring to two or three other criteria from task B which the tool exemplifies well and/or issues raised in task C.
2. If trainees are having trouble thinking of activities, point out that a simple internet search should yield a range of activity suggestions for most established technology tools.
3. Remind trainees to think back to their discussions in task B when listening to other presentations, and to keep the benefits to the learning process at the forefront of their minds.

KEY WORDS FOR TEACHERS

Remind the trainees of the need to be able to use teaching terms confidently and accurately.

REFLECTION

Encourage trainees to complete the sentence stems in a range of different ways, considering all of their discussions throughout the session. Use their answers to summarize key points connected to the use of educational technology, and to emphasize again the importance of prioritizing learning.

This activity provides a final opportunity to demonstrate a tool which collects answers or which enables synchronous editing.

33 Organizing and managing a class

Main focus
To examine some of the principal considerations in classroom management and in facilitating interaction.

Learning outcomes
- Trainees understand the broad scope of issues which can be considered part of classroom management.
- Trainees understand the rationale behind the use of a range of different interaction patterns.
- Trainees understand how to create a supportive classroom environment.
- Trainees understand the principles of how to grade language.
- Trainees understand the principles of effective monitoring.

Key concepts
- organizing learners, monitoring
- board work
- language grading, teacher talk
- group dynamics

Managing an activity is dealt with in unit 34.

Stage	Focus
A Warm-up	defining classroom management and considering what it could involve
B Organizing learners	considering when and why to use different interaction patterns
C Group dynamics	introducing the importance of creating a supportive classroom environment
D Using the whiteboard	considering how to support learning by effective use of the (online) whiteboard
E Grading language	looking at ways of making classroom language intelligible
F Trainees' queries	trainees match questions and answers on a variety of practical points
Key words for teachers	building of specialist vocabulary to talk about teaching
Reflection	trainees consider the implications of what they have learned for their own teaching

5 – Developing teaching skills and professionalism

A Warm-up

Draw trainees' attention to the definition in the quote. You may choose to elicit trainees' own definitions of 'classroom management' first. Tell them that today's session will look at a few key aspects of classroom management, but will of necessity only be an overview as it is such a broad topic. The definition is taken from the introduction to a whole book dedicated to the topic!

1 When setting up this activity, highlight that trainees should focus on what a teacher does which is <u>not</u> subject-specific, and therefore could be done by any teacher.

Alternatives: If you are running a face-to-face course, you could run this activity as a whiteboard race, with two teams aiming to get as many ideas as possible onto the whiteboard. On an online course, you could have two teams using a brainstorming app or online sticky notes to come up with as many ideas as possible.

Possible answers:
- Check attendance.
- Monitor learners during activities.
- Give feedback on performance in activities.
- Use the (online) whiteboard.
- Encourage reluctant learners to participate.
- Set up activities.
- Rearrange furniture in a face-to-face classroom.
- Set up breakout rooms in an online classroom.
- Reduce the dominance of some learners.
- Ask questions.
- Create a safe working environment.
- Manage noise levels.
- Manage materials and resources.

2 Most classroom management is equally applicable to both online and face-to-face classrooms. Some exceptions might be:
- In pair or small group activities online, learners generally can't hear each other. Noise levels online will probably be from beyond the lesson, rather than the noise of learners themselves, for example family members in the background. Teachers may choose to mute learners' microphones if this is a problem.
- In a face-to-face classroom, the teacher can generally monitor all learners at the same time. This has the advantage that they can see what everybody is doing, to some extent and who may be off-task or finished, but the disadvantage might be that the teacher may find it challenging to concentrate on individuals within the whole class.

B Organizing learners

1 Divide trainees into two groups: A and B. Refer them to the relevant page in the trainee book. The first row of the table has been completed as an example.
Here is the completed table, combining the tables which groups A and B can see. It is worth pointing out to trainees that this is just one possible way of completing this table, and that many other interaction patterns are possible, with a wide range of advantages and disadvantages. Encourage them to share any other valid ideas they might have, including other possible example activities.

33 Organizing and managing a class

Interaction pattern	Example activity	One advantage of this interaction pattern	One disadvantage of this interaction pattern
Individual work	Reading comprehension	Learners have some time to concentrate on learning at their own pace.	Learners may be unsure of their answers and therefore not want to share them.
Pair work	Answering discussion questions	Maximizes opportunities for speaking.	Face-to-face classrooms can get very noisy, and it can be a challenge for the teacher to hear individuals.
Small group work	Creating a product to 'sell' to classmates	Learners can bounce ideas off each other and experiment with their English with supportive classmates.	Some learners may be reluctant to participate in small groups, leaving others to do the work.
Two big teams	A whiteboard race	Working as a team can motivate learners to push their English production to higher levels.	If there is an element of competition, learners (and teachers!) sometimes forget the English-related goals of the activity.
Mingle	A survey of classmates' opinions	Learners can speak to lots of different classmates, getting to know everybody better.	This can be challenging to set up in an online classroom, depending on the platform used.
Teacher leads the class	Drilling pronunciation of a new grammar item	All learners are working on the same thing at the same time, which can (sometimes) be easier for the teacher to control.	Depending on how the teacher runs the activity, learners may disengage and lose interest in the lesson.
Learner(s) lead(s) the class	Checking answers to a gap-fill activity	Learners enjoy being given responsibility, and this can help them to feel engaged.	Some learners may think that only the teacher should lead the class, and therefore not listen to their classmates.

2 Answers will vary.
Extra points you may wish to make:
- Varying interaction patterns is one possible way to help learners feel that the lesson is well-paced, and to keep them engaged in activities.
- Pair and group work allow learners to practise without having to perform in front of the whole class, and this may help them to build confidence.
- Additionally, pair and group work allow learners to use a relatively informal style, whereas some may feel the need to be relatively more formal if addressing the teacher.
- In some classes, particularly large ones, pair and group work can lead to a loss of teacher control and sense of disorder. Learners may be uneasy if they feel that the teacher cannot hear what they are saying and that a lot of errors are going uncorrected, and it may run contrary to the expectations of some learners.

5 – Developing teaching skills and professionalism

- If learners feel they are not observed by the teacher, they may resort to the easiest means of achieving a task, including the use of their first language.
- Generally, most teachers tend to feel that the benefits of pair and group work outweigh the potential drawbacks.

C Group dynamics

Answers might include:

- Getting to know learners as individuals, for example by remembering details about them.
- Letting learners know something about you as a person, not just as their teacher.
- Encouraging learners to get to know each other, for example by finding things they have in common with their classmates.
- Creating a supportive environment, where learners can make mistakes without being laughed at or ridiculed.
- Stopping behaviour which might compromise relationships as soon as possible, for example if one learner is bullying another.
- Being inclusive and recognizing diversity, for example of ability, gender, race or sexuality.

You may want to introduce the idea of 'classroom dynamics' to trainees, and point out that the relationships between teachers and students or between students and students are a key factor in the success of lessons.

D Using the whiteboard

Use the pictures to help the trainees understand the most effective way of using the board. If you prefer, you could create a poor example on the board yourself and ask trainees how it could be improved. The following points could be made:

- Plan the use of the board, perhaps leaving designated spaces for different purposes.
- Use upper and lower case appropriately.
- Take care with spelling.
- Generally avoid joined-up writing, as it is harder to read.
- Generally avoid letting the board become too cluttered.
- Consider which colours you are using: it's best to keep red or green for highlighting, and blue or black for main points. Avoid contrasting red and green, as this may be challenging for some colour-blind learners to see clearly.
- Online, choose your fonts and font sizes carefully, bearing in mind that some learners may be accessing lessons on mobile devices. Font size 50+ is best for mobile viewing.
- Online, choose background and font colours carefully to create a clear contrast. An off-white background with a dark grey or black font can be easier for some learners to process.

E Grading language

It is important to point out that it is not necessary for learners to understand every individual word that the teacher says. However, it is important that the learners understand enough to comprehend the overall message. Many researchers would argue that such 'comprehensible input' is a necessary (if not sufficient) condition for language acquisition to take place.

The advice below centres on making language easier to understand, because most trainees have more difficulty in grading language appropriately for lower-level learners than for higher-level learners, where they can speak while making fewer adjustments to their language.

Good advice	Potentially unsound advice
b Use gestures, pictures and other things that will support what you are saying, to make it easier to understand. c Speak with natural rhythm and intonation. e Speak at a natural speed, but pause slightly longer after each 'chunk', if necessary. *A little extra decoding time after each phrase is likely to help comprehension more than pausing after each word.* f Try to avoid 'difficult' vocabulary (for example, very idiomatic language). g Try to avoid complex grammar patterns.	a Pronounce each word slowly and deliberately. *Learners need to get used to hearing reasonably natural-sounding language.* d Miss out small words (articles, prepositions, auxiliary verbs and so on) so that learners can focus on the 'content' words and understand the message. *This will impoverish the input they receive – learners pick up a lot of grammar from hearing it used. Also learners may feel patronized if they feel they are being spoken to in 'baby talk'. However, it is important to be concise at certain points in the lesson. Aim to reduce interjections and unnecessary language, especially when giving instructions or explanations.*

F Trainees' queries

1 Ask trainees to read the comments and to discuss possible solutions to the problems.
2 Ask them to do the matching activity, to compare their answers, and then to compare them with their own solutions from F1.
   Answers: 1–d) 2–f) 3–b) 4–a) 5–c) 6–e)
3 Be ready to answer any other questions the trainees may have.

> **KEY WORDS FOR TEACHERS**
>
> Remind the trainees of the need to be able to use teaching terms confidently and accurately.
>
> **REFLECTION**
>
> You need to ensure that trainees know what lesson they will be teaching next before you do this task.
>
> Allow the trainees to think about the prompts given. Or, if you are short of time, ask them to choose the point that they feel is most relevant to them. You could then put the trainees into small groups to share ideas and suggestions, before asking them to report back briefly in open class.

5 – Developing teaching skills and professionalism

34 Managing an activity

Main focus
To introduce trainees to the activity set-up cycle and help them to apply it to their own planning.

Learning outcomes
- Trainees understand the stages of the activity set-up cycle, and how this can impact on the successful management of an activity.
- Trainees increase their awareness of the connection between lesson planning and effective teaching.

Key concepts
- classroom management
- instructions
- activity set-up
- staging
- demonstration
- monitoring
- feedback

Stage	Focus
A Warm-up	trainees experience the difference between a badly-run and a well-run activity
B Stages of activity set-up	trainees think about the order in which a teacher might set up and run an activity
C Strategies for managing an activity	trainees learn terminology for referring to different parts of setting up and running an activity
D Putting it into practice	trainees plan the stages of an activity they will teach in an upcoming TP and give each other feedback
Key words for teachers	building of specialist vocabulary to talk about teaching
Reflection	trainees reflect on how they can use their new knowledge going forward

A Warm-up

Set up the same activity twice. You could use the information gap activity on pages 181 and 183 of the Trainee Book, or something similar of your own. Set up the activity badly the first time, for example by not telling the trainees the page number for the pictures, giving minimal instructions or giving them all at once without staging the activity, ignoring the trainees during the activity, rushing them, or not following up on the activity by checking answers or upgrading language. The second time, set it up much more carefully, for example by including clearly signposted stages from task B of the Trainee Book or strategies from task C. In both cases, allow two or three minutes for them to do the activity (tell them it would be much longer in a real classroom). The second time, include clear follow-up on the content of the activity and feedback on the language choices trainees made.

In the follow-up discussion, trainees may comment on various areas, depending on what you included in your set-up, for example:

> Activity 1 was less explicit and didn't tell learners exactly what to do.
> Activity 2 used the material to make instructions clear (pointing to the pictures).
> Activity 2 broke down the instructions and checked them throughout.
> Activity 2 demonstrated the activity.
> There was follow-up after both activities, but after activity 2 this included a focus on language items too.

B Setting up and running an activity

1 Trainees work alone to order the stages. They can then compare their orders in pairs or small groups. Encourage them to justify why they have chosen the order they have.

   One possible order:
   1 Get learners' attention.
   2 Give the instructions orally while indicating the relevant areas of the material to be used.
   3 Demonstrate the activity.
   4 Check learners have understood the instructions.
   5 Give a clear signal for learners to start.
   6 Monitor learners' progress during the activity.
   7 Allow learners to compare their answers or ideas with other learners.
   8 Give a clear signal for learners to finish.
   9 Follow up on the content of the activity (for example, by checking answers or eliciting ideas from learners).
   10 Feedback on the language of the activity (for example, by correcting errors or clarifying the meaning of vocabulary items).

2 Refer trainees back to the activity you set up during the warm-up. They could work in pairs to consider how you set up the activity, or you could work in open class to elicit the stages you went through. As an extension, you could ask trainees to memorize the stages from B1, then cover them and remember them, either by saying or writing them.

> **Trainer tip**
>
> If you're running input face-to-face, cut up the stages for trainees to put into order. As an extension, trainees can think of one key word to encompass each stage and use this as a memorization prompt.
>
> If you're running it online, use text boxes on a digital whiteboard to create a similar activity. Trainees can delete the text boxes or turn the text white for the memorization stage.

5 – Developing teaching skills and professionalism

C Strategies for managing an activity

1 You may wish to divide up the four activities between different groups, so that each group is considering different learner and activity types in greater depth and considering which strategies might apply to them. Alternatively, divide up the strategies so that each group is discussing two or three strategies in greater depth and considering which learner and activity types they might be useful for. Encourage trainees to add their own ideas for strategies to enable to smooth running of an activity.
Possible answers:
Adult students completing a gap-fill alone: B, D, E, G, H, I, J
University students preparing a presentation in groups: A, C, D, F (depending on whether students have done this kind of activity before – if they have, some parts of the model might not be necessary), G, H, I, K
Young learners drawing and writing about a monster, guided by the teacher: B, C, D, E, F, I, K
Teenagers design their perfect school in pairs: A, C, D, F, G, H, I, K

2 Give trainees a couple of minutes to think about this alone before discussing it in pairs or open class.
The majority of these strategies are equally applicable online and in the physical classroom. However, when teaching online you may not want to / be able to do A, and G may be more important as it is potentially harder for learners to get the teacher's attention or for the teacher to immediately spot if there is a problem understanding the instructions.

D Putting it into practice

You need to ensure that trainees know what lesson they will next be teaching before you do this task.

1 Encourage trainees to select a more complicated activity, such as a freer practice, or an activity type which they haven't set up before, such as a gap-fill task or an information gap activity. As they are planning, remind them to refer back to the activity set-up stages from task B and strategies from task C.

2 Again, remind trainees to refer back to the activity set-up stages. You may wish to feed in extra ideas to stronger or more experienced trainees, such as different ways to run feedback. If you have time, trainees could rehearse setting up their activity with their partner.

KEY WORDS FOR TEACHERS

Remind the trainees of the need to be able to use teaching terms confidently and accurately.

REFLECTION

This stage will work best if trainees are in their TP groups, so that they can feed in ideas from lessons they have already taught and observed.

35 Teaching young learners and teenagers

Main focus
To introduce trainees to possible differences between adult learners, very young learners, young learners and teenage learners, and the implications that these variations will have on teaching.

Learning outcomes
- Trainees can recognize key characteristics of very young learners, young learners and teenagers, including both linguistic and non-linguistic abilities.
- Trainees begin to understand how variations in these abilities may impact on teaching, with regard to suitable activities for each age group and how to anticipate and deal with potential challenges.
- Trainees are introduced to the idea of project-based lessons.

Key concepts
- very young learners (VYLs), pre-primary learners
- young learners (YLs), primary learners
- teenage learners, secondary learners
- motor skills

Stage	Focus
A Warm-up	trainees reflect on their experiences with different age groups
B Characteristics of different age groups	looking at different age groups to identify key characteristics, activities which might work, and problems which might face teachers working with them
C Sharing projects	sharing findings from the previous stage
D Project-based lessons	trainees identify the features of a project-based lesson, and reflect on their own experience of learning like this
Key words for teachers	building of specialist vocabulary to talk about teaching
Reflection	trainees consider how they might feel about working with learners of different ages in the future

A Warm-up

1 Trainees individually complete the table, indicating which age groups they have prior experience with.
2 Put them in small groups to compare their experiences and how they feel about working with non-adult learners.

5 – Developing teaching skills and professionalism

> **Trainer tip**
>
> You could send the questions from task A out as an online survey before the session. This will enable you to decide on trainee groupings and give you an idea of who already has prior experience, to help you when planning the session. If trainees have no experience with any of these age groups, it may be best for them to be allocated to teenagers, as this is likely to be the easiest age for them to remember from their own personal experience.

B Characteristics of different age groups

Divide trainees into small groups and allocate one of the following age groups to each of them:

- Very young learners (2–6 years old)
- Young learners (7–12 years old)
- Teenagers (13–16 years old)

Mention that in many contexts, students who are 17 and older are likely to be treated as adult learners. It's also worth pointing out that these groupings are somewhat arbitrary, as (for example) a 6-year-old would have more in common with a 7-year-old than a 2-year-old.

Set up the task, then give trainees at least half an hour to create their summaries with their groups. Remind them that they can display their summary in whatever form they choose. You may wish to create a shared online folder before the session for trainees to save electronic versions of their summaries in – this approach can be used on both online and face-to-face courses. Provide resources to help them with their research, but also encourage trainees to reflect on their own experiences with, and knowledge of, each age group, as well as their memories of lessons at these ages.

The Cambridge resources below may be useful to help trainees with their research (links correct at the time of writing). You may also wish to supplement them with other books or websites which you know about. If resources are not available or you feel trainees need more support, you could provide access to the notes in task C of the Trainer Manual.

All ages
Cambridge University Press ELT blog:
https://www.cambridge.org/elt/blog/
Cambridge University Press ELT YouTube channel:
https://www.youtube.com/c/CambridgeEnglishTV

Very young learners (2-6 years old)

Activities for Very Young Learners, Cambridge Handbooks for Language Teachers

Young learners (7–12 years old)
Cambridge World of Fun: https://worldoffun.cambridge.org/

Teenagers (13–16 years old)
Herbert Puchta's 101 Tips for Teaching Teenagers, Cambridge Handbooks for Language Teachers
Language Activities for Teenagers, Cambridge Handbooks for Language Teachers
Cambridge Teacher Development: Teaching Teenagers
https://www.cambridge.org/gb/cambridgeenglish/teacher-development/teaching-teenagers
Top tips for teaching teenagers:
https://www.cambridge.org/elt/blog/2017/11/22/top-tips-for-teaching-teens/

35 Teaching young learners and teenagers

C Sharing projects

Regroup trainees to share what they have learned. For feedback, elicit one or two key differences between different age groups.

Possible answers:

What are the characteristics of this age group? What can they do? What can't they do?

Very young learners: The youngest ones may have a very limited knowledge of their own language(s). As they get older, they may recognize some letters, especially letters in their own name, but otherwise they are unlikely to be able to read or write. They have no descriptive knowledge of language, for example grammar terminology. Children at this age lack fine motor skills, such as holding a pencil to do colouring, and the youngest learners may also lack gross motor skills, such as throwing and catching a ball. They have a short concentration span and need a lot of repetition to remember new language. They also need lots of variety. They are very good at imitation and enjoy anything that involves play.

Young learners: Learners generally have a full grasp of how to speak in their own language, but are developing their ability to read and write throughout this age band. The older ones may know a few grammatical terms, but this depends a lot on the general education system – as a rule, learners of this age still use language instinctively, without being able to analyse it. Young learners have developed a range of fine motor skills, though the youngest ones may still need practice with skills like cutting out or colouring in the lines. Their concentration span is developing throughout these years, though they still need a lot of variety, including both energetic ('stirrer') and calm ('settler') activities. They are focused on meaning, and are generally very curious and enthusiastic about learning new things. They are particularly interested in themselves and their own lives, and are highly imaginative. The youngest ones are good at imitation.

Teenagers: Learners generally have a full grasp of their own language, both written and spoken. They are able to process language cognitively, including understanding grammatical terms such as tense names. As they go through this age band, teenagers are increasingly able to think critically and analyse situations. They can concentrate for a long time on topics or activities which they find interesting. Teenagers are going through a lot of hormonal changes in their bodies, which can lead to mood swings. They are focused on themselves and how (they think) their peers perceive them, working out who they are and how they fit in to society. They often want to express their individuality, but also to feel part of a group. They may want to conform to what teachers expect of them, but they may also want to rebel. Confidence is a big factor for this age group, and can influence what they are willing and unwilling to do in lessons.

What kind of activities work well with them? What don't work?

Very young learners: They appreciate routines, such as question-and-answer chains, or reading the same story multiple times. Activities involving movement work particularly well, such as actions accompanying a song or simple crafts. Activities involving memorizing short conversations, songs or words from flashcards also work. Written grammar activities don't work, nor does anything requiring concentration for more than a few minutes at a time.

Young learners: Concrete, meaning-based activities work well, such as surveys of classmates or creating posters. Stories, songs and chants are also popular. Routines are very useful, particularly to start and end lessons, but also to introduce new language, for example through a range of flashcard games which learners are familiar with. Creative activities such as drawing their dream house or telling a story can also work well. Writing activities depend on the age and confidence of the learners – older ones might be able to do these more successfully. Explicit rule-based grammar study is unlikely to work.

5 – Developing teaching skills and professionalism

Teenagers: Project work allows teenagers to approach topics from different angles and express some of their individuality. As far as possible, give learners a say in the choice of activities or topics you cover to help them engage with their learning, for example by offering them the choice between two different games. Activities which give learners freedom to say or write what they want can work particularly well, such as creating a story from prompts. Activities that rely on having a lot of real-world experience, such as talking about job interviews, or that make learners feel exposed, such as sharing their opinions in front of the whole class, will probably be less successful.

What can go wrong in the lessons? What can you do to prevent/resolve these issues?

Very young learners: Particularly with the youngest children, you may need to do things like take them to the toilet or help them to put their coats on – find out about child protection laws in the country where you're working, and make sure that you are never alone with a child. If learners get bored, this will be very clear – keep them active at all times. Very young learners show their emotions frequently, sometimes including tears and shouting, but also getting very excited – think about what routines you can put in place to deal with these, for example a hand signal to calm learners down, or a chair they can go to when they're upset.

Young learners: It can be easy to feel like you're not control of the group – create clear classroom management rules and routines, be consistent with any consequences for unacceptable behaviour, and praise acceptable behaviour in preference to punishing unacceptable behaviour whenever possible. Learners can be easily bored or get over-excited – include a variety of relatively short activities, mixing 'stirrers' to inject energy and 'settlers' to calm learners down. Older children in this age group may already have had negative experiences with learning in general and English specifically, which can influence how they feel about lessons and sometimes lead to bad behaviour – give specific positive praise and encourage them to participate in a range of activities.

Teenagers: They may not have chosen to be in English lessons, so might be unwilling to participate – agree on classroom management rules with the group at the start of the year, and be consistent in applying these, though always seek to praise acceptable behaviour and look for the positives in learners rather than punishing bad behaviour. Teenagers may be reluctant to express their opinions if they think it will influence how others perceive them – allow them to distance themselves from opinions, for example by talking about teenagers in general or celebrities they like, rather than their own opinions. They might refuse to work with particular members of the group – build in short activities where learners can get to know each other and feel more confident working with everybody; provide variety in groupings so that sometimes teenagers work with their friends, and sometimes they work with other classmates.

> ### Trainer tip
>
> Some trainees probably drew on their life experience when doing this research, such as their experiences of parenting, rather than relying purely on external sources. This session could be a good opportunity to highlight that personal experience is to be valued, especially for less experienced teachers who may feel they need to consult external sources to validate their planning and teaching decisions.

35 Teaching young learners and teenagers

D Project-based lessons

Put trainees into pairs to discuss the questions.
Possible answers:

1 These can be some of the most motivating and memorable lessons for learners and teachers, and learners are often incredibly proud of what they produce. Their language use can surprise us too, as they're generally motivated by the creativity of the project, rather than working on the next language point in the syllabus. Some drawbacks might be the amount of time that project work can take, or a perception from learners or parents that projects are a waste of time.

2 To make the project successful, the trainer hopefully:
  • created a clear framework and end goal
  • provided support in terms of resources (in a lesson, support regarding functional language would also be useful, for example phrases for making, accepting and rejecting suggestions)
  • allowed enough time for learners to create the project
  • (optional) allocated roles to different members of the group, e.g. secretary, presenter, communication manager
  • created some way for trainees to display or share their projects at the end

3 Projects can be used with learners of all ages, including adults, to add variety to the course. Some teachers base all of their teaching around projects.

4 With young learners, this might be topics such as 'My favourite animal', or 'My town', or 'Life in Poland'. With teenagers, topics can be deeper and involve more research, depending on their age and level. 15-year-old beginners might still get a lot out of projects like 'My town', but 13-year-old intermediate students might enjoy researching something like 'Strange inventions from the past' or 'Conservation in my country'. The list of possible topics is endless!

KEY WORDS FOR TEACHERS

Remind the trainees of the need to be able to use teaching terms confidently and accurately.

REFLECTION

1 Encourage trainees to refer back to the projects they have shared with each other, and feed in ideas from the notes for task C in this unit of the Trainer's Manual as required.
2 Refer trainees back to the warm-up, and their feelings about teaching non-adult learners. Allow them time to discuss whether those feelings have changed or not as a result of this session.

Topic 5 – Developing teaching skills and professionalism

36 Teaching at different levels

Main focus
Trainees learn to adapt to teaching different levels.

Learning outcomes
- Trainees understand the needs of learners at different levels.
- Trainees understand how skills-based lessons may vary at different levels.
- Trainees understand how lessons with a grammar focus may vary at different levels.

Key concepts:
- basic user, independent user, proficient user
- beginner, elementary, (pre-, upper-) intermediate, advanced
- language grading
- receptive v productive skills
- accuracy v fluency

Stage	Focus
A Warm-up	trainees are introduced to the CEFR band descriptors
B Adapting to different levels	trainees consider classroom management issues at different levels
C Productive skills	trainees consider how productive skills lessons may vary with level
D Receptive skills	trainees consider how receptive skills lessons may vary with level
E Teaching grammar	trainees consider how grammar input may vary with level
Key words for teachers	building of specialist vocabulary to talk about teaching
Reflection	trainees consider how the issues raised in the unit will impact on their own teaching

This unit could usefully be done at the time when trainees switch to teaching different levels. You could replace the sample material given here with material from books trainees are using in teaching practice. The final (Reflection) task is intended to give fairly concrete and practical advice on adapting to a new class, as trainees move from one level to another.

36 Teaching at different levels

A Warm-up

1–2 Answers:

C1: iii	Can understand a wide range of demanding, longer texts, and recognize implicit meaning. Can express themselves fluently and spontaneously without much obvious searching for expressions. Can use language flexibly and effectively for social, academic and professional purposes. Can produce clear, well-structured, detailed text on complex subjects …
B2: i	Can understand the main ideas of complex text on both concrete and abstract topics, including technical discussions in their field of specialization. Can interact with a degree of fluency and spontaneity that makes regular interaction with users of the target language quite possible without imposing strain on either party. Can produce clear, detailed text on a wide range of subjects and explain a viewpoint on a topical issue, giving the advantages and disadvantages of various options.
B1: v	Can understand the main points of clear standard input on familiar matters regularly encountered in work, school, leisure, etc. Can deal with most situations likely to arise whilst travelling in an area where the language is spoken. Can produce simple connected text on topics which are familiar or of personal interest. Can describe experiences and events, dreams, hopes and ambitions and briefly give reasons and explanations for opinions and plans.
A2: iv	Can understand sentences and frequently used expressions related to areas of most immediate relevance […] Can communicate in simple and routine tasks requiring a simple and direct exchange of information on familiar and routine matters. Can describe in simple terms aspects of their background, immediate environment and matters in areas of immediate need.
A1: ii	Can understand and use familiar everyday expressions and very basic phrases aimed at the satisfaction of needs of a concrete type. Can introduce themselves and others, and can ask and answer questions about personal details, such as where someone lives, people they know and things they have. Can interact in a simple way, provided the other person talks slowly and clearly and is prepared to help.

Council of Europe (2020). *Common European Framework of Reference for Languages*, p.175

You may want to relate these CEFR levels to the names of the levels that trainees are teaching and observing, and which are customarily used in labelling coursebooks, e.g. advanced (C1), upper-intermediate (B2), intermediate (B1), pre-intermediate (A2), elementary (A1–A2).

5 – Developing teaching skills and professionalism

The descriptor for C2 was not included in the task, as this is a level that is rarely encountered by most teachers, apart from those teaching ESP (English for Specific Purposes) or Proficiency classes. For reference, here is the descriptor for C2:

> Can understand virtually all types of texts. Can summarize information from different oral and written sources, reconstructing arguments and accounts in a coherent presentation. Can express themselves spontaneously, very fluently and precisely, differentiating finer shades of meaning even in more complex situations.

You may also choose to mention that the full CEFR documentation includes descriptors for A2+, B1+ and B2+ levels, as well as for pre-A1 and above C2 level. It recognizes that levels are a continuum but that we divide them up for ease of reference, as we do when referring to the colours of the rainbow. (see *Common European Framework of Reference for Languages*, p.36)

3   The aim of this activity is for trainees to apply the descriptors to their TP students, and to assess their usefulness/accuracy.
4   You may prefer to dictate the sentence stems without having the trainees open their books. This would help to create a group atmosphere, rather than having the trainees read and write individually, with each person working at their own pace. If you are running a course online, you may wish to use an application which allows you to gather answers automatically and to display them all simultaneously.

Possible answers might include:
a   At higher levels, learners might need to work on a wide range of different texts / work on understanding implicit meanings / ideas for how to build on their already strong speaking skills / etc.
b   At lower levels, learners might need to practise speaking in a range of familiar situations / phrases to help them in situations where they can't understand what they hear / to build their vocabulary connected to things in their immediate environment / etc.
c   Answers will vary.

B Adapting to different levels

1   Allow the trainees a few moments to read the statements and make their choices. They should find this relatively easy.
Maria: elementary to upper-intermediate:
a   'In the other group, I didn't mind if the learners used their own language a bit – but I try to stop it completely now.'
b   'I realize that the learners I have now can already say a lot of what they want to and my job is partly to give them alternative ways of saying things.'
f   'I really have to work hard to research grammar now. The learners sometimes ask quite difficult questions and my research helps me to feel more confident.'
Salim: upper-intermediate to elementary:
c   'I got a real shock when I started with this new group. I don't think they understood anything I said in the first lesson! There was an activity that was quite easy but I just couldn't get across what they had to do.'
d   'I sometimes found it difficult to explain how to use our online platform. I had to remember to carefully show them what to click on and where to type, not just tell them.'

36 Teaching at different levels

    e 'I've noticed that I have more activities in a lesson and they tend to be a bit shorter – particularly pair and group work doesn't last as long.'
    g 'I can't just chat to this group and find out about them as people so easily. I don't think I have such a good rapport with them.'

  You may wish to highlight that at lower levels teachers need to work much harder at grading their language appropriately. Also, at lower levels, learners often need more thorough preparation for tasks. At higher levels, teachers may need a greater degree of language awareness as explanations become more sophisticated and distinctions more subtle.

2 Again, this should be very straightforward. The aim is simply to help trainees to see the link between these issues and their own teaching practice.

C Productive skills

1 Allow the trainees to look at the first piece of material with a partner.
  a The learners listen to a model, focus on past simple verb forms, and plan what to say based on prompts.
  b The exchanges in activity 5c are fairly predictable – at least to the extent that they are likely to be characterized by just one turn for each learner before the next question is asked, so the exchanges are very short.
    The important thing to emphasize is that at lower levels learners often need a great deal of preparation before a speaking activity, and even then, exchanges may be quite short.
2 a Again trainees could discuss this in groups before reporting back to you in open class. They may suggest that learners are more capable of producing language spontaneously and are able to extend speaking activities with more turns and longer exchanges.
  b Trainees may point out that there is less preparation built into the activity. The learners have to talk about a range of topics (unlike in the first example) and that they are invited to ask each other an unspecified number of questions (rather than just one).
3 If time allows, you might like to encourage trainees to look at writing tasks in published materials to support their discussion.
  At higher levels, writing tasks may be longer. There may be a greater focus on characteristics of the text beyond the sentence level (linking and so on). There may be instruction in different genres of writing (types of letter, CVs and so on). Learners may respond to input data (such as having to write a reply to an email), and the input may be longer and more sophisticated than at lower levels.
  At lower levels, there may be a greater focus on sentence-level writing. Where a longer text is produced, learners are likely to need much more support – for example, the use of a parallel text, which they can adapt using their own information.

D Receptive skills

1 The text was originally published in an intermediate coursebook. Trainees may comment on the length of the text, and its slightly ungraded nature, including an attempt to expose learners to some features of spoken language, such as 'um' and 'anyway'. However, as the next task shows, this does not mean that it could not be used at lower levels.
2 Allow the trainees some time to work in small groups to discuss their ideas before reporting back to you.

5 – Developing teaching skills and professionalism

Lesson a: advanced. There is clear information about the topic, but only a brief context set up. Learners have to listen closely in order to understand the details of the story.

Lesson b: elementary. The learners are 'positioned' as close as possible to the gist of the text with pictures, and the task is a very general one – all they have to do is recognize key words like *wedding, airport* and *party*. They can also collaborate in solving the task, and are given the extra help of the written transcript.

Lesson c: intermediate. The learners are set comprehension questions, which help them focus on the main details of the text. The sequence moves from a general understanding of the text, to a more specific focus on particular phrases used, followed by an opportunity to use those phrases themselves.

3 At lower levels, learners generally need support to help them to understand listening texts, both from their teacher and their peers. It's important to set achievable tasks, especially if the materials are above the learners' level, to ensure that learners don't lose their confidence when listening. This may focus on the 'big picture' of the text, rather than the finer details.

At intermediate levels, learners generally need a framework to help them to access the meaning of listening texts. They can work with texts via a range of different activities, and are more likely to easily be able to make use of language they have heard within their own production than lower-level students.

At advanced levels, learners are independent listeners. While a little support can be useful, learners can generally understand a lot of what they hear, and are able to focus in on the finer points of the listening text.

E Teaching grammar

1 Allow the trainees some time to consider the question in small groups before reporting back. If the following points are not raised, you may like to point out that at higher levels context may be generated through, for example, a fairly long text – but at lower levels this would place too great a burden on learners. 'Rules' typically become more sophisticated and frequently new language is contrasted with existing knowledge at higher levels. It is often assumed that learners have a better understanding of metalanguage at higher levels. More than one form may be presented at one time at higher levels, but this is less likely at lower levels. Practice activities are frequently more extended at higher levels.

2 At this point it may be worth pointing out that the fundamental principles of teaching are not altered. Learners still need to know about form, meaning and the contexts in which new language items can be used.

3 Allow the trainees some time to look at the material.
They should see that at the lower level *be going to* is introduced on its own, but at the higher level it is contrasted with other future forms. The lower-level material also pays more attention to form, whereas this is assumed to be known at the higher level. They should also be able to see that the 'rules' have become more sophisticated at the higher level.

36 Teaching at different levels

> **KEY WORDS FOR TEACHERS**
>
> Remind the trainees of the need to be able to use teaching terms confidently and accurately.
>
> **REFLECTION**
>
> The aim of this task is for the trainees to think about their classes and be able to pass on useful information to another inexperienced teacher.
>
> Tell trainees that they can add additional bullet points, or indeed, leave some blank. You could suggest that in the box marked 'Other' that they think of other useful information that is not directly related to level, for example activities which the class enjoys.

Reference

Council of Europe (2020), *Common European Framework of Reference for Languages: Learning, Teaching, Assessment – Companion volume,* Council of Europe Publishing, Strasbourg, available at www.coe.int/lang-cefr. p.175

5 – Developing teaching skills and professionalism

37 Maintaining learner motivation

Main focus
To raise awareness of the principal ways in which teachers can build and maintain learner motivation.

Learning outcomes
- Trainees understand some of the principal factors that impact on motivation.
- Trainees are able to apply knowledge of motivation to classroom management strategies.
- Trainees are able to apply knowledge of motivation to materials adaptation.

Key concepts
- motivation
- goals
- intrinsic interest
- variety
- personalization

Stage	Focus
A Warm-up	introducing motivation
B Supporting motivation	focusing on principal factors associated with motivation
C Learning from learners	using learner opinions to draw conclusions about motivation
D Putting it into practice	adapting materials to make them more motivating
Key words for teachers	building of specialist vocabulary to talk about teaching
Reflection	trainees reflect on how they can use their new knowledge going forward

A Warm-up

Introduce the lesson by eliciting one or two things that have motivated the trainees during the course. Make sure that the concept of having goals is introduced. After some initial discussion, focus the trainees on the questions and allow some time for them to discuss them in pairs or small groups.
Note: you may want to set classroom observation task 6 on page 195 before the lesson, as this can then be referred to throughout the session. It should indicate the factors that might have led to motivation building or declining in a single lesson.
Invite the trainees to report back their discussions.

B Supporting motivation

1 Focus the trainees on the quote and ask for some suggestions in response to the question. This leads in to the text in B2, where examples are given.

2 The aim of this activity is for the trainees to gain some basic information about things which have been demonstrated to support motivation, while at the same time being exposed to a versatile activity type that they may be able to use in their own teaching.
Explain the mutual dictation activity to the trainees.
One option for setting up the activity is to make it a race between the different groups. When the trainees have completed the text, display the complete version so that they can check the accuracy of their work (and to model how the activity might work with a group of language learners).
After the activity is completed, you may like to briefly discuss the activity type and the reasons for using it. For example, it provides all learners with practice in all four skills and the learner-centred nature of it can bring energy to the classroom. It can be used to practise (or introduce) new language items by ensuring that examples occur in the text, giving learners the opportunity to see language in context.

> There are many factors which can affect a learner's motivation. One of the most important factors is actually teacher motivation. Research suggests that if a teacher is enthusiastic and motivated, they are more likely to have motivated students. Learners are also more likely to be motivated if they feel that their lessons are useful and relevant to them, so clearly teachers have to understand the needs of their learners and tailor lessons to meet those needs. Materials and activities also need to be intrinsically interesting, and this means that teachers are well advised to build interest in activities before doing them. Using a variety of activities and lesson styles can also make classes more interesting. Motivation is further boosted when learners have a sense of control over what and how they learn. Finally, another important contributor to motivation is a sense of success and mastery, so teachers need to help learners see the progress that they are making.

3 Focus the trainees on the questions.
   a Trainees may suggest many examples here. For example, planning lessons carefully, marking homework promptly, taking an interest in the learners, talking about their own experiences as learners with enthusiasm, and trying new teaching ideas. In addition, away from day-to-day teaching, they might take part in professional development activities, such as workshops, or reading about teaching.
   b The teacher might ask learners what they already know about the topic, and ask what learners would like to find out, so that there is goal-setting. They may focus on the visual accompanying a text and invite speculation about the topic.
   c Teachers might ask about learners' needs and expectations for lessons and try to provide content that matches those. They could talk to the learners, or give questionnaires, so that they get feedback on what the learners would like more of and what they would like less of. They could invite learners to choose the type of lesson they will have (e.g. speaking and listening, or reading and writing). They could also encourage learners to be autonomous outside the classroom through, for example, introducing them to appropriate resources.
   d Teachers generally give praise, which encourages learners when it is specific and not overdone. They might give learners short progress tests. They might record learners at the start of the course and then use this as a comparison as learners progress. They could give learners a list of can-do statements for the course ('I can order a coffee in English') and have learners tick them off as they feel confident about achieving them.

5 – Developing teaching skills and professionalism

C Learning from learners

1 The trainees should work individually to complete the sentences. There are, of course, several possibilities but likely responses should be similar to the suggestions below.
   A The teacher should help the learner to set *clear goals/objectives*.
   B This is one way to give learners *choice / autonomy / a sense of control*.
   C This shows how important it is to *build a good rapport in the classroom,* or *create a friendly environment*.
   D It is important that a teacher *is friendly* or *takes an interest in learners*.
   E Ideally the teacher needs to make the classes more *relevant*.
2 You may want the trainees to work with their TP groups for this activity. Give the trainees time to discuss in groups before encouraging them to report back in open class.

D Putting it into practice

One of the most obvious ways in which teachers can promote interest, and therefore motivation, is to make relatively dull, lifeless activities more personal and meaningful (see unit 17).

This material is designed to be an exercise that can be relatively easily transformed into something more meaningful.

Trainees should work in small groups. When they have finished, they can compare their ideas with another group before reporting back in open class.

The obvious changes to suggest are that the material should be personalized by asking about, speaking about and writing about the people in the class. This would also make the activity potentially genuinely communicative (assuming that at least some of what was shared was previously unknown). The current exercise is not really any more than an opportunity to practise using the correct forms.

Emphasize the need to personalize material and make it meaningful as two motivation strategies.

KEY WORDS FOR TEACHERS

Remind the trainees of the need to be able to use teaching terms confidently and accurately.

REFLECTION

This is an opportunity for the trainees to summarize some key factors that can help build and maintain motivation. By prioritizing them, it is hoped that they will be memorable and actually be acted on after the course.

1–2 Give the learners some time to review what they have covered and reflect on the factors that they wish to choose.
3–4 Lead a discussion on how easy these things are to incorporate. For example, in some contexts developing learner autonomy may be difficult, as might adapting or rewriting material. Learners may have very varied interests. A teacher may want to be enthusiastic, but they may also become tired and jaded. Experimenting with new ideas might help in the latter case.

While it is sensible to be realistic, it is also important that trainees feel encouraged and ready to implement a range of things that are likely to help with learner motivation.

38 Introduction to assessment

Main focus
To raise awareness of the reasons for assessment and how it can be carried out.

Learning outcomes
- Trainees understand the reasons that learners are assessed.
- Trainees are able to compare different assessment tools.
- Trainees become familiar with basic terms used in describing assessment.
- Trainees acquire some basic tips on teaching exam classes.

Key concepts
- assessment
- testing
- validity
- reliability
- washback

Stage	Focus
A Warm-up	introducing testing
B Some key terms	using key terms in assessment
C Reasons for assessing learners	introducing the key purposes of assessment
D Ways of assessing learners	introducing some of the key tools used in assessing learners
E How not to assess	highlighting some of the key characteristics of poorly designed assessment
F Teaching exam classes	providing a basic introduction to teaching in an exam-focused context
Key words for teachers	building of specialist vocabulary to talk about teaching
Reflection	trainees reflect on how they can use their new knowledge going forward

A Warm-up

1 Set the activity up as a written test. Tell the trainees that they should not talk to each other. After five minutes, stop the test. There is no need to go through the questions with the trainees unless you think it appropriate, but the answers are:
   1 will + be + ---ing
   2 i) I'm meeting   ii) will work   iii) will win
   3 form (spoken and written), meaning, collocation, degree of formality, grammatical restrictions of use, etc.

5 – Developing teaching skills and professionalism

   4 Various potential points, including how the teacher monitors, the ease with which students can change groups, the ease with which teachers can monitor understanding etc.
   5 Set achievable objectives, plan lessons that have variety, select interesting and relevant material, etc.
2 In open class, discuss whether this would be a fair test of progress on the CELTA course. There are issues of 'content validity'. The CELTA course is very practical in nature and classroom based, so a written test is dubious. Of course, in such a short test it is difficult to include a representative sample of work, and here there is a lot on future forms and little on other language areas studied. Trainees may also discuss issues of timing, mark allocation per question, and so on.

B Some key terms

Part of understanding assessment is understanding the terminology used to describe it. This task introduces simple definitions of the most basic terms. The concepts are referred to in subsequent sections of the lesson, so trainees can be pushed to use appropriate terminology in those discussions.

Trainees can work individually before comparing answers with a partner and then reporting back. You may like to point out that gap-filling exercises such as this are a common language-testing device.

Answers:

1 Assessment   2 test   3 valid   4 reliable   5 practical   6 Washback   7 Formative

C Reasons for assessing learners

1 a for placement purposes
   b for diagnostic purposes – this is essentially forward-looking and helps the teacher plan a relevant and useful sequence of lessons.
   c to check progress – this is essentially backward-looking at things that have already been covered. However, it will give the teacher data about any elements of the course that need to be reviewed and so could contribute to planning.
   d assess achievement over the entire course – similar to c) in that it is backward-looking but over a longer period – potentially the entire course.
2 As well as the reasons included in 1, above, assessments are often used to fit in with expectations of learners and other stakeholders, to screen for entry to public exams, or to help prepare for public exams.

The main drawback is if tests are over-used and end up replacing teaching. Tests may also demotivate learners who do not perform well in test-like conditions. Tests might also lead to unwelcome competition and comparisons between members of the group. Teachers need to guard against these unwelcome effects.

D Ways of assessing learners

1 You will need to ensure that trainees understand the terms used in the questions.
   a **Individual (discrete) language items.** Although multiple choice questions can be used to assess a range of language, each item is discrete. Sentence transformations also tend to test individual language items, as would the sentence production exercise. Gap-fill exercises can be used to test one language point (if, for example, only auxiliary verbs are removed) but can also be used to test a range of language. Self-assessment and portfolios may focus on discrete language items, but could also be used to assess tasks (e.g. *I can make a reservation for a hotel room.*)
   b **Integrated language items.** Direct tests of productive skills (writing a composition and learners describing pictures) will involve integrated language. Observation, portfolios and self-assessment can also be used.
   c **Objective marking.** Multiple choice questions and gap-fill exercises will be marked objectively. The sentence transformations will also be fairly objective, but judgements about acceptability may have to be made in some cases, and the same is true for the sentence production exercise.
   d **Subjective marking.** Direct tests of productive skills (writing a composition and learners describing pictures) will involve some degree of subjectivity in the marking and will therefore require assessment criteria, so that performance can be graded with some degree of consistency. Conclusions drawn from observation, portfolios and self-assessment are also likely to be subjective to a large extent.
2 You may like to assign groups to look at the different areas, to ensure that they are all covered. The table below shows probable answers, although arguments for other uses could be made. Virtually everything will involve vocabulary and grammar to some extent, and the brackets indicate where this is tested indirectly. Multiple choice questions can be used to test writing skills indirectly (for example, by choosing the most appropriate linking word).

	Receptive skills	Productive skills	Vocabulary & grammar
Observation	✓	✓	✓
Portfolios	✓	✓	✓
Self-assessment	✓	✓	✓
Multiple choice questions	✓	(✓)	✓
Gap-fill exercises	✓	(✓)	✓
Sentence transformations		(✓)	✓
Writing a composition		✓	(✓)
Oral interviews		✓	(✓)
Sentence production		✓	✓

3 You may wish to omit some or all of this activity if you are short of time.
   Trainees may identify:
   Success at communicating, which may in turn be influenced by:
   - fluency – the ability to keep going without undue hesitation
   - accuracy of language production, including prosodic features of pronunciation and individual sounds

5 – Developing teaching skills and professionalism

- range of vocabulary and structures used
- strategies for dealing with communication breakdowns

Trainees will then need to further break these down for their criteria. For example:

Fully able to communicate intended meaning	Able to communicate most of intended meaning	Unable to communicate significant parts of intended meaning
Little unnatural hesitation	Noticeable pausing and hesitation	Pausing and hesitation, putting an undue burden on the listener
Few noticeable errors	Some errors, but rarely interfere with meaning	A number of errors, some of which interfere with meaning
A good range of vocabulary and structures, allowing communication on a variety of topics	An adequate range of vocabulary and structures	An inadequate range of vocabulary and structures to communicate effectively
Can repair breakdowns in communication	Can repair breakdowns in communication for the most part	Unable to repair breakdowns in communication

Of course, criteria will vary with level and trainees may devise criteria with more than three points on the scale. Trainees may argue that a mark should be given for each criterion, or that a single mark is awarded on a 'best-fit' basis.

This task may take some time. You may prefer to assign two or three areas to each group, rather than ask all groups to do all categories. Alternatively, you could do one on the board in open-class to serve as a model.

E How not to assess

Allow the trainees a few minutes to complete their sentences before comparing with each other. Obviously, answers will vary but possible answers are included below:

1. Instructions need to be clear. (Examples are useful to achieve this.)
2. The content of the test should reflect the content of the course.
3. Input data needs to be easy to understand (i.e. in this example, if the aim is to assess writing, then relatively few demands should be made of reading). Input texts can be selected/written to ensure this.
4. Feedback should be constructive and clearly point learners towards attainable short-term improvement goals.
5. Markers of assessments should standardize their practice before marking scripts. For example, they could mark a few scripts together and discuss those scripts. This is important where there is subjective scoring (e.g. of an oral interview or a piece of writing). Markers of assessments should also use clear marking criteria.

F Teaching exam classes

Explain that the trainees simply have to write each number on the cline. They can do this individually before comparing in groups and then reporting back. Depending on the context of the exam class, answers may vary slightly. The main point to emphasize is that there will be a balance between language development and exam practice.

1. This may be useful, particularly if the course is quite short. On the other hand, it may be quite anxiety-provoking if the learners are unable to perform at anything like the required level.
2. Yes, this is generally true. The goal-orientation should support motivation.
3. The learners need to know basic information about duration and question types. However, this should not come to dominate the time available.
4. While it is reasonable to focus on exam strategies to some extent, the main focus should probably remain the improvement of the language level of the learners.
5. Learners may be highly motivated but this cannot be taken for granted. Motivation can be quite fragile and learners may feel demotivated if they feel they are not making sufficiently quick progress towards their goals. Motivation may also be negatively impacted if the learners do not want to do the exam, but it has been externally imposed, which may be the case in some education contexts.
6. While this is important, the most important thing is to try to improve the language level of the learners.
7. This can be a good idea, as it will help learners to become familiar with the criteria by which they will be assessed and also helps develop learner autonomy.
8. This is almost certainly true.

KEY WORDS FOR TEACHERS

Remind the trainees of the need to be able to use teaching terms confidently and accurately.

REFLECTION

1. Answers:
   a. Regular assessment can help to set short-term goals (and hence maintain motivation) and can also encourage learners to review what they have done. It can also help to give a sense of progress. Diagnostic and progress assessment will give the teacher information that can be used to plan future lessons.
   b. Teachers can give guidance on what to improve and (importantly) concrete steps that could improve performance, rather than simply pointing out errors.
   c. This can lead to a sense of independence and therefore support motivation.
   d. Essentially, teachers should guard against overusing testing tools and be sure that testing does not replace teaching.
2. If time is short, this could be reduced to identifying appropriate content and identifying appropriate question types.

Topic 5 – Developing teaching skills and professionalism

39 Developing as a teacher

Main focus
To explore how to continue developing as a professional teacher.

Learning outcomes
- Trainees appreciate the importance of professional development and understand the different kinds of development opportunities on offer.
- Trainees know how to make the best use of these opportunities.

Key concepts
- experiential learning
- reflection
- in-service development opportunities: observation, workshops, webinars, conference participation, etc.
- diplomas, MAs

Note 1: This unit could feed into trainees' preparation for the written Assignment 4 – Lessons from the Classroom. The reflection task could be adapted to suit the assessment rubric of your centre.

Note 2: Another way of approaching this unit is to set a pre-session task, with different groups of trainees researching various aspects of professional development that they can then share with the group. Topics of research might include, but are not limited to:
- professional organizations, such as IATEFL
- websites that provide teaching material
- websites with forums and discussion opportunities on issues that concern teachers
- Diploma level qualifications, and their pros and cons
- MA qualifications, and their pros and cons

Stage	Focus
A Warm-up	introducing the nature of development
B Professional development	reviewing elements of the course and how they may be taken forward
C Learning from experience	discussing reflective practice
D Case studies	introducing some key ways teachers develop
Key words for teachers	building of specialist vocabulary to talk about teaching
Reflection	trainees reflect on how they can develop going forward

A Warm-up

1 You may like to lead in with an example from your own experience. The focus should be on how expertise was developed over time, rather than the initial phase of learning. When the students have had a chance to consider this, they can exchange stories. Elicit parallels between the narratives that the trainees volunteer and developing expertise as a teacher (e.g. talking to more skilled others, reflecting on experience, etc.).

39 Developing as a teacher

  2 The aim is that trainees recall some of the elements of the CELTA course in a fun way as a lead into task B. Ensure that trainees understand the activity. Put some prompts (such as the categories from task B below) on the board. Again, you may like to demonstrate with one of the trainees.
  3 It is likely that it could be used to review learning in a warm-up activity, or to close a lesson in a fun way.

B Professional development

  1 Ensure that the trainees understand that there are no 'wrong' answers. The purpose of this task is not to evaluate the course, or provide feedback on it, but simply to encourage trainees to think about how learning opportunities may be viewed and used differently by different people. It is not expected that trainees will necessarily concur, although there may be a preference for the more practical aspects of the course, in terms of their learning potential. Allow trainees time to work individually before comparing with a partner.
  2 The task anticipates others that follow, so it is not necessary to go into any detail at this stage.

C Learning from experience

  1 You may like to introduce this by sharing an experience from the course that you have reflected on, and the consequences of that reflection. Ask learners to reflect on their course so far: the obvious parallel with the learning cycle is the teaching practice experience, which follows a cycle of planning, teaching, reflecting, drawing out principles, and planning again. Trainees should try to be as specific and detailed as possible in the events they recount.
  2 Allow the trainees some time to read the quote and ask any questions that they wish to. You may want to give an example of a belief about teaching. For example, a teacher might believe that a lot of repetition practice is highly useful. However, we should all be open to questioning these beliefs and changing our practice as a consequence. A change in beliefs may come about through reflection on experience, or through reading evidence-based articles, for example.
     The trainees can then work in groups to discuss the questions.
     a Practice may change as a result of beliefs about learning and teaching changing. Also, teachers may develop a wider repertoire of techniques as they become exposed to more materials and teaching contexts. Beliefs may change because teachers develop greater understanding. This may be through 'what works for me'-type learning, or through reading and discussion. It may also be that a particular teaching context demands different approaches. The key thing for trainees to appreciate is that they will continue learning as they question their practice and make modifications for the particular learners that they teach.
     b There are several possibilities. For example, teachers may keep a reflective journal or annotate lesson plans with post-delivery comments. They could set themselves reflective tasks, such as those on pages 189–191 in the Trainee Book, to help structure their thinking.
     c Teachers might not change their practices for a variety of reasons. They might not question their beliefs, or be motivated to develop as a teacher. If the context in which they work does not change, they might feel that what they have done in the past continues to work for them. They might work in a context where the teaching style is prescribed for them, allowing for little variation and development.

5 – Developing teaching skills and professionalism

3 The aim of this activity is to give trainees some practical ideas for how they might continue to develop as teachers. You could modify the phrases to suit you and your group. Dictate the following words and phrases, and ask trainees to write them in the column which is relevant to them.
The trainees should then compare in groups and report back ideas afterwards.
- writing a reflective journal
- writing a blog about your teaching experiences
- reading and discussing articles about teaching
- observing other teachers
- being observed by others
- conducting classroom research
- taking part in webinars
- attending conferences
- contributing to discussion forums
- team-teaching
- asking learners for feedback

D Case studies

1 You may prefer to set this up as a jigsaw reading.
Answers will vary. Broadly speaking, all the teachers see their development as involving other people to some extent. George seems to favour experiential learning and trying things out. Cara has benefited from working alone to an extent and from reading and developing her sense of expertise and confidence. However, her pride in sharing her knowledge in the staff room offers a social dimension. Like Jane, she is now considering further courses/qualifications. Ayala has tapped into the things the school offers (an observation programme and workshops). This again sees development as a social activity. Jane is looking at further development through certified courses, and those options are further discussed below.
2 Allow the trainees to ask their questions. One key feature of both Diploma and MA courses is that they are best done when a teacher has gained some experience. You could take this opportunity to point out that there are plenty of shorter courses, many available for free online, that might be useful for teachers before they do a more formal further qualification, demanding more commitment.

KEY WORDS FOR TEACHERS
Remind the trainees of the need to be able to use teaching terms confidently and accurately.

REFLECTION
Ask trainees, working individually, to draw up some action points for their first few months of teaching. Obviously, their action plans will be dependent on the situation they find themselves in (which may still be unknown), but they should be able to sketch out some broad strategies for development after the course.
Allow trainees to compare their plans in pairs or small groups.

40 Preparing for the workplace

> **Main focus**
> Finding work as an ELT teacher, and considering how to manage wellbeing to avoid burnout.
>
> **Learning outcomes**
> - Trainees learn where they can find information about ELT positions.
> - Trainees have strategies for handling a job interview.
> - Trainees are aware of potential stressors for teachers and how to handle them.
>
> **Key concepts**
> - work contexts: state sector, private sector; in an English-speaking or non-English-speaking country
> - pay and conditions
> - employment: CVs, job interviews
> - wellbeing, burnout

Stage	Focus
A Warm-up	introducing the topic of looking for work
B Finding a job	helping trainees learn where teaching positions may be advertised
C Job interviews	preparing for and practising job interviews
D Maintaining health and wellbeing	considering how teacher wellbeing can be affected positively and negatively, and strategies for maintaining positive wellbeing
Key words for teachers	building of specialist vocabulary to talk about teaching
Reflection	re-capping the main areas covered in the unit

There is one optional activity which supports the unit, in which trainees consider the layout and content of a sample CV.

If possible, you may also wish to invite guests to this session who could answer some questions trainees might have. These guests could be previous CELTA trainees, potential employers, or teachers from the organization running the CELTA course.

A Warm-up

Allow the trainees a little time to choose the three points that are most important to them. They should then speak to as many other trainees as they can, in a mingle if face-to-face, or moving between rooms if online. They should see if they can find anyone who chose the same points as them. Allow a little time for them to report back at the end of the activity.

5 – Developing teaching skills and professionalism

B Finding a job

Provide trainees with a list of four or five websites which they could use to look for teaching positions after the course. Some international websites (available at the time of writing) include:

- TEFL.com
- ESL Cafe
- International House
- British Council
- English First

You could also add local websites, or ones more suited to contexts which your trainees are likely to move into, for example university teaching positions.

You may wish to show trainees around the websites first, highlighting where to find jobs and what a typical job advert looks like. Alternatively, give them time to explore by themselves.

When you are ready, set a time limit for trainees to choose a position they would be interested in applying for. Highlight that this is for the purposes of this session, and it's OK if they don't really want to apply for the position they select.

Allow a couple of minutes for trainees to share which position they have selected and why.

If time allows, you could extend this activity by asking trainees to choose one advert and make a bullet point list of things they would address in a covering email.

Note: Depending on your trainees, you may wish to discuss the issue of organizations advertising for 'native speakers only'. This is considered discrimination under some legal systems. The number of schools including this line in their adverts is decreasing over time, partly due to pressure from within the industry and lobbying groups. Most ethical employers would only look at relevant skills, including the ability to use English, regardless of when and how it was learned.

C Job interviews

For both C1 and C2, you may wish to divide the suggested topics between different pairs, or have some pairs work on C1 and some work on C2. This could be a good opportunity to demonstrate a technology tool, allowing trainees to pool their possible questions into a single resource which they could then refer back to after the course. The lists of suggested questions are not intended to be exhaustive, and you may wish to extend them.

1 These are some of the areas which applicants may be asked about at interview:
   - professional development, including qualifications
     CELTA; English language proficiency certificates; further qualifications, such as certificates in teaching young learners or business English; other professional development, such as attending workshops or conferences, professional reading, or observations; degree
   - experience
     teaching experience (online/offline, age groups, English teaching or other subjects); language learning experience; other relevant work experience; other relevant life experience, such as volunteering, particularly for early-career teachers
   - language awareness
     for example: how to clarify the difference between similar words such as *sensitive* and *sensible*; problems learners may have with grammar points selected by the interviewer; challenges for learners of English from different language backgrounds (such as Thai or Croatian learners of English)

- soft skills, such as teamwork or time management
  ability to work in a team; time management strategies; ability to complete administrative requirements such as writing reports; stress management strategies
- strengths and areas to develop
  areas highlighted by CELTA trainers; areas trainees have identified themselves when reflecting on their teaching, perhaps addressed during the interview by asking trainees to describe particular lessons; trainees' developmental needs

2 Trainees may think of a range of questions. Here are some suggested topics:
  - learners
    the types of learner in the school (age, backgrounds, needs, etc.); typical group sizes
  - teachers
    the size of the teaching team; the management structure and who the trainee would report to; how much contact teachers have with each other and the management team
  - syllabus, materials and resources
    the syllabus and system of assessment; the material used, e.g. coursebooks; the availability of resources such as whiteboards, computers and internet connections within the school (if teaching face-to-face); the platform used (if teaching online)
  - pay and conditions
    teaching hours (length and number); administrative hours; what is and isn't paid for; travel costs, holiday, benefits, etc.; contract type (full-time, part-time, ad hoc, etc.)
  - professional development
    the support available for new teachers; the school's professional development programme for all teachers; other professional development opportunities such as additional certificates or the opportunity to attend conferences; opportunities for career progression within the school
  - safeguarding
    requirements for criminal record checks; safety policies, including online; safeguarding requirements for teachers and other staff
  - (if applicable) relocating to another country
    travel arrangements and expenses; organizing visas and work permits; accessing healthcare; taxes; finding accommodation and covering initial costs such as deposits; help with settling in and meeting people

3 Allow a little time for trainees to compare their lists.
  At this point, you may wish to tell trainees a little more about the typical application process for an English teaching job, and what it might include apart from an interview. For example, some schools ask teachers to teach a demo lesson, do micro-teaching, or create a lesson plan as part of their application.

4 Divide the group into interviewers and applicants. Set a short time limit, for example five minutes, for each interview to be conducted. Allow a little time afterwards for interviewers and applicants to provide feedback.

5 – Developing teaching skills and professionalism

D Maintaining health and wellbeing

The aim of this activity is to highlight the importance of caring for our own wellbeing as teachers, and the impact that this can have on our lessons and our learners. It is hoped that by addressing this during the CELTA course, trainees will be somewhat better prepared to face the inevitable challenges of being a (new) teacher and be aware of some strategies to deal with these challenges.

Allow a few minutes for trainees to read the quote and discuss the questions. Trainees may discuss a wide range of ideas, including but not limited to:

1 High workload, blurred boundaries between professional and personal lives, large amount of emotional labour (for example, dealing with their own and others' confidence issues), feeling responsible for their learners' progress and achievement, precarity of working conditions (for example, zero-hours contracts or last-minute-cover classes), large classes, lack of support from management, demanding students or parents, etc.

2 A teacher who is feeling under stress will be more likely to spend mental energy addressing those areas of stress, rather than focusing on their lessons or their learners. They may feel tired, distracted, frustrated, or any number of other negative emotions, which can create a negative environment if they bring those feelings into the classroom.

On the other hand, 'emotional contagion' means that a teacher who is feeling positive will be more likely to pass those feelings onto their learners, and therefore create a more positive working environment. They are likely to have more mental space to consider how to plan engaging lessons, and therefore learners will be less likely to cause discipline issues. Teachers will also probably have more awareness of learner progress and achievement, and be able to provide better quality feedback, if they have more mental space available to dedicate to this, rather than dealing with stress.

3 Possible ways to maintain wellbeing might include:
- staying physically healthy: eating a balanced diet; taking regular exercise; maintaining a regular sleep pattern
- time management: creating clear boundaries between work and home life; using lists, diaries or planners to block out specific times for planning, marking, or professional development; getting into routines; being aware of screen time
- professional and personal relationships: knowing who to go to when help is needed; building a support network, for example friends to talk to, or colleagues to offer advice; maintaining positive relationships with managers, for example through clear communication, or asking for and offering constructive feedback
- leisure activities: regularly engaging in enjoyable activities, such as doing hobbies, watching films, or doing sport; mindfulness

KEY WORDS FOR TEACHERS

Remind the trainees of the need to be able to use teaching terms confidently and accurately.

REFLECTION

1 Put trainees into pairs. Demonstrate how they can play 'tennis':
  The trainer gives the topic of the round. In pairs, trainees take it in turns to say one opinion, fact, or piece of advice connected to the topic. They cannot repeat something which has already been said. If they can't think of an idea, that round ends. There are three rounds, echoing the main areas covered in this unit.
2 Allow trainees time to think of their tips, before comparing them with a partner.

5 – Developing teaching skills and professionalism

Optional activity

1 Work in pairs. Look at the following curriculum vitae. Discuss these points.
   1 Do you like the layout of the CV?
   2 Are these the same sections that you would include on your own CV?
   3 Are they in the same order that you would put them in?
   4 Would you include more or less detail?
   5 What information can you include on your own CV?
2 Write your CV. Then compare with a partner. How could you improve your CVs?

Eva Veselá

Profile
A keen and enthusiastic teacher. Able to work on own initiative or as part of a team. Good language awareness and a dedication to helping others meet their objectives. A background in business and offers business English as a specialism.

Career history
September 2017 – present: English Language Teacher (including for Cambridge Main Suite exams – PET, FCE, CAE)
Hello English School
Prague
Summer 2017: English Language Teacher
UK Summer School Scheme
Bournemouth
2016 – 2017: Temporary office work

Qualifications
Certificate in English Language Teaching to Adults (CELTA)
(Inside Track School of English, Brighton)
BSc. Business Management and Finance,
Masaryk University, Brno
Maturita: Czech, English, Mathematics – passed with distinction
Cambridge C1 Advanced (CAE): Grade B
Cambridge C2 Proficiency (CPE): Grade C

Personal details
Date of birth: 03 October 1995
Full driving licence

Interests
Reading, going to the cinema, and sport

Contact details
Valtická 15
628 00, Brno-Vinohrady
Czechia
+420 602 743 515
evaveselateacher@gmail.com

Reference
Ms Ally Foster
Director of Teacher Training
Inside Track School of English
21–25 Grays Road
Brighton, UK

Photocopiable   © Cambridge University Press & Assessment 2022

Trainer's notes for optional activity

Trainees could look at the CV produced here in small groups and compare it to their own. They could brainstorm the sections and information that they think would be relevant and also discuss the amount of detail that they think is necessary. If you have time, for example on a part-time course, this could lead into the trainees producing their own CVs.

Teaching practice

Teaching Practice (TP) is a core component of the course, and provides trainees with immediate, ongoing, and hands-on experience in classroom practice. TP is an opportunity to try out practical approaches that have been described in the methodology sessions. Also, through the feedback and reflection that follows TP, it acts as a stimulus to the development of trainees' personal and practical theories of teaching. For the maximum benefit to be gained from TP, the trainer's involvement is crucial, both before and after TP, and also during it. Although all trainers will have their own preferred styles and routines, here are some points on the setting up and conducting of TP that you may like to consider. The trainer's role in TP typically involves the following functions:

- preparing and assigning 'TP points', i.e. the guidelines for each trainee's TP lesson (at least at the start of the course)
- supervising guided lesson planning
- observing the TP lessons
- conducting a feedback session after TP, usually with all the trainees involved
- evaluating the lessons and writing up, for each trainee, a post-TP report
- where appropriate, integrating reflection on the TP experience into the scheduled methodology sessions

Each of these functions will be dealt with below and in turn. But before we look at the trainer's role, it is important to emphasize the importance of establishing a good group dynamic between the members of the TP groups. Without such a dynamic, the learning potential of TP may be adversely affected. Factors that promote a good dynamic in groups include:

- *having a shared purpose:* It is important that the group members understand that TP is not a competition or 'talent quest', but that, by collaborating, they have a better chance of succeeding than if they don't
- *time spent together:* Form the groups as soon as possible, and give them as much time as is possible in the timetable to work together
- *learning about each other:* Encourage trainees to share experiences, e.g. by talking about previous teaching and/or learning experiences
- *interaction:* Set up activities which require trainees to interact, e.g. group planning, group feedback
- *proximity:* Make sure that the trainees can work together, always in a circle and preferably away from other groups, and ensure that no single member is 'out of the group', e.g. sitting apart from the group, not able to participate in group messaging, or simply not participating

TP points

Usually, the TP lessons are based on published coursebook material. The coursebook is chosen because it is representative of published materials and because it is suitable for the level of the learners. Trainees will normally have access to the standard coursebook components, including any recorded listening material, the workbook and the teacher's guide. Trainees may also be encouraged to adapt and supplement the material that they are using, but at the same time they should be able to demonstrate that they can exploit existing materials without spending an unrealistically excessive amount of preparation time.

Trainer's Manual

The purpose of setting TP points (rather than asking trainees simply to follow the book) is mainly to ensure that each trainee gets to teach a variety of lesson types – including some with a language focus, and others with more of a skills focus. At the earlier stages of the course, the TP points serve to show how coursebook material might be segmented and adapted by an experienced teacher. They are also a way of introducing and explaining activity types that might not yet have been covered on the course. Perhaps most importantly, they pinpoint the main focus of the lesson for the trainee.

The TP points should be distributed sufficiently in advance of TP to allow trainees reasonable planning time: this may be two or three days in advance in the case of intensive courses, and more in the case of part-time courses. TP points tend to be more detailed and explicit at the beginning of the course, but less so as the course progresses. By the end of the course, trainees should be able to plan their lessons unguided and unassisted, although some collaboration with colleagues will still be necessary so as to ensure cohesion between lessons, and to avoid undue overlap.

Here are two sets of TP points, taken from Day 2 and Day 6 of a 20-day (four-week) course, based on the same upper-intermediate coursebook. Note that initially the TP points are detailed and explicit, and that each is assigned to a particular trainee. By Day 6 the trainees are simply given broad suggestions. Some centres encourage trainees to segment and allocate the material themselves.

Material: *Evolve 5* Unit 1

5 × 20 mins each

1. **TP focus: Speaking. Materials: Page 1: Start speaking**
   Show learners the picture of Hayley. Put them in pairs to discuss A. Show them the caption to check their ideas. Put them into two groups: improvements / problems; each group discusses one of the questions in B. Re-pair them so one improvements and one problems person are working together to share their ideas. Give them a couple of minutes to think before working in pairs to discuss C. D is a back-up if you finish early (without the video).

2. **TP focus: Reading. Materials: Page 4: Language in context 1A / 1B**
   Show learners the pictures and get them to discuss the questions in A in pairs. Ask learners to briefly report back on their ideas. Show them the title of the article and ask them to predict what it might refer to and why Amy is writing about it. They read the article quickly to check. Tell them not to worry about the words in bold – they will look at them later. Ask them to complete a table with now / the 80s for bikes, phones, music (note: make it clear there's no answer in the bikes/now box). They reread to complete the table, then compare their answers in pairs. If time, they can discuss whether they agree that a TV is a time machine.

3. **TP focus: Vocabulary. Materials: Page 4: Vocabulary 2A / 2B / 2C / 2D, SB p.141 1.2 A or 1.2 B**
   Refer learners back to the blogpost they read with the previous trainee. They work in small groups to remember what they can. Then allow them to look back at the post to add to what they remembered. Form: learners divide the words into adjectives / verb phrases. Meaning: they use dictionaries to complete 2B and check meanings. Pronunciation: they listen (to you or the audio) and repeat the words briefly. Choose one exercise from SB p.141. Ex 1.2 A or 1.2 B – learners complete alone, pair check, then whole class. 2D in pairs.

4. TP focus: Grammar. Materials: Page 5: Grammar 3A, 3B, 3C, SB p129 Ex 1.2 A

Refer learners back to the blogpost they read earlier in the lesson. Ask them to find the four sentences in the 'Past habits' box in the blogpost and underline them. Alone, they complete the rules in 3A, then pair check and whole class. Ask them to underline more examples of this grammar in the blogpost. Ask questions to check their understanding if necessary. In pairs, learners complete SB p.129 Ex 1.2A. During whole-class checking, make sure they can see the answers, not just hear them. 3C: give them prep time alone, then time to compare with a partner. Ask them to share ideas in whole class and give them feedback on their use of the target language.

5. TP focus: Speaking. Materials: Page 5: Ex 4A

Set up an activity in which the learners discuss the question in Ex 4A. To do this, you may want to talk about your memories first, and elicit some of the possible follow-up questions the learners might ask. Alternatively, show Jacqueline's video as a model – ask them to note interesting language they could 'steal' from her. The speaking activity will work best in small groups. Afterwards, ask learners to share their ideas in whole class, and give them feedback on one or two good uses of language, and one or two areas they could improve. If time, put the learners into new groups to repeat the activity.

Material: *Evolve 5* Unit 3.1

3 × 40 minutes each

Theme: Personality types

Language point: Relative pronouns; reduced relative clauses

Trainee 1

TP focus: Listening. Materials: Page 21: Start Speaking, Page 22: Ex 1A–C

Use p.21 as inspiration for the lead in. 1B/1C – learners only read if necessary after they've completed the listening tasks.

Trainee 2

TP focus: Grammar. Materials: Page 23: Ex 3A–C, Page 131: grammar bank

Practise clarifying this grammar with another trainee to help you feel more confident with it. Don't forget the pronunciation!

Trainee 3

TP focus: Vocabulary. Materials: Page 22: Ex 2A–2C, Page 23: Ex 4A

Check with trainee 1 whether learners will have a copy of the script or whether you need to give it to them. Don't forget the pronunciation! You might do 2C and 4A or choose just one of them.

Guided lesson planning

The setting up of guided lesson planning varies greatly between centres. However, the following points may prove useful where there is sufficient time. Particularly in the early stages of the course, the trainer is usually available to advise on lesson planning, whether done collaboratively or individually. Such guidance can take various forms, including:

- helping the trainees to understand how the TP points relate to the materials and how to set up activities they may not have come across before: this is generally only appropriate for the first one or two TPs
- observing the process of group planning, based on the TP points, and making suggestions only when the trainees seem to be in difficulty
- directing the trainees as they 'walk through' their lessons, using the other trainees as 'dummy learners': this can be useful at the earlier stages of the course
- talking through a draft of the trainee's lesson plan with the individual trainee: this is often appropriate at the later stages of the course

Observing lessons

When observing TP, trainers need to be able to see and hear the trainees and the learners, while not being too obtrusive themselves. Trainers should have a copy of the trainee's lesson plan (although this may not apply for the very early stages of the course), and any materials that accompany it.

Most trainers make notes while observing, and will refer to these during the feedback session and when writing up a TP report. One way of organizing these notes is to record the stages of the lesson, and, at each stage, to note both strong and weak points, as appropriate. These notes can be useful when reminding trainees of particular incidents within the lesson.

On some courses, trainers choose to create a live messaging backchannel, allowing trainees to discuss the lesson as it happens. The trainer may be part of the backchannel, feeding in occasional questions or highlighting critical incidents for trainees to pay attention to. However, they may prefer to leave the discussion between the trainees, as the trainer already has quite a lot to pay attention to during TP. In either case, it's important for ground rules for the backchannel to be laid out before the TP, for example:
- Be constructive and supportive – consider the kind of comments you would like to read about your own teaching and remember that everybody in your TP group can see the discussion
- Keep comments focused on TP – don't discuss other matters during the lessons
- Narrow down your feedback – choose a focus to avoid being overwhelming, for example focus only on strengths of the lesson, or the teacher's personal objectives for that lesson, or two or three of their action points from their previous TP feedback

Opinion is divided as to the extent trainers should intervene during TP. The conventional wisdom is that they shouldn't, as, among other things, this might create a lack of confidence on the part of the learners. At the same time, *not* to intervene when a trainee is clearly in need of advice – such as when it is obvious that learners don't know what they should be doing in group work – may seem unnecessarily heartless, especially at earlier stages of the course. There are grounds for arguing that the learning of any new skill, including teaching, is a *mediated* experience. That is, it is best achieved by working in close collaboration with a more experienced other. This collaboration can take the form of 'coaching from the sidelines', as when the trainer prompts the trainee from time to time, or even *team-teaching*, when the trainer and trainee take turns to teach the stages of the lesson. The latter model of training is especially appropriate in training contexts where the trainee is sharing a class with the supervising teacher. It is important to stress that any such mediation should be progressively withdrawn over the duration of the course, and that in the last observed lessons the trainees should be both planning and teaching their lessons independently.

Conducting TP feedback

Feedback on TP is typically conducted as a group, with the trainer guiding the discussion. It may take place immediately after TP, or on a subsequent day. In either case, the feedback can be usefully structured around a *reflection task* that the trainees who taught in TP have been given, and around an *observation task* that the observing trainees have been given. A selection of such tasks can be found in the sections on Teaching practice and on Classroom observation in the Trainee Book. The choice of task will depend on such factors as: the stage of the course; the developmental path of individual trainees; the kind of lessons taught (e.g. whether there was a focus on language or on a particular skill); and the particular focus of the current methodology sessions. Even when TP feedback follows immediately on TP, it is important that trainees have taken the time to write a short self-evaluation of their lessons. Below is an example of the self-evaluation rubric that is used by one centre.

Self evaluation of teaching practice

After each teaching practice session, you should take some time to consider your lesson and complete this form. If you wish to write more for any section, continue over the page.

Name: .... **Date lesson was taught:** ....

Main aim of lesson: ....

To what extent do you think you achieved this aim? Put a cross on the line: 0% _____ 100%
What did you like about the lesson? What did the learners seem to like about the lesson? Why?
What would you change about the lesson if you taught it again?
Are there any questions you would like to ask your tutor?

In situations where feedback occurs on a subsequent day the use of journals can be useful, as long as the trainees have sufficient time to complete them. For journal writing tasks, see pages 191–192 of the Trainee Book.

When discussing individual lessons, try to focus trainees' attention away from simply what 'went wrong' in the lessons, and towards drawing some concrete conclusions as to how they can improve their practice. This may take the form of:
- **description:** ask the trainee to quickly recap the stages of the lesson
- **positive evaluation:** ask the trainee to say what went right, and what their role was in making this happen – many trainees will only mention the learners' role in positive parts of the lesson

- **techniques or activities to recycle:** ask the trainee to say what they tried in this lesson which they would do or use again in the future
- **problem identification:** ask the trainee to identify any problematic moments
- **explanation:** ask the trainee to try and account for the problem(s)
- **possible solutions:** ask the trainee to say what they might do differently in the future

The other trainees should be involved in the feedback as well, especially at the *possible solutions* stage. However, it is very important that they should not be encouraged to make negative criticisms about a trainee's lesson. One way of structuring peer feedback so as to reduce the risk of negative criticism is to provide a rubric that helps 'accentuate the positive', such as:

Complete this sentence: *What worked well in your lesson was … .*
Complete this sentence: *What I wondered about was … .*

(There are more TP Observation tasks in the Trainee Book.)

One possible framework for conducting TP feedback (particularly at the start of the course) might be:

1 **Prepare to share:** Trainees take a few minutes before they speak to make notes about positives and questions based on their colleagues' TPs. Trainees who taught during that TP may also want to reread their post-lesson self-evaluation. If there is feedback from the learners, this can be read privately at this point.
2 **Teacher impressions:** In pairs or small groups, trainees who taught during that TP have a designated amount of time to share their reflections on their lesson. Observers may reassure or feed in brief comments or questions, but should allow the trainee to say what they want to at this point.*
3 **Observer feedback:** In the same groups, observers share what they noted from their observation task. Trainees ask questions and make comments, with the aim of finding out more, rather than defending their decisions.*
4 **Trainer summary:** The trainer then briefly summarizes strengths and action points from the TPs, particularly anything important which hasn't been discussed during stages 2 and 3. They may also choose to feed in a little reactive methodology input, or demonstrate a useful technique.

*Stages 2 and 3 can be run simultaneously, with each TP teacher paired with a different TP observer, or consecutively, with each TP teacher's lesson discussed one after another.

Some alternative ways of conducting TP feedback include:
- The trainer leaves the room / online session. The trainees conduct their own feedback in a group. The trainer returns and the trainees report on what they have each learned from the group discussion.
- Initially, each trainee writes on the board one thing they liked about a lesson, and one question about it – these comments and questions then form the basis of the feedback discussion.
- the trainer conducts the feedback individually, rather than in a group (this is useful in the case of trainees who are not meeting the required standard).

While it is important to maximize group participation in TP feedback, the trainer should not abdicate responsibility entirely. The trainer's role is to orchestrate and guide the discussion, to defuse any incipient aggression or defensiveness, and to draw out action points that can be applied in future lessons, as well as to provide explicit suggestions and advice. When making suggestions, these may be more easily accepted if framed, not as *You should do X*, but as *What I find helps is …* or *The learners might be more engaged if …*

One important role for the trainer is to *listen* to the trainees. Listening with attention and understanding can help mitigate the disappointment that often accompanies post-TP feedback.

TP Reports

There is no set format for writing TP feedback reports, although centres are expected to adopt a pro forma which they should use consistently. Most reports tend to comment on the following broad areas:
- the planning of the lesson (including the plan itself, and any language analysis)
- the execution of the lesson, including such aspects as classroom management, pace, interaction with learners, use of materials and aids, dealing with problems and error, and the trainee's manner and rapport

As in the giving of verbal feedback, it is important that the written report is selective, i.e. it should not include so many points that the trainee is either demoralized or confused; and that it provides a useful summary of the trainee's progress, including concrete advice as to how to continue developing as a teacher.

Here, for example, is a trainer's TP report for a trainee at a point early on in a course:

Teaching practice feedback form

NAME	TUTOR	LENGTH OF LESSON
Katya Sokolova	SM	40 minutes

DATE	LEVEL	TP SESSION
29.04.22	Upper-intermediate	5

LESSON TYPE

Functions - agreeing/disagreeing

PLANNING

Your plan is very clear, Katya. There is a nice balance of activities - and I really like the idea of starting with a discussion, then presenting the new language and then having another discussion. I think it worked well.

The analysis of the forms you are teaching shows an appropriate level of detail and was useful to you in the lesson.

My only reservation is that you seem to have planned enough here for 90 minutes!

ACTIVITY	COMMENTS
Teacher sets up survival game	You got into the discussion very quickly – perhaps you could have 'sold' the activity a little more at the start to build interest. Still, the mountain situation worked well and the items for discussion were all credible – well done.
Learners discuss items to take with them	This is generating a lot of language. Your monitoring is generally good, but try not to spend too long with any one group. Be aware of what is happening in all of the breakout rooms.
Teacher elicits / Teacher's language for (dis)agreeing	Good to start with the exponents that the learners volunteered and then feed in some extra ones – this kept things learner-centred but expanded their knowledge too. You covered the forms very efficiently – great. But … I think you also needed to spend some time on the contexts in which each would be appropriate – how formal are they? What are the differences between them? etc.
Teacher sets up second discussion	Very nice – instructions were excellent and good to move learners into new groups. Again, pop into all of the breakout rooms to be aware of how everybody is doing.
Teacher leads class feedback	You handled this very confidently. You were very enthusiastic and prompted very well. Excellent to do some correction, and to focus on good use of language too.

OVERALL

This was a very engaging lesson, Katya – well done. There were lots of opportunities for learners to communicate and you did some really useful work with language at the end of the lesson. Your planning was very thorough, too.

Action points:
- **Monitoring**: Keep in mind the whole class and don't get too involved with one individual/group.
- **Language focus**: Consider how bits of functional language are different (e.g. formality) as well as similar.

To standard for this stage of the course. Well done, Katya.

Integrating TP

It is important that the TP experience is not viewed as being divorced from the content of the input sessions, especially the **classroom teaching** component. There are a number of ways of integrating TP into the input, including:
- at the beginning of a session, asking trainees to briefly recall occasions during TP that are relevant to the topic of the session. For example, if the session deals with the listening skill, ask trainees to recall TP lessons that involved the use of audio or video recordings, and to reflect on both the pros and cons of using such material

- anticipating when the language area that is the focus of the current session is coming up in TP, and asking the trainees to use what they have just learned about this area to plan a presentation or a practice activity for it
- asking trainees to get into groups with trainees from other TP groups to say how the content from the input session might be relevant to working with their TP groups, how this might differ based on the learners' levels, and what else they might need to know to put into practice what they have learned during the session with their TP groups

Classroom observation

Classroom observation of experienced teachers should be scheduled so that it occurs at regular intervals throughout the course. It is important that this observation has a focus. For this purpose, the TP observation tasks (in the Classroom observation section of the Trainee Book) have been designed for use in both TP and in classroom observation. The observations can provide useful data for both reflective activities during input sessions and written assignments.

In advance of classroom observation, trainees should be reminded of some basic courtesies when visiting someone else's class. Draw the trainees' attention to the guidance given on page 193 of the Trainee Book.

Trainees often express surprise that the observed teachers sometimes 'break the rules', that is, that they do not always follow the same teaching procedures that are promoted on the course. You could point out that the routines that are appropriate for novice teachers are often adapted and even rejected by experienced teachers, once these routines have outlived their usefulness. For this reason, too, trainees should be discouraged from simply criticizing the observed classes; the purpose of observation is to gain new insights into learning and teaching, and these insights may be more readily acquired if trainees approach observation in a spirit of enquiry, rather than a judgemental one.

Observation Tasks

The observation tasks in the Trainee Book can be used for any observation during the course (of TP, video lessons, or of experienced teachers). There are more tasks than the trainees will probably be able to use during the course, and for this reason the trainer should select those which are considered appropriate for the stage of the course, for the trainee's own developmental needs, and for the type of lesson that the trainee is going to observe (if this is known). The tasks have been sequenced to follow the approximate order of the kinds of concerns that trainees will have as they develop, starting from such basic issues as the teacher's body language, through classroom management concerns, to more learner-oriented concerns such as treatment of error. The tasks focus primarily on what is *observable*, that is, what are called 'low-inference phenomena', such as the teacher's actual behaviours and speech, rather on 'high-inference phenomena' such as what the teacher or the learners might be thinking or feeling at any point in the lesson. Likewise, the tasks avoid encouraging the trainees to form value judgements on the observed lessons – or at least not until they have gathered sufficient observable data. Where possible, trainees are encouraged to corroborate any inferences they make by, for example, comparing notes with the teacher after the lesson. This 'anthropological' approach has been deliberately chosen so as to discourage trainees from the kinds of snap judgements they sometimes tend to make, such as *The learners were bored* or *The milling activity didn't work*. Whenever trainees make this kind of assessment, they should be challenged to provide concrete evidence (as opposed to unsupported opinions) from their observations.

Review quiz

48 FINISH	47 You have been asked to teach an EAP class. What does EAP stand for?	46	45 On the Common European Framework scale, which is higher: A1 or C1?	44	43 Think of three different ways in which you could give advice in English.
37 Write *cat* in phonemic script.	38	39 Give two ways in which you can continue developing as a teacher after the course.	40	41	42 'What do you do?' Explain the difference between the first and second *do*.
36	35 A student asks: 'What's the difference between *mustn't and don't have to?'* Explain.	34	33	32 Why might someone who has already learned two additional languages have an advantage over someone who hasn't learned any?	31 You have to teach phrasal verbs with *get*. Think of four.
25 You have to teach the second conditional. Think of a model sentence.	26 Think of two minimal pairs for /v/ and /b/.	27 What is one key difference between a PPP lesson and a task-based one?	28	29	30 Why is it a good idea to integrate skills in lessons?
24	23 'Practise *have got* using realia': what could you use?	22 Think of two things a teacher could do to build and maintain learner motivation.	21	20 How could you check that learners have understood the gist of a dialogue?	19
13	14 An elementary student asks: 'When do you use *some*, and when do you use *any?*' Explain.	15 Give two advantages of online teaching and one disadvantage.	16	17 Use intonation to say the word *tonight* with three different meanings.	18
12 How could you finger-correct this mistake? 'She is doctor.'	11	10 Think of a way of presenting *there is/there are* to elementary learners.	9 Give two ways in which using a learner's first language can be beneficial.	8	7 'I wish I was home'. Think of two concept questions.
1	2 Give two ways in which a teacher could give support to learners during a communication activity.	3	4	5 A student asks: 'What's the difference between *Do you like … ?* and *Would you like … ?*' Explain.	6 What is a placement test?

Trainer's Manual

Trainer's notes

Trainees work in groups. You will need a copy of the board and a dice for each group of players.

Rules

1. Each player needs a different coin or counter.
2. Players take turns to throw the dice.
3. Players landing on a question must answer it to the satisfaction of the other players. Players who cannot answer a question lose a turn. In case of doubt or dispute, the tutor may be called to decide.
4. Players landing on the bottom of a ladder, go up the ladder. Players landing on the head of a snake, go down the snake.

Suggested answers

2. e.g. supply vocabulary, prompt, ask questions, encourage
5. *Do you like* = present simple, a question about facts, habits; *Would you like* = conditional construction, invitation/offer
6. entry test, to assess the level a learner should start in
7. Am I home? Do I want to be home? Am I thinking of the present, future or past?
9. e.g. clarifying instructions, making presentations of new language clear, checking understanding, comparing and contrasting to English, using translation as practice
10. e.g. using a picture showing objects, e.g. furniture in a room; describing the classroom
12. Hold up four fingers, sound out *she, is, doctor*, indicating the first, second and fourth fingers respectively, and point to the third to elicit *a*.
14. Very generally, *some* tends to be used in affirmative contexts, and *any* in negative contexts and questions.
15. e.g. Advantages: ease of access and saving of time, can be anywhere in the world, possibility of personalized, private dialogue. Disadvantages: need for good wifi connection, some loss of social aspects of meeting people in person
17. e.g. giving of information, asking a question, invitation/suggestion
20. Ask some general *wh*-questions, e.g. *what is the dialogue about?*
21. e.g. make content relevant, personalize content, give praise, build rapport with learners, be enthusiastic in their job
22. things that the learners are carrying or wearing, e.g. keys, watches, pens, etc.
25. e.g. *If I was a millionaire, I'd buy a big house.*
26. e.g. *ban, van; berry, very; kerb, curve*
27. A PPP lesson begins with presentation of a pre-selected grammar item; a task-based lesson begins with a communicative activity.
30. Because skills are typically integrated in 'real life' communication outside the classroom.
31. e.g. *get over, get back, get up, get on (with)*
32. Because they will have already developed successful learning strategies, they will be confident and expect success.
35. *Mustn't* is used to talk about obligation, whereas *don't have to* implies a choice and lack of obligation.
37. /kæt/
39. e.g. reflecting on lessons, being observed, observing others, reading about teaching, further courses
42. The first *do* is an auxiliary verb, and has solely a grammatical purpose (required in the question as an 'operator' to form a present simple question); the second is a lexical verb, meaning (in this context) *work at*.
43. e.g. *you should, why don't you, if I were you, I'd … , you ought to …*
45. C1
47. English for Academic Purposes

Acknowledgements

The authors would like to thank Karen Momber and Jo Timerick at Cambridge University Press for their support and guidance throughout the project and also Hugh Moss and his team for their valuable input. Indeed, we are sincerely grateful to all those behind the scenes at Cambridge University Press and Assessment for their contributions to all aspects of this work. Our thanks are also due to David Bunker for his editorial expertise and all those who commented on drafts of the manuscript.

The authors and publishers acknowledge the following sources of copyright material and are grateful for the permissions granted. While every effort has been made, it has not always been possible to identify the sources of all the material used, or to trace all copyright holders. If any omissions are brought to our notice, we will be happy to include the appropriate acknowledgements on reprinting and in the next update to the digital edition, as applicable.

Key: U = Unit, TB = Trainee Book, TM = Trainer's Manual

Text

TB – U4: Ryôkan, ["In the empty doorway many petals are scattered;"] from *One Robe, One Bowl: The Zen Poetry of Ryôkan, translated and introduced by John Stevens*, First edition, 1977. Protected by copyright under the terms of the International Copyright Union. Reprinted by arrangement with The Permissions Company, LLC on behalf of Shambhala Publications Inc., Boulder, CO, shambhala.com; **U6:** Project Gutenberg. (n.d.). Retrieved February 21, 2016, from www.gutenberg.org; **U8:** Consonant chart taken from *Cambridge International Dictionary of English*. Copyright © 1995 Cambridge University Press. Reproduced with kind permission of Cambridge University Press via PLSclear; **U15:** Polish language presentation and translation by Monika Grządka. Reproduced with kind permission; **U33:** Cambridge University Press for the text from 'Nurturing the relationships in our classrooms' by Sarah Mercer. Copyright © 2020 Cambridge University Press. Reproduced with kind permission; **U36** Council of Europe for the adapted text from 'A Common European Framework of Reference for Languages: Learning, Teaching, Assessment – Companion volume'. Copyright © 2020 Council of Europe. Reproduced with kind permission; **TM – U36:** Council of Europe for the adapted text from 'A Common European Framework of Reference for Languages: Learning, Teaching, Assessment – Companion volume'. Copyright © 2020 Council of Europe. Reproduced with kind permission.

Photography

The following photos are sourced from Getty Images:

TB – U13: funnybank/DigitalVision Vectors; Caiaimage/Chris Ryan; **U17:** arh-sib@rambler.ru/iStock Editorial/Getty Images Plus; Hans-Peter Merten/Photodisc; Tue Nguyen/EyeEm; Fergus O'Brien/The Image Bank/Getty Images Plus; Steve Allen/Stockbyte; Fotosearch; James D. Morgan/Getty Images News; **U20:** Jim Vecchion/Photo library; Harold M. Lambert/Archive Photos; **U21:** Spiderplay/E+; Siri Stafford/Photodisc; pop_jop/DigitalVision Vectors; **U25:** Jane_Kelly/iStock/Getty Images Plus; MicrovOne/iStock/Getty Images Plus; **U36:** Juanmonino/E+; ajr_images/iStock/Getty Images Plus; **U37:** ShutterWorx/E+; Juanmonino/E+; **U23:** Jose Fuste Raga/Corbis; **TM – U13:** filadendron/E+.

The following photos are sourced from another libraries:

TB – U5: imageBROKER/Alamy; **U21:** Superstock; **U36:** Steven May/Alamy.

TB – U21: Commissioned photography by Trevor Clifford.

Illustrations

TB – U8: Felicity House; Johanna Boccardo; Pat Murray; Tony Wilkins.

Typeset

Typesetting by QBS Learning.

Corpus

Development of this publication has made use of the Cambridge English Corpus(CEC). The CEC is a computer database of contemporary spoken and written English, which currently stands at over one billion words. It includes British English, American English and other varieties of English. It also includes the Cambridge Learner Corpus, developed in collaboration with the University of Cambridge ESOL Examinations. Cambridge University Press has built up the CEC to provide evidence about language use that helps us to produce better language teaching materials.